MICHAEL PALIN
SAHARA

To John —

MICHAEL PALIN
SAHARA

Mcavadon

PHOTOGRAPHS BY BASIL PAO

WEIDENFELD & NICOLSON

CONTENTS

For Helen, Tom, Will and Rachel

120 MALI

160 NIGER

192 ALGERIA

210 LIBYA

227 TUNISIA

241 ALGERIA

252 GIBRALTAR

INTRODUCTION

My father was in charge of the Export Department of a steelworks and every Christmas he received an enormous box of dates from their agent in Algeria, addressed to a Mr E. M. Palm. I remember wondering if he should tell them, but he never bothered. Perhaps he thought the supply of dates might dry up if they discovered his name wasn't Palm.

I didn't want them to stop coming either, not because of the dates, but because of the box they came in. The illustration on the packet fuelled powerfully romantic fantasies of somewhere hotter, drier and even more exotic than south Yorkshire; a place where men with turbans, baggy velvet pants and wicked moustaches reclined under palm trees with veiled and sequinned ladies, whilst their faithful camels stood in picturesque silhouette against the setting sun.

The first 'proper' book I was ever given was *Tales from the Arabian Nights*. Its seductive illustrations, by A. E. Jackson, combined with the date boxes to fan a precocious fascination for things of the desert. Curved swords, soft silks, tassels and see-through skirts. Mirages and genies, huge jellies and lubricious oils and unguents. The desert world seemed, apart from the odd beheading, to be a place of complete sensual fulfilment. Even delight itself was Turkish.

Almost fifty years later there came a chance to expose my childhood fantasies to the harsh glare of reality.

In the first spring of the new millennium I met up with Roger Mills, director of many of the travel programmes I've done, at a pub opposite Notting Hill police station. Over a pint or two he suggested a journey through Francophone Africa, those huge and empty countries from Cameroon northwards, once loosely federated as part of the French empire. Rarely visited by British television, they might provide fresh pickings and new discoveries.

I got home, unfolded a map, and saw one word spread across most of these countries. Sahara.

The French empire was interesting, but it had come and gone. The Sahara is a potent, evocative reality. It is one of the world's great brands. No one name so completely epitomises an environment. Oceans can be Atlantic or Pacific or Indian, mountains can be Himalayas or Andes or Alps, but if you want to convey desert, you only have to say Sahara.

It embodies scale and mystery, the thin line between survival and destruction, the power to take life or to transform it. A self-contained, homogenous, identifiable world, uncompromising and irreducible.

In other words, a challenge. And by no means an easy one.

As big as the United States, with a population the size of Norfolk, the Sahara is only 15 per cent sand, and though the great ergs, the sand seas, are among the most exquisitely beautiful landscapes I've ever seen, there is a dark side. The Sahara is also a killer, scorching the life out of crops, people, and all but the most tenacious living creatures. It's growing larger every year as drought turns pasture back into sand, which the remorseless desert wind carries into towns and villages until they die of suffocation. It has its share of war and conflict. Many areas we wanted to see were inaccessible because of minefields and military activity.

Yet how close it is to us. The Sahara lies just beyond the borders of Europe. The heart of the desert is three hours' flying time from Paris, four hours from London. This proximity is not lost on the many thousands of sub-Saharan Africans who cross the desert to escape what they see as poor, unstable and oppressive regimes back home.

Today, the Sahara, far from being a cosy date-box illusion, has become a bridge from Africa into Europe, and a bridge that is increasingly well used by those prepared to risk their lives for a better life on the other side of the Mediterranean. If the Sahara was my fantasy, Europe is theirs. Perhaps they will learn from their journey, as I did from mine, that fantasy and experience never quite match up.

Michael Palin, London, 2002

www.palinstravels.co.uk

Sahara was filmed between February 2001 and February 2002. For various reasons, it was impossible to shoot it as one continuous journey. Summer heat and all-year-round bureaucracy forced a number of breaks upon us. The diary days in the text represent days at work, give or take the very rare day off, and not time spent travelling out to the desert.

PAGE 1
Timbuktu sign, Zagora, Morocco.

PAGE 2
Arched doorway at Chefchaouen, Morocco.

CONTENTS PAGES
Holiday snaps. Left to right: Iron Ore Train, Zouérat, Mauritania; St-Louis, Senegal; Djenné, Mali; Timbuktu, Mali; Train at Carthage, Tunisia; Oran, Algeria; Background picture: Sand sea at Chinguetti, Mauritania.

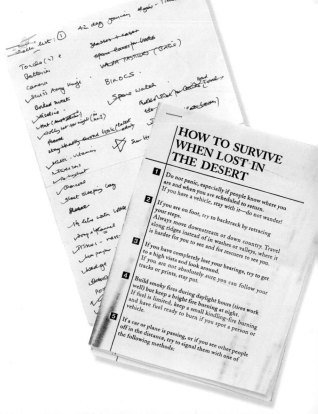

ACKNOWLEDGEMENTS

The filming of Sahara lasted a little over four months and covered nearly 10,000 miles. The preparation for the journey and the process of welding it into a series took the best part of a year. No-one had an easy job.

At our home base in London, Anne James steered the boat through choppy waters, from launch to final anchorage, with diligence, energy and enthusiasm. Natalia Fernandez dealt with every detail of our travel plans, which, considering the bureaucratic complications in this part of the world, deserves more than your average respect. Janina Stamps, who set us on the road, and Gina Hobson, who brought us back and saw the programmes to their conclusion, applied skill and experience to some nightmare situations, and Lyn Dougherty rode expertly through the minefields of cash flow.

Paul Bird and Alison Davies at the office helped preserve my sanity, without apparently losing their own, and Alison tucked and tidied the manuscript.

Elizabeth Parker wrote music for the series and Bernard Heyes designed our maps and titles. George Foulgham and all the team at VideoLondon made it sound wonderful and the amazing Alex Richardson took on the task of editing all four hours. Though he and his family may be regretting it, I, quite selfishly, am delighted. Nicola Moody at the BBC gave us generous encouragement and great support.

It's impossible to thank everyone who helped us out on the road.

Many of those to whom I owe my thanks are mentioned in the text. Of those who are not, but without whom we could never have made such a journey, I must not forget Marie Gloria Macedo, Richard Stanforth, Alan Keohane, Bob Watt, Djadje Ba, Violet Diallo, Barry Halton, Mike Lord and Stirling Security Services, Mr Ahmed Faci, Kahlifa Airways, Simon Khoury at Arab Tours, Judith and Fanta and Tidene Expeditions in Niger.

Our core filming team, whose average age, we were shocked to find, is well into the mid-fifties, were nevertheless a credit to Saga Filming. Nigel Meakin on camera and John Pritchard on sound (and putting anything back together again within five minutes) took to the desert with cool authority. Peter Meakin, apart from bringing the average age of the crew down by a good ten years, loaded, unloaded and shot film in quite horrendous conditions, without ever once complaining. Except when his father wasn't looking.

RIGHT

On the road in Gibraltar. Left to right: Peter Meakin, Nigel Meakin, Aaton Super 16 XTR Prod (aka 'The Baby'), MP, Roger Mills, Gloria Macedo, Natalia Fernandez, John Pritchard.

LEFT

On the road in Djerba, Tunisia. Standing left to right: Basil Pao, John Paul Davidson, Peter Meakin, Claire Houdret. Sitting: Pritchard, Meakin, Mohammed (Driver), Man With Grin.

BELOW

The famous Green Jobs.

John Paul Davidson ('J-P') led our motley group through Senegal, Mali and Niger and always had a bit of goat ready for us at the end of a long day, and, even more miraculously, a bottle of very warm red wine to wash it down. His enthusiasm was wonderful to behold and his investments in the local economy were much appreciated.

Roger Mills directed my first steps out of the Reform Club fourteen years ago, when *Around the World in 80 Days* was a new and nervous departure for me. The fact that we still travel together shows not only how unadventurous we are, but how much we trust each other and how much we still enjoy it. The fact that Roger took on the extra responsibility of Series Producer this time shows a fine streak of masochism.

Vanessa Courtney, another veteran of previous travels, scoured remote parts of Africa on a gruelling recce with Roger and saw us safely through Morocco. Dudu Douglas-Hamilton in Mali, Jane Chablani in Niger and Claire Houdret in Tunisia buttered up the locals and generally made wheels run smoothly in often difficult situations. Simon Neatham provided me with a tent.

My thanks to Bobby Birchall at DW Design for all the time he's put in to make the book look so good. At Weidenfeld & Nicolson Claire Marsden has been the most sympathetic and conscientious of copy editors, and Michael Dover the most generous, supportive and hospitable of editors. Thanks too to David Rowley and to Angela Martin for all her work in ensuring that someone actually read the book.

Finally, thanks to my good friend, gastronomic adviser and stills photographer Basil Pao for bringing back as fine a set of holiday snaps as you could wish for. What the world doesn't know is that the secret of his success is a constant supply of certain throat sweets to which the whole crew became addicted. These Valda Pastilles, or Green Jobs, as he called them, became essential morale boosters on an adventure low on luxuries.

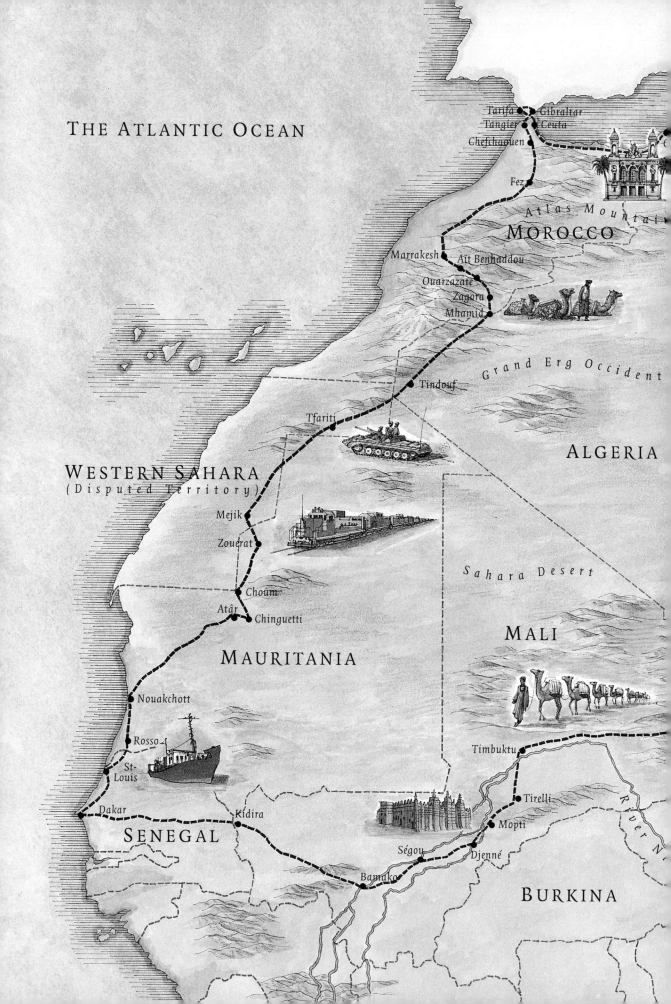

THE ATLANTIC OCEAN

MOROCCO

Atlas Mountai

Tarifa   Gibraltar
Tangier   Ceuta
Chefchaouen

Fez

Marrakesh   Aït Benhaddou
Ouarzazate
Zagora
Mhamid

Grand Erg Occident

Tindouf

Tfariti

WESTERN SAHARA
(Disputed Territory)

ALGERIA

Mejik

Zouérat

Sahara Desert

Choûm
Atâr   Chinguetti

MAURITANIA

MALI

Nouakchott

Rosso

St-
Louis

Timbuktu

Dakar   Kidira

Tirelli

Mopti

SENEGAL

Ségou   Djenné

Bamako

BURKINA

River N

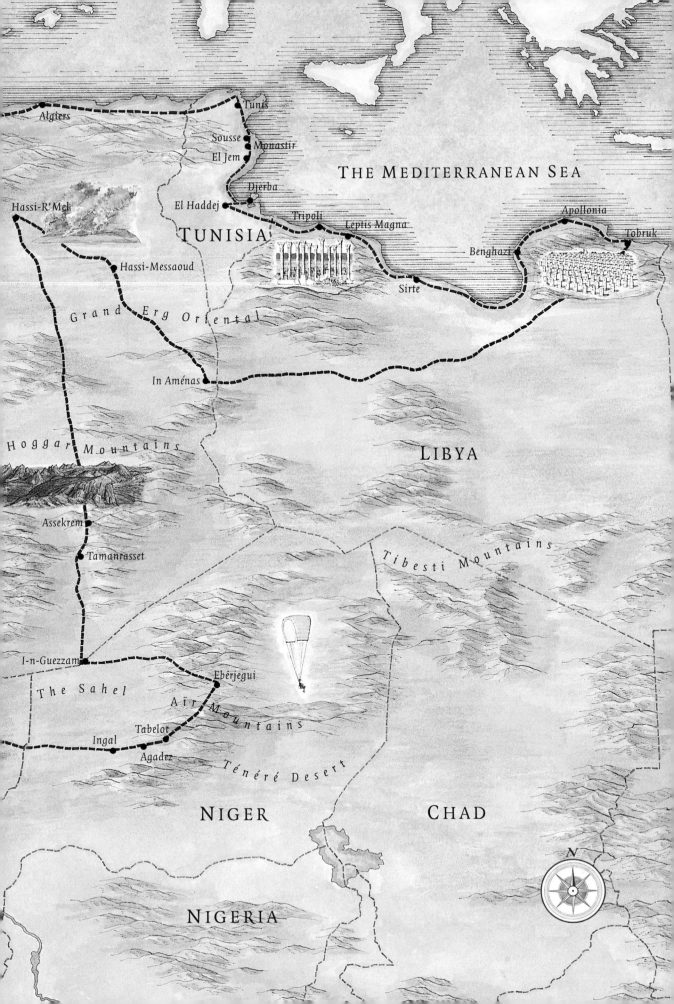

DAY ONE GIBRALTAR

Only 300 miles from the Sahara Desert there is a place where brass bands play, warm beer is served and a blue lamp marks the police station. Where people shop at Marks & Spencer and twenty-one gun salutes sound on royal birthdays. Where Noel Coward played cabaret and John Lennon got married.

This corner of a foreign land that seems forever England is a gnarled limestone rock, nearly 4 miles long and 1400 feet high, tucked into Spain's lower regions like a prostate, dominating the dozen miles of ocean that separate Europe from Africa.

For the Berber chief Tariq Ibn Ziyad, who first settled on the Rock thirteen centuries ago, it held the promise of escape from the hostile Sahara and a stepping stone to the rich underbelly of Europe. It became known as Jebel el Tariq, Tariq's mountain, which, eroded down to the single word Gibraltar, it has remained ever since.

The Britishness of Gibraltar, which began with Admiral Rooke's invasion in 1704, is well entrenched. Contemplating my map of North Africa outside Pickwick's Pub, I order a coffee. No messing with *latte* or *machiato* here.

'Coop or Moog?' I'm asked in a thick Geordie accent.

I choose cup.

12

Cars are squeezed into a pleasant shady square beside me. Buildings are squeezed around the cars: an attractive colonial house with deep balconies and freshly painted wrought-iron railings on one side, the handsome Georgian façade of the garrison library on the other and, next to it, the offices of the *Gibraltar Chronicle*, the veteran local newspaper, which broke the news of Nelson's victory at Trafalgar.

For me, a first-timer in Gibraltar, there have already been surprises. First of all, that there are buildings of quality which are not just selling duty-free booze or fish and chips, and secondly, that Gibraltar's Britishness is one layer of a deceptively international cake. The balconied, green-shuttered cottages that stretch up the steep alleyways leading off Main Street were largely built by Portuguese and Genoese, and the Catholic cathedral was converted from a mosque by the Spanish. There are, I'm told, more working synagogues on Gibraltar than in the whole of Spain. The Alameda gardens reflect Andalusian taste. The uncharitable view is that Gibraltar is an ordnance depot reinventing itself as a tax haven, but the reality is more complicated and a lot more attractive.

Nevertheless, it is Britishness that holds this polyglot community together. Sitting on the terrace of the Rock Hotel as the day fades, it is quite possible to believe that the sun will never set on this tenacious shred of Empire. Sipping a cocktail, surrounded by comfortable, chintzy, Home Counties decor and the soft sound of *Daily Telegraph*s slipping from snoozing laps, I imagine the Rock of Gibraltar as a liner, loosing its moorings and sailing slowly off, bearing inside its crumbling white flanks the last traces of the old order. This, I must admit, is after a couple of quite generous whiskies, of the sort I am unlikely to find elsewhere on this trip, together with marmalade, eggs and bacon, cups of tea, pints of beer, *Match of the Day* and all those things that I miss idiotically when I'm in foreign parts – and parts don't come much more foreign than the Sahara Desert.

Later, I settle into bed and with one long, last, loving glance at the Corby trouser press, turn out the light.

BELOW

The Royal Gibraltar Regiment is the Rock's own army. Here they put on a ceremonial parade in Casemates Square.

DAY TWO ACROSS THE STRAIT

At the highest point of the Rock of Gibraltar, where a sheer cliff face plunges 1400 feet into the Mediterranean, there is a gun emplacement called O'Hara's Battery capable of lobbing artillery shells from Europe into Africa. I'm assured it's never been used in anger and, indeed, as I climb the last few steps on this idyllic Mediterranean morning, the only signs of anger are from seagulls swooping at my head to warn me off their nests.

From up here, the confrontation of the continents is quite a sight to behold. The two land masses don't just meet, they rise to the occasion. The white cliffs of Gibraltar

facing up to the serrated black crest of Jebel Musa on the Moroccan shore. The Greeks and Romans were aware of the symmetry and called the twin peaks the Pillars of Hercules, the end of the known world, beyond which lay outer darkness.

Gibraltar remains protective to the last, as if testing my resolve to take on something as bleak and inimical as the Sahara. Since the beginning of human history people have been trying to leave the desert behind, from Tariq Ibn Ziyad and the Islamic armies who crossed the Strait in the eighth century, to the African migrants trying to cross it today. On the morning news there is a report of a boat-load of immigrants capsizing in the Strait last night. Amongst them were three pregnant women. They were only saved from drowning because one of them carried a mobile telephone. I try to find a Spanish newspaper for more details, but no Spanish dailies are sold anywhere in Gibraltar. I sense a glimmer of paranoia here, as if the natural siege mentality that seems to hold Gibraltarians together might be threatened by too much information.

So I'm not persuaded to linger, not by the fine books and leather armchairs of the garrison library, nor by the sound of the British Grenadiers, nor even by the sight of the midday flight back to London roaring across the airport runway, which also happens to be the main road out of Gibraltar.

Once the plane has raced past us and soared out over the Atlantic, the barrier opens and it's a short walk to the frontier. This is not a happy place, for either side. Spain has never concealed its irritation over what it considers British occupation of Spanish territory, and the referendum of 1967 in which Gibraltarians voted overwhelmingly to remain British was followed by closure of the frontier for sixteen years.

Now things are less confrontational but just as niggly. The Spanish examine drivers' papers with elaborate care, causing huge traffic jams, and the Gibraltarians reply with a large sign pointing out who's to blame: 'Gibraltar regrets the inconvenience caused to you due to frontier restrictions imposed by the Spanish authorities contrary to your European rights to free movement'.

The next sign we encounter reads 'Policía', and after a perfunctory going over we're out the back door of a long, low, anonymous customs shed and into Spain, where a huge welcoming billboard directs us to the nearest McDonald's.

The ferries that cross the Strait of Gibraltar leave from Algeciras, 3 miles from the frontier. We board a solid, ponderous old vessel called *City Of Algeciras*, which will take one and a half hours to cover the dozen nautical miles between here and Africa. As the new generation of lightweight ferries has clipped the crossing time to thirty-five minutes, I'm not surprised to hear that this is her final voyage.

I'm puzzled, though, by the lack of any ceremony. If this had been, say, the last journey of an Isle of Wight ferry, it would surely be full of people in anoraks pointing cameras and tape-recording the last blasts of the ship's horn. Instead, it's like a ghost ship. In the saloon the television screens beam American basketball to rows of empty seats. In the main lounge 'Don't Let the Sun Go Down on Me' thuds out to a few thin Moors with wispy beards and close-cropped black hair.

A vigorous westerly rips in as we reach the open sea, where the bottle-neck entrance to the Mediterranean shrinks to a mere 9 miles. This is dangerous water, a tide race of accelerating currents and a thousand ship movements a day, a difficult stretch to navigate at the best of times, but in a tiny boat, at the dead of night, potentially suicidal.

The bonus of this urgent west wind is a panorama of dramatic clarity. The fingers of Europe and Africa almost touching and between them, dead centre, the sun merging slowly with the horizon. I feel for a moment a jubilant sense of freedom, of being in limbo, beyond tribal loyalties, national boundaries, anthems, flags, customs, papers, permissions and prejudices, free from all restraints except the elements themselves. I feel positively Homeric. Then a particularly fierce gust picks me up and hurls me, bodily, into the bar.

MOROCCO

DAY THREE TANGIER

ABOVE

Moorish arched
gateway in the
casbah, Tangier.

'When I meet fellow Americans travelling about here in North Africa, I ask them, "What did you expect to find here?" Almost without exception, regardless of the way they express it, the answer reduced to its simplest terms is a sense of mystery.'

Thus wrote Paul Bowles, the American writer who adopted Tangier, in the book that lies where it fell from my bed last night.

Earlier in the evening, a group of elderly Moroccan musicians had played a thin, tinkling version of 'Happy Birthday' for me in the hotel restaurant. It was such an uncompromisingly Arab sound that it was only halfway through that I realised it was 'Happy Birthday' at all, and for that reason alone I shall treasure the memory of it.

It's six o'clock now and I'm trying to shake off the first hangover of my fifty-ninth year. The new day glows cruelly bright behind the curtains and I can't ignore it. I swing myself out of bed, surprised by the cool touch of a marble floor, and throw open the curtains. But the smarter the hotel the less easy it is these days to throw open the curtains, and by the time I've found the right cord to pull and disentangled the net from the main drape I'm seriously irritated and irreversibly awake.

The view is less spectacular and much friendlier than I'd expected. It's a painter's view. Below me is a small verdant garden, dominated by the luxurious crown of a palm tree and a solitary Norfolk pine standing with its branches out like a cake stand. Running roughly in line from west to east are a harbour wall, with a ferry boat

alongside, a distant beach already covered with tiny figures and, rising gently behind the curving bay, the headland, beyond which a pipeline dives beneath the Strait, carrying 10,000 million cubic metres of Algerian natural gas into Europe every year.

The town is compact. Narrow streets rise and fall around low hills and their damp cobbles catch the morning sun. The buildings look more French than Spanish, with red roofs and white-plastered walls, sooty and streaked by the rain, from which sprouts a canopy of television aerials and satellite dishes. The sharp clarity of the light is softened by the drowsy mix of early morning sounds – dogs barking, doves cooing, a fishing-boat engine springing to life.

I'm excited. I know there's a way to go before we reach the Sahara but I'm on the starting grid. Tangier, where Europe clings onto Africa and Africa clings onto Europe, has a fine record for great departures. Among my birthday presents from the crew, piled up beside a bottle of duty-free champagne (empty), are two books about Ibn Battuta, one of the greatest travellers of all time and a Tangerine, born in this town in 1304. At the age of twenty-one, he set out on the first stage of a 75,000-mile adventure through most of the known world, across the Sahara to Timbuktu, up to Spain and through Europe to Persia, Arabia, Sumatra, India and China, returning home thirty years later to write a book about it.

Not a bad role model.

The El Minzah Hotel opens onto a busy street leading up from the port and the market. There are cars, but they're well outnumbered by human traffic. Berber women, tough, pugnacious and wide, plod up the hill as if wearing all the clothes they own at the same time. Their low centres of gravity allow them to carry virtually anything. I wouldn't be surprised to see one of them with a small car on her back. The men, by contrast, don't carry, they push. Covered from head to foot in thick woollen burnouses (the wind that's keeping the clouds away is brisk and chilly), they steer rubber-wheeled handcarts full of bits of this and that up the centre of the road. Among the crowd are men in sharp suits doing nothing but standing and looking around. The admirable Alan, our fixer, tells me they're probably policemen. At dinner last night a local man went out of his way to deny that Morocco was a police state.

'Not at all,' he insisted, 'it is a *well-policed* state.'

There's an Anglican church nearby which was painted by Matisse, one of a number of artists, from Delacroix to Francis Bacon, drawn to Tangier by the quality of light and the tolerant hedonistic atmosphere, which also attracted writers like Bowles and Joe Orton and William Burroughs. Putting thoughts of hedonism aside for an hour or two, I fish out my only tie and walk over there for Sunday Service. My parents would have been proud of me.

Walking to church in Sheffield was never like this. The entrance to St Andrew's, Tangier is virtually obscured this morning by a Berber street market. Doughty ladies from the mountains have taken over the pavement, spreading in front of them a fragrant assortment of fresh cheeses, onions, carrots, thick sheaves of mint, coriander, sage and rosemary.

Somewhere behind the piles of food I locate two white gateposts, which mark the way into the churchyard. Once inside, I feel like Alice in Wonderland. Nothing is quite what you expect it to be.

Down by the gatepost, squeezed into a corner of the wall, is a makeshift wooden construction that I take to be a kennel, but which, on closer examination, proves to contain a bearded old man, who glares back at me. A moment later an attractive Arab woman pops in through the gate, squats down and begins to dictate a letter to him.

Leaving the boxed scribe behind, I walk up the shaded path. On either side of me is a thick, entangled, but artfully managed secret garden of cypress, gum and false pepper trees, jacaranda and creepers and assorted thick bushes, in the recesses of which I can dimly make out graves and headstones. On closer inspection most of these bear the names of people from the Scottish Highlands. Curiouser and curiouser.

Then there is the church itself. It emerges from all this greenery looking like something out of the Cotswolds, except that the tower from which the blue cross of

St Andrew flies is decorated with Moorish tiles. The church porch has an Islamic horseshoe arch and inside is a chancel arch, around which the Lord's Prayer is picked out in Arabic.

I'm warmly welcomed by a manic garrulous Moroccan, in white *djellaba* and black astrakhan hat, given to fits of giggling, lunging kisses and a curious staccato English punctuated regularly by the phrase 'thank you very much'. He introduces himself as Mustapha Chergui, the church caretaker. Thank you very much. For thirty-eight years, thank you very much. In between pointing out such features as the coffered chancel ceiling, carved from cedar wood by master craftsmen from Fez, and the display of arum lilies, which he fetches every Sunday from the market, he has to rush away to help Mary Evans, one of the churchwardens, prepare the hymn books.

Mustapha Chergui and Mary Evans are not really off the same menu. She is quintessentially English, pronounces lost 'lorst' and, very much in the tradition of Tangier travellers, is just back from Syria and Jordan.

The congregation begins to assemble. Only a smattering of the 150-strong British community comes to church, one of them being an engaging Australian-born journalist called Jonathan Dawson.

Thanks to him, I soon know all the dramatis personae, that Mrs Evans, the churchwarden, married 'one of the few straight chaplains the church ever had' and that by far the greater proportion of the congregation are Nigerians involved in getting themselves and others across the Strait of Gibraltar.

So here we all are: the British upper-class ladies, the Nigerian migrants, Mustapha the sexton and myself, all leafing through our books to find Hymn Number One Hundred and Forty-Four and in our own ways, and often our own keys, giving voice to 'Glorious Things Of Thee Are Spoken'.

The Nigerians treat the service as a moveable feast, coming and going according to the demands of their mobile phones, which go off frequently, often in the middle of prayers. (Jonathan tells me that the Christmas service was constantly interrupted by mobiles playing 'Jingle Bells'.) No-one seems to mind them nipping out to do business during Matins. Their attendance rate today is impressive, if variable, rising from eight before the collection to twenty-five afterwards.

At the end, when we've filed out and the chaplain has shaken hands with everyone, I ask him about the Nigerians. He says life is precarious for them here. The Moroccans arrest them and then dump them back at the Algerian border. The chaplain introduces me to a young man called Regis, a Catholic with a plastic rosary around his neck. He has just walked back from the border by foot. It took him four days, but he didn't dare take public transport in case he was arrested again. Once again, I find myself wondering what it is about their own country that makes these young men risk arrest, beatings, drownings and the Sahara Desert.

Then something reminds me I'm still in Wonderland.

Hobbling out behind Regis is a tiny Englishwoman with a fierce stare. Her name is Lady Baird. She must be well into her eighties and yet has come to live here relatively recently. When I ask her what brought her to Tangier, she replies crisply, 'A garden! The most beautiful garden in Morocco.'

I'm about to ask her whether this wasn't a lot to take on at such a late age, when, on seeing Jonathan Dawson pass by, Lady Baird indignantly indicates her right leg.

'You see that?' she cries. 'Birdie did that!'

'Birdie?'

'His bird. Bit me on the leg.'

Birdie, it transpires, is a cockerel who lives in Jonathan's apartment.

He doesn't attempt to deny it.

'Bit a great hole in her leg,' he confirms.

I said he was lucky not to be sued. Jonathan looks uncharacteristically sheepish.

'Well, he did bite a very distinguished American woman and she thought it was rather funny, but after three courses of antibiotics and massive doctor's bills, I'm afraid it was a bit of a strain on the friendship.'

We walk down the path away from the church. Through the trees, across the road, I can see a façade with the faded lettering, 'Grand Hôtel Villa De France'. Green louvered shutters swing in the wind. It was from one of those rooms, Room 35, that Matisse looked out and painted this unique Anglo-Arab church and the trees and the sea beyond, as it all looked ninety years ago.

'He is a misogynist, I'm afraid,' says Jonathan, by way of explanation. 'Only ever bites women.'

I don't think he meant Matisse. But who knows.

The day ends on twin notes of anticlimax, both football related. Roger wants to film activity on the town beach, the public playing fields of Tangier. To integrate me in this happy recreational scene he has persuaded a local team to let me have a kick around with them. Considering their average age is about sixteen and there are distinct language problems, they do everything to make it easy for the elderly

Englishman thrust into their midst, and I'm eager to show that, despite being two years short of sixty, I still know a few tricks.

One of these is the sliding tackle, which, together with the hefty up-field boot,

was the basic essential of football as I was taught it. I win the ball, but, this being sand and not the Wembley turf I'm used to, I'm unable to move it, and as one of my legs sprints off the other one stays firmly beneath the ball. As my groin is prised apart I have no option but to fall flat on my back. I see the camera crew chuckling away on the touchline. Good old Michael, really entering into the spirit. This gives me fatal encouragement to get up and race off after the action. One more kick and something goes twang internally, and I hobble around, cursing. More laughter from the camera crew, and it's several minutes before they realise that this is not an Equity performance, but for real.

To have so recklessly disabled myself so early in the journey could pose all sorts of problems, but at least I satisfied the first rule of filming – if you're going to get hurt, get hurt on camera.

DAY FOUR TANGIER TO CHEFCHAOUEN

Woken again by the intensity of the fresh-risen sun, a glare so fierce I think there might be a blaze outside my window. But it's bright rather than hot, and in the shaded street outside the hotel I can understand why the men are wearing thick jackets and have the hoods of their burnouses pulled up.

'Morocco is a cold country with a hot sun.' Jonathan Dawson squints into the light. 'That's what someone told me when I came here. If you're sitting in the shade over there you might be freezing your tits off, but when you're sitting out here it's hot, you know.'

We're on the terrace of the Café Tingis in the Petit Socco, a square once renowned for all sorts of naughtiness. Jonathan, with his piercing blue eyes, swept-back silvery hair and air of languid amusement, seems to thrive on Tangier. He came here in 1992 to do a piece for the *Evening Standard* and stayed.

He sighs a little regretfully as his *café au lait* arrives.

'They used to sell booze, all these caffs.' In 1956, after Morocco won independence, liquor was banned from the medina and the party, if not over, at least went underground.

'So Tangier is a shadow of its former racy self?'

Jonathan rakes the square with a half-smile. 'Everything is here if you want it. You can have boys, girls, cockerels or anything you want...'

'Drugs?'

'It's not, er...legal, but it's sort of slightly not illegal. I don't encourage it,' he says, before adding cheerfully, 'I've got a great friend coming to stay. She's a dope-smoking grandmother. You should be interviewing her.'

For Jonathan, Tangier remains a tolerant place, where you can be what you want to be. He likes the sea and the beaches and the freshness of the food, the fact that it can get cold enough for open fires and, of course, the prices.

'You can buy a villa here for less than the cost of a London basement.'

We finish our coffees. The noise levels in the square are rising. Laughter, argument, the booming of a television set from the darkened interior of a café opposite. It's time for us to move on south, but Jonathan won't let us go just yet.

'I've got some lovely wine. Come back for a quick gargle.'

Jonathan lives not in a villa but in a top floor apartment crowded with books, paintings and fine furniture. Across this fine furniture struts Birdie, the confident comb-tossing, lady-pecking cockerel with whom Jonathan lives.

Jonathan shouts at him frequently, but Birdie takes very little notice.

'He's not an egg-laying bird. He's not house-trained. He's a liability.'

'So why do you keep him?'

'Oh well, I'm alone and he's alone and we keep each other company, I suppose. He likes a bit of telly actually. He likes a cup of tea and a bit of telly.'

'Does he like a gargle?'

'Well, he used to have a bit of wine with porridge, but I stopped that. He got a bit fond of it.'

OPPOSITE

(ABOVE) *Jonathan and Birdie enjoy a quiet moment.*

(BELOW) *Tangerine children play on a cannon commissioned by Sultan Moulay Hassan of Morocco in 1882 and built in Newcastle.*

23

ABOVE

*Trio of fine buildings
in the Plaza Uta El
Hammam,
Chefchaouen: (left
to right) casbah,
medersa (Koranic
school) and mosque.*

At this point Jonathan notices my empty glass and shouts towards the kitchen.
'Mr Lassan!'

Mr Lassan, the third member of this ménage, is Jonathan's manservant and a compulsive kleptomaniac.

'I had a remote control bell for Mr Lassan, but he sold it when I was in Marrakesh.'

Mr Lassan turns out to be a middle-aged Moroccan with a curious lopsided leer, which Jonathan puts down to the fact that he has a new set of teeth.

'He can't stop smiling because they won't close.'

Apparently, Mr Lassan keeps losing his teeth. He says they go missing when he takes them out in the hammam, the public baths, but Jonathan suspects him of selling them. 'I mean what sort of man takes his teeth out at the hammam?'

Mr Lassan tops up our glasses, turns on his heel and leaves with a slow, insolent swagger. Jonathan looks after his retreating figure and sighs heavily.

'He's a terrible tosser, but I'm afraid I'm fond of him.'

He pauses and breaks into a smile.

'He's like Tangier. He's an addiction.'

Heading south and east out of the city, on the road to Tétouan, my guidebook notes what could be a good omen for the journey. Outside the football stadium we shall pass the only memorial to the great traveller, Ibn Battuta, which stands on a plinth beside it. The plinth is there but unfortunately the statue is gone. Our driver thinks it was stolen some time ago.

He doesn't know why.

Skirting the city of Tétouan, we follow the road up a broad rising valley. The green and wooded landscape with flocks of sheep and cattle could be Wales or Scotland save for the red-capped French kilometre posts by the side of the road and the occasional vivid glimpse of Berber shepherdesses in scarlet hats, white tops, boots and bright red knickerbocker leggings.

Late in the day we come to a town spread dramatically across the steep sides of a jagged limestone ridge. It's called Chefchaouen. As in Tangier, there is an old and new town. The French never attempted to fuse the two together, so the old town, the medina, remains pretty much as it must have been when it was founded at the end of the fifteenth century as a mountain retreat for those Moors and Jews expelled from Spain by the Catholic Monarchs.

It is said that up until 1920 only three Christians had ever found their way into Chefchaouen, and until 1937 slaves were openly traded in its market.

Now it's on the tourist trail as a picturesque mountain town and the hippie trail as a fine place to enjoy the much sought-after local marijuana, known as *kif*. Or as the rock and roll bands used to call it, Moroccan Red.

Around the long rectangular central space, the Plaza Uta El Hammam, are grouped an elegantly harmonious cluster of old buildings: the mosque with its delicately beautiful six-sided minaret of brick and plaster, the low white walls and fine doorway of the *medersa*, the Koranic school, and the crumbly, toffee-coloured walls of the casbah, the old castle, from whose gardens rise palms and cypress trees.

LEFT
Lounging around in the funduq. *Out-of-town traders mull over marketing strategy.*

25

At one end of the square is a *funduq*, or caravanserai. These were originally intended to be stopovers for those coming into the town to buy and sell goods. Around a whitewashed courtyard two arcaded storeys provide room for unloading and quartering of the animals, with sleeping accommodation for their masters above. This *funduq* has not yet been tarted up for the tourists. A bed frame, painted silver, sits in the middle of the yard, mangy cats slope around bales of straw, a chicken, one leg tied by a string, is at the end of its tether, pecking at the ground. Robed men from out of town recline on plastic chairs, arms behind their heads, doing nothing much. The place smells, not unappealingly, of skins and leather and horse dung.

We are not allowed to film anything in Chefchaouen until we have a police escort, so we kill time in the Plaza eating minced lamb and sipping non-alcoholic drinks. The mint tea is good but dangerous, as it immediately attracts a crowd of bees. These are apparently a serious nuisance, especially in the warmer months, when special covers are provided for the tea, but the honey they make up here is much sought after. General Franco had his private supply of it airlifted to Spain.

A man in wrap-around dark glasses, straight-line moustache and a black suit approaches. The sort of man who could only be one of two things, a policeman or a pimp. He turns out to be our official escort. Throwing himself into the job with gusto, he shoos away anyone within a hundred-yard radius of the camera, creating the impression that the town has been hurriedly evacuated.

Despite protestations that my hamstring is getting better, Roger is keen for me to attend the public baths tomorrow and have it massaged. I have to buy something to wear. My guidebook advises shorts for men, knickers for women. Walk into the souk, down whitewashed alleyways, past buildings painted an almost fluorescent, swimming-pool blue, an effect created by mixing lime and water with the paint. Blue, in many striking variations, is the predominant colour of old Chefchaouen. Apparently it's good for keeping evil spirits at bay.

Find a shop with a comprehensive display of shorts. The shopkeeper is obliging, and I pass a complimentary remark on the popularity of the place.

'Many people here. Many people in your town.'

He smiles thinly.

'Too many,' he says.

Before turning in, I walk into the Plaza. By night, the great space is very different; more mysterious, but more personal. Irregular stabs of light pierce half-closed doors and shuttered windows. There is subdued chatter, some music, faces at upper windows, figures silhouetted on back-lit balconies. If this had been a town in Britain the noise would surely have been growing by now; there would be laughter, fights, shouting and raucousness. Then a familiar smell drifts across from the half-lit balconies, spicing the cold night air with a sweet aroma and bringing on a flush of nostalgia.

Now I understand why it's so quiet. Everyone's stoned.

DAY FIVE CHEFCHAOUEN TO FEZ

Wake feeling distinctly queasy in the digestion department. Bowel control will be essential this morning as the prospect of being washed and scrubbed and massaged before the cameras looms. Am tempted to take a tab of Immodium, but this turns intestines into Elgin Marbles and I'm not ready for that. I'll have to rely on mind over matter, never one of my strong points.

It turns out I'm not the only one affected this morning. Anyone who had the minced lamb in the main square last night is feeling similarly delicate.

The hammam is neither health club nor massage parlour. Its function is primarily religious; to provide ritual cleansing and purification. Before attending prayers in the mosque, every good Muslim must wash hands, lower arms, nose, mouth, ears, feet and ankles. If he or she has had sexual intercourse that day, a complete body wash is expected.

The abundant amounts of hot water required for such ablutions were, and often still are, beyond the means of most households, hence the importance of the public facility.

I'm not surprised to hear that there appears to be difficulty in obtaining permission to film. In fact, I feel slight relief.

But our police escort manages to talk them into it, provided we film before the baths open for men at eleven. Women's hours are in the afternoon.

This raises the question of who will be there if it's closed to the public. Our drivers and our police escort sportingly agree to be extras, though, to my deep concern, they assure me that I will be stretched by a professional.

The baths are located in an old building at the bottom of a steep, cobbled street. You wouldn't know they were there, except for a blackened hole high on the outer wall, from which a telltale plume of steam issues from the boiler.

The door is low, studded and painted pale blue. It gives onto a cool stone-flagged passageway, at the end of which is an open changing area, laid with coloured raffia mats and lit by daylight from above.

My Chefchaouen shorts, though long and suitably modest, are a trifle narrow at the waist, not helping an already delicate digestive situation. I put my clothes in a locker and heave open a hulking metal door. A concrete counterweight on a rope slams it shut behind me. I find myself in the first of three chambers graded by heat. Gentle in the first, stronger in the second and in the third and final room, where the action takes place, powerful enough to send the sweat surging. The rooms are dimly lit, with vaulted ceilings and white tiles halfway up the walls. There are alcoves in the first two rooms, for resting and cooling down, and in the hot room a series of partitioned stalls where the intimate parts may be washed in some privacy.

As the heat pumps up through the floor the washing begins. You can wash yourself or be washed. In my case, Ali my driver, round as a Buddha, takes on the task of cleaning me up, first with extensive lathering and shampooing, then by rubbing me with a viciously abrasive mitt, which reduces my outer skin to thin rolls of dirt.

Meanwhile, the masseur, thin and wiry, with a villainous slash of a moustache, is at work on one of our other drivers. By rocking him backwards and forwards, with legs and arms interlocked, he seems intent on elongating Youssef even beyond the 6 foot 5 he already is.

LEFT
The calm before the storm. On my way to the hammam clutching my new shorts.

29

Then it's my turn on the human rack. As I slither into his clutches it occurs to me that this could be dangerous. My Arabic is of no help. 'Good morning', 'Thank you' and 'Tea, please' are the only three phrases I can remember, and none of these is going to help me here. Anything useful, like 'pulled hamstring', 'food poisoning' or 'I confess!', will require a dictionary, which I don't have.

He indicates to me to lie flat and works thoroughly but compassionately, body on body, stretching, bending and using a lot of what the late great Charles Atlas used to call 'dynamic tension'. His manipulations remain this side of agonising but our intricate couplings leave me feeling pleasantly loose-limbed.

After the massage, Ali dumps several buckets of warm water over me. He aims each one at the crown of my head and the force of the water leaves me gasping. But as I sit and recover in a marble-tiled alcove in one of the cooler outer chambers, head back, staring up at the peeling plaster, it occurs to me that not only have I survived what could have been a dreadful embarrassment, but also my stomach feels much better. I mean, much better.

Our drivers go back to being drivers, but there's a sort of camaraderie amongst us that didn't exist before the hammam. I'm quite blasé, especially about the massage. It was nothing. Just a scratch. They grin knowingly, and it's only when we're on the road again that I hear they had specially asked the masseur to go easy on me. Roger, very amused, tells me the exact words they used translate roughly as 'treat him like a virgin'.

The mountains of Morocco were formed millions of years ago by the collision of the land masses of Africa and Europe, which created a series of folds, running southwest to northeast and providing a spectacular roller-coaster landscape. The road we take to Fez crosses the first of these great ranges, the Rif. Rising over 8000 feet, the mountains are creased and cracked into an often inaccessible network of valleys and peaks, providing cover for local warlords, who have always been more powerful here than central government. Though we pass cork forest and olive groves and flocks of goats along the way, the mountain soil is not fertile. The only crop that grows anywhere is *Cannabis indica*, kif.

It is illegal to possess, deal in or move kif within Morocco, yet somehow it's always available, and there's a big demand for it abroad (the chaplain at St Andrew's in Tangier told me that part of his responsibilities were to administer to the dozen or more English and Americans currently in prison on smuggling charges).

All of which makes these mountains potentially dangerous and lawless places, and we are warned not to stop under any circumstances. Any accident or breakdown will usually have been arranged as a trap.

Occasionally I see young men loitering, but mostly the road is empty, curling round dark and craggy outcrops, high enough at one moment to see eagles wheeling below, then falling steeply down through pine and cedar forest to meadows and verges thick with oleander.

As we emerge from the Rif the land ahead of us opens out into a panorama of rolling hills and fields, a wide Moroccan prairie. From this, in turn, emerges one of the great cities of the Arab world.

Five hours after leaving Chefchaouen, the city of Fez appears due south on the horizon. Low, treeless and compact.

DAY SIX FEZ

To an ear disoriented by deep sleep it sounds like bagpipes warming up or a very ancient siren being cranked into life. Then, after a moment of struggling wakefulness, it coalesces into a rough approximation of a voice, albeit weirdly stretched and distorted. Just as it seems to grow clear and explicable another voice chimes in, at a different pitch and much further away, then another, close by, hard, hooting and metallic, then another and another, until waves of overlapping, over-amplified exhortation burst from the darkened city. If I knew Arabic I would know they were saying, 'God is Great. There is No God But God. Prayer is Better than Sleep.'

I check my watch. It's 4 am.

Soobh Fegr, the dawn summons, is one of five calls to prayer that mark the Muslim day. I have heard it many times, but never anything as spectacular or prolific as the prayer calls of Fez, a rolling wall of sound rising from over fifty mosques, cradled in a bowl of hills.

Infidel that I am, I fall to sleep rather than prayer, and by the time I wake sunlight is thumping against the window and the only sound is the trilling of birds.

I step out on my fifth-floor balcony. All the trees in Fez seem to be clustered in the hotel gardens below me. Three enormous jacarandas, wispy casuarinas, orange and lemon trees, fat, spreading palms and amongst them a great congregation of birds, rushing from one tree to another, perching, pecking, preening and darting away. It occurs to me that they may well be birds from Lincolnshire or the Wirral down here for the winter. They recently tagged an osprey that had flown from Rutland Water to Senegal, over 3000 miles, in twenty-one days. Which is a lot quicker than we're going.

Like Chefchaouen, old Fez was a security-conscious city. Until 1912 and the arrival of the French, no-one could enter without a pass, and even then they would be expected to conduct their business and leave within forty-eight hours. The city gates were locked at sunset and those who failed to abide by the rules would likely as not end up, along with others who fell foul of the law, with their heads on spikes outside. And all this well into my own father's lifetime.

As was their wont, the French built their own separate new town and left the medina alone. Thanks to this enlightened, if crafty, policy, it remains, according to my Cadogan guidebook, 'the most complete Islamic mediaeval city in the world'. It's also a mysterious, labyrinthine place, enclosed and secretive. I need an interpreter. To interpret not just the language but the city itself.

Which is how I meet Abdelfettah Saffar, known to his English wife as Fats and to his friends as Fettah.

'Like the cheese,' he says with a well-worn smile.

He has a house in the old town, which he's been restoring for three years, speaks impressively good English, once lived on a houseboat on the Thames and at one time designed a Moroccan-style bathroom for Mick Jagger's house in Richmond.

He's shorter than me and about twenty years younger, with a neatly trimmed black beard, white *djellaba*, bare feet tucked into a pair of *babouches*, backless yellow slippers, and an efficient black briefcase.

Twenty-first-century Fez may look mediaeval, but it's a working town. Thousands live, shop, worship and do business without ever having to leave the medina. The streets are narrow, and though all motor traffic is forbidden, you're quite likely to be run down by a mule or squashed against the wall by an overladen donkey. In the Arab

fashion, domestic life is discreet and hidden away, but commerce is open, visible and upfront. It's also organised traditionally, into guilds of craftsmen. Each guild area announces itself with a distinctive scent, what Fettah calls 'a geography of smell'. The acrid whiff of pigment in Dyeing Street, cedar wood shavings in Carpenters Street, leather in Tanners Street, the fragrance of fresh-made sweets and nuts in Nougat Street, the seductive sizzle of grilling meat along Butchers Row.

A traffic jam in old Fez can be a treat for the nostrils. At one point on Talaa Kebira (Main Street) I'm thrust to one side by a man with a tray of freshly baked bread on his head, who is trying to avoid a woman carrying a basket of fresh vervain, who, like him, is trying to avoid a mule laden with fresh oranges.

We pass along an alleyway of open-fronted stalls, which rings with the sound of metal beating. The din is cacophonous and comforting, and through the smoke from their fires I can see men and boys, forging, beating and shaping copper and brass into an inexhaustible supply of low-tech utensils. There are huge bowls, some 3 or 4 feet wide, in which meat, dried with salt and spices, will be preserved through the winter (a throwback, says Fettah, to the siege days, when the city gates sometimes remained shut for months). There are tall fluted instruments for distilling perfumes like rosewater, crescent moon and star fixtures for cemeteries and mosques, and stacks of teapots. Down the street a young boy and an old man with thick gold-rimmed glasses are stooped over a low table, stitching together pointy-toed leather slippers like the ones Fettah is wearing, and a little further on a man is turning table legs on a spindle, using one foot to drive it and the other to guide a chisel tucked between his toes.

An arched gateway, sandwiched between two small shops, gives onto a courtyard where lime is being daubed on animal hides to strip them clean. This *funduq* is a monochrome world, full of ghostly surfaces so thickly coated with white lime and plaster that it's difficult to see where the layers of paint end and the buildings begin. A tall black African stirs a vat of fresh lime with a wooden pole, as stocks of fleeces sway through the archway on the backs of donkeys.

There is not a single piece of machinery here. It is a glimpse of a pre-industrial age.

Fettah says he has something special to show me. It doesn't look promising. We squeeze up narrow stairs covered in threadbare red carpet into a shop packed tight with leather goods of all kinds. We pass through ever smaller and more claustrophobic

33

ABOVE

Panorama of old Fez, with a stretch of thirteenth-century ramparts in the foreground. Until 1912 it was a closed city. Outsiders who overstayed their welcome often ended up with their heads on stakes at the gates. The French occupied Morocco in 1911, but never touched the old town, building their own Ville Nouvelle nearby.

rooms, until, without warning, we're at the back of the building and light is spilling onto a wide terrace.

With a dramatic flourish, this tight, concealed old city, is thrown wide open. Below us, like a giant paintbox, is a honeycomb of fifty or sixty stone vats, each one around 4 feet across, filled with pools of richly coloured liquid ranging from snow white through grey, milky brown and pale pink to garnet red, metallic blue and saffron yellow. It is a complete and immaculately preserved mediaeval tannery.

Water, heaved up out of the Fès river by a massive wheel, is distributed amongst the vats, in which the tanners mix the heavy combination of water, hides and dye using only prehensile feet and the pressure of the muscles in their legs. This is a young man's game. The tanners have no protection from the sun, and temperatures can rise above 50°C/122°F in high summer. For a day's work in these conditions Fettah reckons they take home 100 deram. Around £6.

And it's not only the heat they have to endure. A sharp acidic stench rises from the kaleidoscope of colours below, a combination of the sheep's urine and pigeon shit used in the dyeing process. The tanners have had to get used to it. A tour group watching them from an adjacent balcony are offered sprigs of mint as nosegays.

Apart from the slow, rumbling creak of the water wheel, there is no sound other than voices, splashes and the sound of wet hides slapping on the side of the kilns. If I close my eyes I could be in a great open-air bathhouse.

Fettah reminds me that the Fez of 600 years ago would have had 200 such tanneries, as well as 467 *funduqs*, 93 public baths and 785 mosques.

There is a minor jam along one of the passageways on our way out of the medina, caused by a donkey shedding a load of mattresses. No-one seems impatient to pass, nor to pass comment on the Laurel and Hardy-like attempts at reloading. It's the way life is in this extraordinary city. The walls of Fez have kept the modern world at bay. What I have sensed today is little different from the impressions of two French travellers, the Tharaud brothers, who came through here in the 1930s.

'In Fez there is only one age and one style, that of yesterday. It is the site of a miracle. The suppression of the passage of time.'

Paintbox effect at the mediaeval tanneries in Fez. Skins are treated and dyed in stone vats, as they have been for hundreds of years, by individual human effort, most of it gruelling leg work. There were once 200 tanneries like this.

Today Fettah has asked me round to his house.

The entrance gives nothing away. A discreet little doorway set into the high walls of one of the warren of passageways in the medina. This gives onto another much narrower passage, dimly lit and smelling of cool, damp plaster, another modest doorway and then, a revelation. A covered courtyard, its walls decorated with intricate arabesque patterns and glazed *zellij* tiles, rises 60 feet to the roof of the house. This soaring space opens onto a blue and white-tiled terrace, almost as broad as the courtyard is tall, with a garden beyond, full of flowers, shrubs and various fertile trees, which are pointed out to me in detail by Narjiss, one of Fettah's two young daughters, with occasional promptings from her mother.

'We've got lemon, we've got orange...we've got, er...'

'Pomegranate...'

'Yes...we've got pomegranate...'

'Olives...'

'Yes, we've got olives.'

'Kumquat...'

'I know! I know!'

As at the tanneries yesterday, the contrast between the close-packed streets outside and the airy spaciousness inside is more than remarkable; it's almost an optical illusion.

'Doors within doors within doors,' is how Fettah describes the phenomenon of public and private Fez. 'The more you get into it, the more you're lured into it.'

BELOW

Abdelfettah in his
workshop, carving
designs in white
plaster. 'Islamic art
is an abstract,' he
tells me. 'It's all
about the use of
the line.'

His property has a floor space of 22,000 square feet, but it's by no means the largest private house in the medina. Many of them are in poor condition, and it is only over the last three years that there has been much interest in restoring them. In London, such a mansion would be worth many millions. It cost Fettah £60,000.

Abdelfettah is proud of his city. As the craftsman son of a craftsman father, he believes passionately in the preservation of the medina and the traditional styles and skills of the craftsmen within it. He does not see his enthusiasm as narrow or nationalist. Since he and his wife returned here after seven years in England they have welcomed people from twenty-eight different countries to a house which they see as a meeting place for musicians, writers, film-makers and, of course, artists from all over the world.

Off to one side of the property, through small rooms where lunch is being

prepared by smiling relatives, is another spacious courtyard with workshops set around it. Among them is Fettah's studio, where he works on elaborate and complex plaster-work decorations.

I ask him why Islamic art has to be abstract. Is representation of nature and the human body really forbidden?

Fettah thinks there is no express ban in Islam but that creating the likeness of man and nature is, as he puts it, stepping into God's field.

'Islamic art,' he says, 'is the story of the line...the Muslim artist just exploits it to the maximum.'

His own work is painstakingly and meticulously carved by hand. He starts with a blank space and fills it up as the ideas come to him.

'I'm interested in the accident,' he says. 'I find English people plan too much. The accidental is not there.'

He should know, for he married an English girl, Naomi. Slim, angular and a head taller than her husband, she's articulate and down-to-earth, as befits a Suffolk farmer's daughter. Besides Narjiss they have another daughter, called Emily, and a cat called Compost, who lies in the garden bed where he's not meant to. I ask her why they decided, after seven years together in England, to come and live in Fez.

'Fettah's a Moroccan man,' she says, as if explaining something she's had to explain to herself often enough. 'He didn't take on some of the roles that Englishmen take. When he realised what child-rearing was, he's going, "Where's your mum? Where are your sisters? Where are your friends?" I was going, "No, no, you've got to do it, you've got to do it."'

Figures flit by in doorways behind her.

'Life here's very much a community thing. You're never on your own, you're always surrounded by family and friends. And they all help and there's a real teamwork going on. So, in that respect, life's easier.'

Fettah is one of seventeen brothers and sisters. His father had three wives, and for a while, siblings were arriving at the rate of two a year.

Naomi smiles and loops a rogue strand of hair back over her ear.

'The two younger wives are still alive. They live together in one house and they're both called Fatima and they get on fine.'

This must account for all the smiling ladies in the kitchen, preparing food, playing with the children, helping here and there. It must account for why Fettah can find time for work, teaching, restoring the house and running music festivals, and why sometimes Naomi misses privacy and space of her own.

'Fez is quite a traditional city and people are fairly conservative. If you go out in the street you have to have a reason for going out, for shopping and visiting...you don't just sort of amble. Women are at home, cooking, cleaning, looking after children, that's their role.'

This is said with a touch of regret but no malice. Anyway, Naomi thinks that attitudes have changed in the three years she's lived in Morocco. People are less frightened of expressing themselves, of talking about politics.

'Holding hands and kissing in doorways. That's all changed since I've been here.'

This day of peace and quiet, walking around Fettah and Naomi's garden, eating a vast couscous around the table on the terrace, hearing of their plans for the house and their affection for these unique surroundings, has lulled me into a dangerous sense of contentment. I haven't thought of the Sahara all day.

It's all about to change. This time tomorrow, *inshallah*, we'll be in the city of Marrakesh, beyond which sand and mountains merge into the edge of the void.

Ring Jonathan Dawson in Tangier to thank him for his hospitality, only to hear that Birdie has broken his beak. Apparently he pecked at some phantom delicacy on the terrace and bit hard on a floor tile. His beak has gone black at one end and may have to be removed.

ABOVE

Fettah and Naomi's daughters, Emily and Narjiss, play with their cat, Compost, who, naturally, prefers lying in a garden bed.

DAY EIGHT   FEZ TO MARRAKESH

Fez and Marrakesh, the two most important cities of old Morocco, lie in the centre of the country, built to guard ancient trade routes through the Atlas Mountains. Modern Morocco has moved to the coast, around the capital Rabat, and Casablanca, the country's biggest city, with a population twice that of the old towns – Tangier, Fez and Marrakesh – put together.

This is why we find ourselves accelerating south by heading west, using the fast motorway system around Meknès, Rabat and Casablanca as the quickest way to get to Marrakesh.

South of Casablanca the main road slims down to a poorly surfaced single carriageway, choked with trucks and buses. Quite suddenly, some 80 miles north of Marrakesh, the landscape undergoes a transformation. Maybe I was asleep and just woke up, but as we pull up out of a dip beneath a railway bridge I notice Morocco has changed colour. The greens and golds of the fertile northern plain have been reduced to a line of pale yellow wattle trees running beside the road. Beyond them, the land is brick-red and bare.

The walls of Marrakesh reflect this red land with a beguiling rosy glow which deepens as the afternoon light fades. Running unbroken for over 6 miles, their towers and battlements throw a spectacular cloak around the city. But if Fez was enclosed, almost hidden away behind its walls, Marrakesh is bursting out of them. The new town pushes right up close. It's colourful and expansive, with broad avenues and a Las Vegas-like dazzle and swagger. Slab-like resort hotels, with names like Sahara Inn, jostle alongside a brand new opera house. This is an old city desperate to accommodate the modern world.

I'm disappointed. I'd expected something exotic and unpredictable. After all Marrakesh has the most romantic connotations of any city in this romantic country. Perhaps it's because the snow-capped range of mountains that frames the city in every tourist brochure is virtually invisible in the haze. Perhaps it's because almost everyone I've seen so far is white and European like me, or perhaps it's because I feel, on these tidy tree-lined streets, that I could be anywhere.

Then someone suggests the Djemaa el-Fna.

To get to it I have to leave the wide streets and bland resort hotels of the New Town and pass inside the peach-red city walls through the twin arched gates of Bab er Rob and Bab Agnaou.

ABOVE

*Early evening in the
Djemaa el-Fna.
Street theatre and
fast food attract the
crowds, but
compared with what
happens after dark,
this is sedate.*

Once inside the gates the atmosphere is transformed. Tourist buses prowl, but they have to move at the pace of a largely African throng. The tallest building is not an international hotel but the elegant and decorative minaret of the Koutoubia mosque, rising to a majestic height of 230 feet, from which it has witnessed goings on in the Djemaa el-Fna for over 800 years. There is an entirely unsubstantiated story that because the minaret directly overlooked a harem only blind muezzins were allowed up it.

The Djemaa el-Fna is not a beautiful space. It's a distended rectangle, surrounded by an undistinguished clutter of buildings and lines of parked taxis. Its name translates as 'Assembly of the Dead', which is believed to refer to the practice of executing criminals here.

It's bewildering. There's so much noise that they could still be executing criminals, for all I know. There seems no focal point to the commotion – no psychic centre. At one end, where gates lead into the souk, tourists take tea on café balconies and overlook the action from a safe distance. The locals favour the food stalls, which are drawn up in a circle at the centre of the Djemaa, like Western wagons waiting for an Indian attack. They are well lit, and the people serving the food have clean white coats and matching hats. This concession to First-World hygiene is deceptive. The rest of the Djemaa el-Fna is a realm way beyond protective clothing.

A troupe of snake charmers with wild hair and staring eyes tries to provoke old and tired cobras into displays of aggression, playing pipes at them with ferocious intensity. A squad of lethargic transvestites dances lazily, clicking finger cymbals without much conviction. Not that they need to do much more than that. Judging by the size of the crowds around them, the very fact of a man dressed as a woman is deeply fascinating to Moroccans. There are fortune-tellers, fire-eaters and boxers prepared to take on all-comers. Performing monkeys, chained and skinny, will be thrust on you for photographs. Berber acrobats hurl each other around while their colleagues work the crowd with equal agility. There are self-taught dentists, astrologers and men who let scorpions loose across their faces.

Women do not seem to take much part in these entertainments, but they form the majority of the beggars, moving silently through the crowd, sleeping children on their shoulders, palms outstretched.

The Djemaa el-Fna is part fairground, part theatre, part zoo, underscored with a frisson of mysticism and primitive ritual.

Despite my appetite for all things strange and wonderful, I feel more and more of an outsider as the evening wears on and the hysteria mounts, stoked by the constant thudding of drums, squealing of pipes and blasts from brass horns. Repetitive, remorseless rhythms shred away the layers of consciousness until you either give in or, as I did, flee the whole madness and retreat to the wonderful world of bland resort hotels.

DAY TEN MARRAKESH

The grandest hotel in Marrakesh, and one of the most famous in the world, is the Mamounia, named after the exotic gardens around it, which were laid out by Pasha Mamoun, a governor of Fez, in the eighteenth century. It was once the official residence of the crown prince, until the French turned it into a hotel of great style, sophistication and expense.

The shopping arcades of the Mamounia do not deal in take-home gifts, unless there's someone you know who might want a 6-foot silver lion sinking its claws into a 5-foot silver antelope, and the shopkeepers are not the sort who will fish out a box of matches and an evening paper from under the counter for you. In fact, they would not dream of calling themselves shopkeepers. They are dealers in and connoisseurs of fine things. Determined not to be intimidated, I enter one of these emporia hoping to find something useful, like a leopard-skin satellite dish or a lapis lazuli shoe-horn, and end up making the acquaintance of an exquisitely jewelled Spaniard called Adolpho de Velasco. He is not even a dealer, he is a designer.

'A big designer,' he corrects me. 'I launch the oriental look in the whole world,' he claims, before adding, endearingly, 'I'm not modest. When I do something that I like, I like people to appreciate it.'

He sees no contradiction between the jet-set playground Marrakesh has now become and the spartan fortress founded nine centuries ago by Abu Bakr and his holy warriors, fresh out of the southern desert.

Marrakesh, he says, has always benefited from a trade in fine things from across the Sahara. 'An enormously rich trade – glass, jewellery, precious stones, spices, silks.'

I ask him if he has spent much time in the desert himself. He rolls his eyes theatrically.

'Yes.' He pauses. 'And it's terrifying.'

Beneath a shock of carefully coiffured hair Adolpho's lean, leathery face takes on the aspect of an early Christian martyr, racked by some distant anguish.

'It's something that takes you, as it were, into another dimension.'

Cheered by this, I bid Adolpho goodbye, only to receive an expansive invitation to come to his home for a drink at the end of the day. He gives me an address.

'Next to Yves Saint Laurent.'

And he's not referring to the shop.

I visit the souk, the old market in the medina, for a dose of reality, but even here the modern world seems to have won the day. I'm drawn with dreadful inevitability into a carpet emporium, an attractive vaulted interior off a muddy back street. The salesman has lived in London for many years.

'Marloes Court.'

Then, as if I don't believe him, he adds, in quick succession, 'Andy Williams was my best friend. Do you know the Sombrero Night Club?'

His name is Michael.

'Same as yours,' he adds, warmly if unnecessarily.

I hover over an undoubtedly tempting Berber rug, bearing a Star of David motif, a reminder that it was not just Moors but the Jews as well who were thrown out of Spain by the Catholic Monarchs.

'I'm going south, across the desert. I can't take things like that with me.'

He shrugs, as if to say how could anyone who knows the Sombrero Club be going south across the desert.

There are some bewitching sights. Lengths of freshly dyed cotton are hung to dry across one alley, forming a swirling indigo canopy above us, and in the yard that leads off it I catch a glimpse of the men who dye the cloth, bent to their task, arms and torsos stained deep blue.

By the time I leave the souk the sun's going down, and so are my energies. Then I remember that I have to find Yves Saint Laurent.

Yves, as I like to call him, lives in and owns the Majorelle Garden, a botanical garden in the New Town, and Adolpho de Velasco lives in a house surrounded by tall trees just over the wall from the great man. Adolpho is more than a neighbour; he is one of Yves' forty 'favourites', which, amongst other things, means being privileged to receive one of his specially painted Christmas cards. Adolpho has a set of them, all framed, of which he is very proud. He's proud too of how he has expanded his cottage by converting a loggia into a conservatory, with an open fire crackling at one end and the stout trunk of a false pepper tree rearing up and through the roof as if an elephant's foot had just come through the building.

Immaculate in a gold-trimmed *djellaba* and stroking a very large citrine medallion around his neck, Adolpho smokes imperiously, talks flamboyantly and orders his servant to replenish my glass of pink champagne with such frequency that almost every sentence of my interview ends with the words 'don't mind if I do'.

ABOVE

*Keeping moving in
the souk at
Marrakesh. Not an
easy thing to do, as
tea and carpets are
always on offer to
slow you down.
Allow at least a week
to see everything.*

Adolpho is a hot-blooded, passionate Mediterranean of the sort our fathers warned us about. He does not like things, he loves things. Himself, Morocco, his neighbour, emeralds, whatever. In fact, the only thing he doesn't love appears to be tourists from Birmingham, one of whom had complained of having her bottom pinched while walking in the souk. Adolpho was indignant.

'"What she look like?" I ask my friend. "Well, she was like this, she was like that."

'I say, "Bill, was she ugly?" "Yes," he say. "Yes. Very." I say how lucky girl she was. Never in England, in Birmingham, will ever, ever, her bottom be pinched.'

His eyes swell with pride for his adopted land.

'Lucky country. Lucky country.'

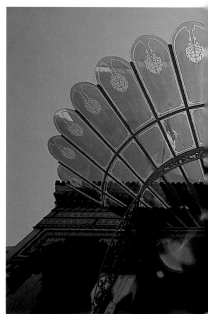

DAY ELEVEN MARRAKESH

I meet Amina Agueznay at a scrubby patch of wasteground outside the city walls, where taxis, donkeys and minibuses have worn the grass bare as they come and go touting for business. Names of destinations are shouted out and horns blasted to announce the imminent departure of buses, which everyone knows will not leave according to any timetable but only when they're full to bursting.

Amina is very much a modern Moroccan, a jewellery designer in her mid-thirties, unmarried and independent. She's short, bespectacled, articulate and possessed of an attractive self-confidence. She has lived and worked in New York and her English accent is more Mafia than Moroccan.

When we met yesterday I put it to her that the Atlas Mountains, the world-renowned backdrop to Marrakesh, are a computer-generated image to fool the tourists, for strain my eyes as I have these past forty-eight hours, I have seen nothing more than a dim grey blur in the hazy skies to the south.

According to Amina, the mountains not only exist, but they're less than two hours away, and she will show me villages more breathtakingly beautiful than anything else I've seen in Morocco.

She picks her way coolly through this frenzied transport market until she finds a *grand taxi*, an old Mercedes of the sort I remember in Munich in the 1970s, which she judges to be safe and sound. As we make to get in, an old man deftly intercepts us and stretches out a hand for some money. Amina gives him a coin. Very important, she says. Moroccans are very superstitious, especially about journeys, and a coin to a beggar will help ward off the evil eye.

We head south, passing low, flat-roofed houses with rough-textured, dried-mud walls. Storks circle above them, carrying food to nests high on chimneys or tall trees.

BELOW LEFT
The grand portals of the Mamounia Hotel.

BELOW *Haggling for a pair of backless slippers they call 'babouches'. The sign of quality is the number of stitches round each one. The yellow pair had 350 on each slipper. Not my colour, but I bought them all the same.*

Our taxi driver has perfected a technique of roaring up to the vehicle in front, hugging its slipstream, but not overtaking until he can clearly see an oncoming vehicle.

Around 30 miles from Marrakesh we stop, to my relief, at a large village called Asni. Outside the cafés, tagines simmer on charcoal braziers, salesmen offer us an assortment of knives, rings, fossils and crystalline rocks, and Berber women, wearing long green cloaks and white headscarves with lacy fringes, pass by with loads of undergrowth on their backs.

I learn from Amina that the Berbers (the word comes from the Greek for barbarians) were the original inhabitants of Morocco. Some say they came from the Caucasus Mountains but no-one disagrees that they moved into Morocco long before the Arabs. Ibn Khaldun, the great fourteenth-century chronicler of Arab history wrote of the Berbers: 'the men who belong to these family of peoples have inhabited the Maghreb since the beginning'. The Arab word Maghreb means 'the lands of the west' or 'the lands of the setting sun'.

Public transport in the High Atlas.

BELOW

The local truck is the only way to reach the highest Berber villages.

BELOW RIGHT

The air gets cooler and fresher as we leave Imbil far below.

Despite the fact that Berber speakers make up 40 per cent of all Moroccans, they have been traditionally repressed by their Arab conquerors and largely confined to rural mountain areas like the High Atlas. Amina says that things are different now. There are Berbers in the cities. They're hard-working, ambitious and creative. She seems uncomfortable with direct questions about Arab-Berber relations. Maybe it's because Morocco is anxious to avoid any equivalent of the recent violent protests by Algeria's Berbers over the suppression of their culture. Maybe it's because Amina, it transpires, is a Berber herself, from the south on her mother's side and from the Rif Mountains on her father's side.

Beyond Asni the road rises so steeply that we have to exchange our Mercedes for a pick-up truck, squeezed in the back with a group of villagers.

The road coils along a gorge beside a riverbed, bone-dry today but bearing the scars of fierce torrents of the past. In two places the concrete highway has collapsed and been washed away, and they have been waiting since 1975 to have it repaired. We

pass a precipitous village called Imbil, which sells postcards and has a government centre for hikers. From here a dirt track climbs steeply through a landscape of dry stone-walled terraces, which support sturdy vegetable plots and cherry orchards. The air cools and bubbling streams race down the mountain.

The dusty white hairpin bends are becoming so tight that the hard-worked pick-up, unable to make them in one, negotiates a series of death-defying three-point turns, leaving us at times backed up to the very edge of a precipice, with only a handbrake between us and a 1000-foot drop.

At last we pull up onto a flat saddle of land offering temporary relief and a breathtaking view down the valley. To the south, a dizzy succession of interlocking spurs, and to the north, a spread of horizontal terraces and rooftops. This is the village of Aremd, 8000 feet high, overlooked by jagged raking ridges and wedged in a fold of the mountains, with this narrow, gravelled track as its only lifeline.

The silence of the mountains amplifies any sound that breaks it. The cracking of a twig for a fire, a dog's bark, a child's shout identify the village long before we reach it. A picnic is laid for us on carpets and cushions set on a terrace shaded by walnut trees. After washing our hands in water from a silver salver, a meal of couscous and tagine, the name of the food and also the conical earthenware pot it comes in, is served, with Amina and myself as guests of honour. This brings its own problems. There are no knives, forks or spoons and I have to learn to eat Berber-style, using my right hand only – the left being traditionally reserved for ablutions. This is not without its own very strict etiquette. One does not stick ones hand in and pick out what one wants. Oh dear me, no. One uses one's thumb and two fingers, the thumb squeezing the food into a ball solid enough to dip carefully into the sauces and return to one's mouth. All this from ground level.

I find it hard enough even to reach the rice without swaying most ungracefully off balance, and the rolling of it into a ball using only three digits is a damn sight harder than it sounds. Especially as the rice is hot.

Mercifully, a small band starts up, creating a diversion and enabling me to use an extra digit to grab some of the wonderfully tender chunks of lamb soaked in the juice of olives.

Oranges, mint tea and a rosewater finger bowl are brought round and our *déjeuner sur l'herbe* continues with the performance of a courtship dance. Men and

women form up in two lines facing each other. The men, all in white *djellabas*, chant, yodel and beat out a rhythm with hand-held drums, whilst the women clap their hands and respond with their own chant. One from each side dances in the middle. The man struts and shakes his shoulders in passable imitation of an animal ruffling its feathers and scratching the ground. The dancers never touch each other, yet it's performed with a flash of the eyes and a boldness of movement that makes it highly charged. Something chaste and wild at the same time.

DAY TWELVE   MARRAKESH TO OUARZAZATE

Marrakesh bus station, romantically known as the Gare de Voyageurs, is not the sort of place to arrive at the last minute.

The details on the departures board are predominantly in Arabic, and in the busy central hall mine is one of the few heads moving from left to right as I try to decipher the scant French translation.

The depot is modern, concrete and functional, and beside the '*Horaires de Départ*' a large portrait of the old king, Hassan II, looks down on the confusion from a veneered wooden frame. The king is the supreme civil and religious leader of his country, and remembering Amina's words yesterday about the superstition attached to any journey, I suppose it is reassuring to have the Commander of the Faithful gazing down on you as you look for the right destination, even if he has been dead for two years.

I must have forgotten to add '*Inshallah*' (God willing) when I bought my ticket, for once through the gate, I narrowly avoid being mown down by two departing coaches before I locate the Express Nahda service for Ouarzazate, Zagora and the south.

The last few seats fill up in an atmosphere of increasing anxiety amongst the squad of young men who appear to run the bus company. Lists are checked, cross-checked and checked again, with deepening frowns.

Eventually, with a valedictory fart of thick black smoke, our elderly Daf pulls out of the yard and begins a slow crawl round the outskirts of Marrakesh in heavy morning traffic.

At one stop I watch a man in a *djellaba* and straw hat scraping up donkey droppings from the middle of the road with two boards. I can't work out if he's from the council or just an opportunist. When I was growing up in Sheffield the police horses used to pass our house on some sort of exercise, and if any dung was left behind I had to watch in profound embarrassment as my father and our next door neighbour, both keen rose-growers, raced out with shovels and fought over it.

When we're finally clear of the city the driver shoves a dusty cassette into a slot on the dashboard and the bus fills with the sound of chanting. It's a tape of the Koran, played to invoke Allah's protection on our journey and recited, I'm told, by an Egyptian who is considered such a star that he intones the Holy Book at Mecca itself.

The driver seems a placid, reliable sort, rarely using his horn in anger and seemingly undistracted by a plastic vine which trails up one side of the windscreen, dangling its faded black grapes over a photograph of a woman, veiled in white, hands raised in devotional gesture, which is stuck on the windscreen above his head.

The mountains begin to close in, and, as the driver hauls the coach round a dizzying succession of hairpins, the prevailing colour of the countryside changes from rufous maroon to brown and grey. Convoys of four-wheel drive vehicles, carrying their affluent tourist cargoes towards the Desert Experience, hover impatiently behind us.

Some four hours after leaving Marrakesh the coach pulls in to the small, noisy town of Tademt, the last truck stop before the Tichka pass. The smoky aroma of fresh-grilled kebabs is irresistible, though obtaining one isn't quite so simple. Helpful locals point me to a roadside butcher, from whom I buy the meat, before taking it over to the fire, where I pay again to have it cooked. As I tuck into it, a truck, on its way down

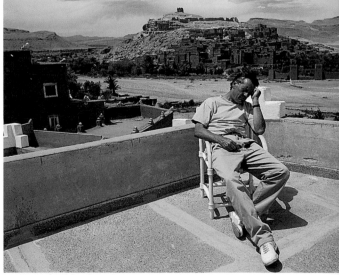

from the pass, air brakes hissing, comes to rest opposite me. It carries a load of cattle and one little old man, gripping the sides and peering impassively from a long line of bovine backsides.

After Tademt it isn't long before we run clear of the last agricultural terraces and climb slowly and steadily upwards between bare, fractured rock until we reach a plateau covered in short spongy grass and pools of standing water, where a few sheep graze. This is harsh inhospitable land, watershed country, whose melting snows feed rivers that will run either north to the plains of Marrakesh or south to die out in the desert.

We're at the pass (*tizi* in Arabic) moments later. A bristle of communications masts and a sign, around which some European boys are draped for a photograph, announce that we are at the top of the Tizi n'Tichka, at 7500 feet, the highest pass over the Atlas Mountains.

An hour or so later, I leave the coach near the town of Aït Benhaddou. We're still on the flanks of the Atlas Mountains, but for the first time on the edge of real desert. The landscape reminds me of Arizona, flat-topped mesas turning red, gold and purple as the sunlight moves over them. Yet this small town we've come to, some 15 miles off the main road, is one of the most familiar on the planet. Anyone who has seen *Gladiator* will have seen it. Anyone who has seen *Lawrence of Arabia* or *Romancing the Stone* or *The Four Feathers* will have seen it.

Almost the only time I went to the cinema with both my parents was to see biblical epics. The last one I remember us enjoying was called *Sodom and Gomorrah*, which, with lines like 'Beware the Sodomite patrols', was perfect for a young adolescent about to go away to an all-male boarding school. Only today do I find out that the Sodom that so impressed me in Sheffield forty-five years ago is the village I'm in today.

Like so many settlements on the old trade routes south, Aït Benhaddou was fortified by the warlords who controlled the High Atlas, the most famous of whom was T'hami El Glaoui, who ran southern Morocco as his own fiefdom right up until independence from the French in 1956. A multitude of picturesque towers rises from a rocky bluff overlooking a wide dry riverbed, at the top of which are the prominent ruins of an *agadir*, a fortified granary, its bastions now so eroded by the rain they look like melted candles.

This was a wealthy town, renowned for the beauty of its women as well as the splendour of its buildings, and when the clear sunlight catches the elegant tapered towers with the richly decorated patterns on their upper walls and archways I can understand why the tourists, and the film-makers, keep coming back.

I enter past the recently demolished arena from *Gladiator* and up into the streets, tapping walls every now and then to make sure they're real. The hardened clay pathways are narrow and picturesque and eerily tidy. There are no motor vehicles and, it seems, very few residents. The only shops are selling souvenirs and gifts for tourists. Aït Benhaddou is a sort of Sleeping Beauty – pretty, well preserved and oddly sterile, waiting for the next movie to bring it back to life.

It is late in the afternoon, and as we near Ouarzazate the landscape is spectacular

in the declining sunshine. Rock faces twisted like muscles in spasm are scoured by a low sunlight that picks out every nuance of colour until they glow like smouldering coal.

And all at once I see my first mirage. It's an ancient and glittering citadel rearing up out of nowhere, part fortress, part palace. On closer inspection it proves to be the city of Jerusalem, and on even closer inspection it proves to be held up by scaffolding.

Shouts of 'Dino!' and the smell of fresh paint fill the desert air as an Italian construction crew go about their business putting the finishing touches to marble urns, copper braziers and plasterboard loggias.

'Jesus and Judas,' reads the windscreen sticker on one of their vans.

At the Berber Palace Hotel in Ouarzazate this evening a young Englishman introduces himself. He's an actor, playing John the Disciple in an ABC television version of the New Testament currently being shot in the Moroccan Jerusalem. A short curly haired American, naked save for a towel around his waist, passes through the lobby exclaiming loudly, 'Boy, that hammam has knocked me out! Wow!'

My friend calls him over.

'Michael, meet Jesus.'

ABOVE

Aït Benhaddou. Impressive and elegant towers below, thanks to Hollywood and UNESCO, but the negelected old fortification at the top of the hill is half reduced to ruin by rain and wind.

This is a historic moment, but all I'm worried about is that if he shakes hands his towel will fall off.

So we just say 'Hi!', and Jesus hurries away to change.

'There's a whole lot of us here,' says my friend. 'We're all disciples.'

Sure enough I notice them later in the restaurant, all with identical beards. At a table for twelve.

DAY THIRTEEN OUARZAZATE TO TINFOU

Ouarzazate recedes into the distance. A town of substance, a regional capital, a centre for the increasing trade in tourists who want the Desert Experience without having to go too far into the desert. It has an airport and some big hotels and a military garrison but not much else to hold us up.

The mountains are not quite done with us yet. We may have crossed the High and Middle Atlas but there's still the Anti-Atlas ahead of us. As the road climbs towards yet another pass the Land Rover coughs and splutters and we pull in to the side. Our driver opens the bonnet and releases a hissing cloud of steam. Like a priest wielding a censer, he scatters a couple of bottles of Sidi Mansour mineral water over the radiator and we set off again. A few miles later the knocking from the engine becomes so insistent that I wonder if there might not be someone trapped inside. Our driver tries manfully to ignore it, but you might as well ignore a broken leg, and reluctantly he brings us to another, and I suspect more permanent, halt.

As we're staring into the engine, two very sleek Toyotas, coming fast out of the desert, bowl down the hill towards us. Seeing our plight, the occupants stop, offer greetings in the Arab fashion, right hand lightly touching the heart, and a man in a cotton robe, face shrouded in a blue veil, comes across to us. His skin is dark and tight across his cheekbones. He appraises us with a fierce unblinking eye before reaching into his robes.

'I am a nomad. Here is my card.'

It's a kind offer, and reminds me of the Monty Python sketch of a cliff-side full of hermits, chatting, gossiping and offering to do each other's shopping.

Squeezed into one vehicle, we toil without further incident up to the pass, the unforgettably named named Tizi n'Tinififft, 5500 feet above sea level. To the north, east and west the crests of a half-dozen mountain ranges extend to the horizon. A gorge splits the earth and we follow the curving walls and rock-stacks of the canyon down toward the incongruous green ribbon of palm trees and cultivated land that marks the course of the River Drâa.

The Drâa was once one of the great rivers of North Africa, mentioned by Ptolemy as running from the Atlas Mountains to the Atlantic Ocean. As the desert has spread the river has shrivelled and, in this last hot decade, has disappeared into the sand without even reaching the sea.

Here, beyond the town of Agdz, the Drâa is fresh off the slopes and shows how barren desert can be transformed if there's water around. A carpet of palm trees extends for up to a mile across the valley floor, providing a livelihood for a string of towns and villages along its route. It is, in effect, one long oasis, with glimpses of silver-green water amongst the trees, and brightly coloured clothes drying on bushes, through which flocks of black goats pick their way. The valley provides the best dates in the world, so they say, and we stop to buy some from a boy of nine or ten who stands by the side of the road holding a basket in outstretched hand.

Within seconds a crowd of competitors, none older than fourteen or fifteen, engulfs me.

It seems fun, but the force with which they fight to get near me, the intense clamour for a sale and the almost studied indifference of my driver to these skinny jostling boys give me the feeling that this is as much about survival as free enterprise. Perhaps all is not as well as it looks in the picturesque villages of the Drâa valley.

It's early afternoon when we drive into Zagora through a horseshoe-arched gateway and down Avenue Mohamed V, which, with its arcades and long line of shaded shop-fronts, has the atmosphere of a Wild West frontier town. Children walking back from school hold exercise books up to their faces to keep the sun off.

There is a scuffed, crudely painted, concrete road sign here, a child's-eye view of desert sands, camels and gleaming-eyed Touareg grouped around a grubby arrow and the words '*Tombouctou 52 Jours*'. It's a reminder that Zagora is the largest town we shall see for another 1000 miles and that its tourist hotels and hard-topped roads may seem like rare luxuries in the days ahead.

After Zagora the palm groves thin out and the casbahs become fewer and farther between. The Drâa reduces to a trickle, then ceases to flow altogether. A fierce gusty wind springs up from nowhere, gathering the sand and dust into clouds that cover the sun and plunge this dazzling landscape into anonymous greyness.

Progress slows and we rest up for the night at Tinfou, 20 miles south of Zagora and a few miles short of the end of the road at Mhamid.

The Auberge du Repos de Sables has great character, if limited comforts. The building is a small casbah, complete with four clay-brick towers at its corners, at the top of one of which is my room. The *auberge* is family owned and run in very laid-back style by the El Faraj family, painters and potters whose work covers the walls. The rooms are small, whitewashed and simply furnished with bamboo and beam ceilings.

I open out my Michelin map, 'Africa North and West', until it covers most of the bed. I look at the route we've taken so far – blue sea, then red and white roads that have carried us across the green and brown of mountain and valley. From here on there is only one colour: golden yellow, stretching 1000 miles, south, east and west. The size of many Moroccos.

Except for the single word Sahara in bold black type, there is hardly any print across this emptiness apart from a number of faint blue inscriptions: '*Mejaouda, Peu d'Eau à 4m*', '*Hassi Tartrat, Potable*', '*Oglat Mohammed, Eau Bonne*'. I realise that not only is this the first map I've used which has sources of water specifically marked, but that their names are often hundreds of miles apart.

In the night a fierce wind bursts open the shutters behind my bed and I'm aware how much cooler I feel. By morning I'm reaching for a sweater.

DAY FOURTEEN TINFOU to TINDOUF

Wake at six as a muezzin's cry rends the stillness. Fortunately, I can control this one, as the voice comes from a pink alarm clock bought in the bazaar at Marrakesh. Click it off and lie there idly speculating whether any Muslims have ever been woken by the sound of the Bishop of Bath and Wells.

Examine the day. It looks perfect. Clear skies, translucent desert light. I climb down the ladder from my turreted refuge and take in the beauty of the morning. Just outside the main gate, three camels sway their heads towards me before resuming their chewing. I watch a couple of sparrows perching on swaying palm fronds and can't help noticing how chubby they are for birds on the edge of a desert. The road is empty, save for a slowly advancing figure on a moped.

The only shadow in this sub-Saharan Eden is a dry cough that I picked up yesterday.

A persistent, gritty, welcome-to-the-desert cough.

By the time we're packed and ready to go the wind has started to rise. The last Moroccan road quickly runs out and we're off piste, swerving and twisting as the drivers search out the hard surfaces. A screaming wind is scything sand off the dunes and hurling it across our windscreen. As we enter the Sahara, it's as if we're entering a storm at sea.

Beyond Mhamid the desert stretches away into Algeria, the second largest country in Africa. It is not best friends with neighbouring Morocco, and one of the reasons lies beside the solitary tarmac road that runs across this flat and rubble-strewn landscape. Above a walled compound on the outskirts of Tindouf, a flag slaps and cracks in the wind. The flag – a chevron, three horizontal bands and the moon and star of Islam –

belongs to none of the countries whose frontiers meet in this desolate spot. Not Algeria, Morocco nor Mauritania. It is the flag of the Saharawi Arab Democratic Republic, and you will scour the atlas in vain for its name, for officially it doesn't exist.

Inside the compound there is an almost cloistered hush. The wind has dropped and the stillness of the surrounding desert deadens noise like a fresh snowfall. In the middle of a quadrangle of sand and stones people are meeting and talking softly in the shade offered by an open-sided thatch-roofed shelter. Around the walls of the compound runs a single-storey block of rooms providing accommodation and other facilities. The writing on the walls provides a clue to the mystery of the Saharawis. '*Tienda*' above the shop, '*Comedores*' above the refectory. Another clue is in the faces of those talking. Over half are clearly not African. They're light-skinned, with chunky moustaches and round, earnest faces.

There's a WC prominently indicated, one of a row of privies in an ablution block. As I push open the door I'm hit by a sharp whiff of uric acid rising from the damp sides of a hole in the mud floor. We who are used to having our body waste disposed of instantly forget that in the desert flushing lavatories appear only in mirages.

Our host for the next few days is a short, wiry man of middling age, eyes creased and narrowed. With his hands sunk deep in the pockets of a thick quilted jacket and his body angled forward as if braced for the next sandstorm, everything about him suggests stoic defiance.

His name is Bachir Mehdi Bhaya and Algeria is not his home. He was born and brought up in the contentious territory of Western Sahara, a land of long coastline

BELOW

Southern Morocco. Bedouin tribesmen secure their camels in the teeth of a gale. Many now depend for their livelihood on the demand for camel safaris from increasingly adventurous tourists.

and hostile desert, larger than the United Kingdom, which once comprised the Spanish colonies of Río de Oro and Saguia el Hamra. When the Spanish abruptly left in 1975 taking everything including the bodies in their cemeteries, they offered what was left to Morocco and Mauritania.

The Polisario Front (Frente Popular para la Liberación de Saguia el Hamra y de Río de Oro), acting on behalf of the half million inhabitants, known as Saharawis, who wanted to be neither Mauritanian nor Moroccan, began a guerrilla offensive. They were encouraged by the judgement of an International Court of Justice, which upheld the right of the locals to self-determination and scored early guerrilla successes against the Mauritanians, who have now abandoned claims to Western Sahara. The Moroccans are less amenable. They regard Western Sahara as having pre-colonial ties with the rest of Morocco. Its acquisition would almost double the size of their country, and the exploitation of valuable phosphate deposits would be a huge boost to their economy. To this end they encouraged 350,000 settlers to move in to Western Sahara during the 1970s.

Rather than accept this 'invasion', almost half the Saharawis fled to Algeria, who offered them land on this bleak military exercise area to set up temporary camps.

But, as the saying goes, 'there is nothing more permanent than the temporary', and, twenty-five years later, this compound near Tindouf remains the first port of call for anyone wanting to do business with the Saharawis. This includes many NGOs from all over Europe, but predominantly Spain, which explains the sallow men with moon faces and chunky moustaches, drawn here by the old colonial connection.

They are anxious to offer what help they can until the United Nations, which has monitored a ceasefire between the Moroccans and the Polisario for ten years, can come up with some permanent solution to the problem.

Bachir, who has lived as a refugee for nearly half his life, is the personification of the embattled exile. He will not compromise. He and his people will not rest until things are done the way they want them done. I recognise the syndrome. It's like being a Yorkshireman. As it turns out he has spent time in Leeds and learnt his English there, so he takes this as a compliment.

'I like them,' he says, grinning.

'We're very stubborn,' I remind him.

He nods approvingly.

'I like stubborn people. I'm one of them. Even if I'm wrong, I'm right.'

He won't hear of us staying here with the other foreign visitors.

'You will all stay at my house,' he insists.

And I know there's no point in arguing.

BELOW

Saharawi women outside a weaving school. Women virtually run the camps. They cook, build, administrate and run the children, whilst many of the men are in the army.

ALGERIA

DAY FIFTEEN SMARA REFUGEE CAMP

ABOVE
*Night falls over
Smara Camp. Dust,
blown constantly
into the air, creates
this diffuse lemon-
yellow sunset.*

The extraordinary thing about Bachir's house is that we all fit in. How many of us would be able to accommodate seven extra people and forty-five pieces of luggage and equipment when you've already got a wife, four children and a constant influx of relatives? It's not as if his home is that much larger than any of the others in Smara. Exile means equality. Within its low, mud-brick walls are the standard small courtyard, kitchen, single squat toilet, two rooms and a tent.

The tents are of traditional design, with tall peaks and wide rectangular bases. According to Bachir, they are not only practical but also symbolic, a reminder to the Saharawis of their nomadic inheritance, and a reminder too that this cheerless landscape is only a temporary resting place on the journey back to their homeland.

The sun's up around eight. Two of us have slept in the tent and the other five, including myself, are squeezed into a room at the opposite end of the courtyard with the equipment strewn around us like the spoils of a pirate raid. Three of Bachir's children, including the two five-year-old twins, stand at the door, eyes wide, watching us folding up sleeping bags, cleaning teeth, combing hair, taking this, that and the other pill, and washing ourselves as best we can in small bowls of water, filled from the communal can.

Smara, a dozen miles into the desert from Tindouf, is, like the three other refugee camps, named after a town in Western Sahara. Though the camp has roughly the same population as the city of Winchester, it has neither mains water nor electricity. The communal water can for drinking, cooking, washing and sanitation is filled from metal cisterns half a mile away, which are in turn filled by old Volvo tankers, supplied by the UN, which shuttle between the camp and its nearest water source, an artesian well 16 miles away.

No-one in their right mind would choose to live in this sun-bleached, rubble-strewn wilderness, which makes the self-belief of the Saharawis seem all the more impressive. Despite the fact that they have few influential friends, 170,000 of them are content to remain in someone else's desert waiting for a breakthrough.

Bachir is proud of this solidarity, but aware too that it will not last for ever. He clutches at any straws to raise morale. The recent decision of the Spanish government to honour the pensions of those Saharawis who served in the Spanish army is seen as a major benefit, putting a little money into the pockets of those who have too often relied on UN hand-outs, and creating a small but growing private market in the camp.

We walk down the main street, where the shops are little more than makeshift stalls, fashioned from branches hung with whatever coverings can be found. This results in some bizarre combinations: a shack entirely covered by an ancient German wall map of South East Asia, another dominated by a poster of a Cuban beach resort. Out front are small amounts of oranges and onions, car tyres, clothes, a few plastic buckets. A butcher's shop has a dismembered camel carcass on the floor and, outside, on the ground in front of the shop, is its head, complete and looking strangely serene.

BELOW LEFT
Cosmopolitan future for the Saharawis. Metou, the partly Welsh-educated woman who showed me round the camp, sporting her traditional melepha *and less traditional jeans and Doc Martens.*

BELOW
Abstract patterns are important, as Islam discourages figurative art. Here just a glimpse on a melepha *and tent covering behind.*

This evening, as a fat full moon rises over the camp, Bachir's wife Krikiba produces a meal for all of us and her family, cooked, as far as I can see, on one primus stove on the mud floor of a tiny kitchen.

We slip our shoes off and enter the tent. A white strip light, powered by electricity from a solar panel, casts a harsh glare. There are no chairs, and, unable to lounge and eat with nomadic nimbleness, we contort ourselves awkwardly on the mats, carpets and cushions, providing a continuing source of entertainment for family, relatives and

ABOVE
(LEFT) *Bachir,*
Krikiba
and the children.
(CENTRE LEFT)
Outside the room
we shared.
(CENTRE RIGHT) *All*
building materials
welcome. I find
myself leaning on
the Far East at one
of the shops that
have recently sprung
up in Smara.
(RIGHT) *In the school*
playground.
Hamstring fully
recovered.

neighbours as we tuck into camel casserole and rice. This is the first time I've knowingly eaten camel. The meat has a slightly sweet flavour, more like mutton than beef, and I can't stop myself wondering if any of this was ever attached to the head I saw in the market, with its inscrutable Mona Lisa smile.

DAY SIXTEEN SMARA CAMP

The children are getting bolder now, especially Sidi, the more hyperactive of the five-year-old twins. In between fetching water and preparing breakfast, Bachir tries to call him to order, but the lure of thirty pieces of film equipment is too much and he spends most of his time in our room shrieking with excitement at each new discovery.

Though I hear the muezzin's call in the morning, religion does not seem a big issue here. Education and political discipline are more important. Bachir and Krikiba's children are educated at the primary school nearby, after which they will go to one of the two big boarding schools that serve the camps. The literacy rate amongst the Saharawis is now 90 per cent, far higher than in Morocco or Algeria. The Hispanic connection is strong and many of the teachers are from Cuba. Some of the brighter pupils go over there to complete their education.

Bachir introduces me to a young woman called Metou. She is in her early twenties, was born in the camps and has never seen her homeland. She's bright, well educated, lively and attractive, a modern girl. She wears a light, but all-encompassing, purple sari called a *melepha,* which doesn't attempt to hide the imitation leather jacket, jeans and Doc Marten boots beneath. Metou is a cosmopolitan Saharawi. She has travelled in Europe, speaks fluent Spanish, French and English and spent time at university in Wales. Beneath the blazing Saharan sun we discuss the knotty problem of getting from Machynlleth to Aberystwyth by public transport.

She takes me to a workshop in a collection of mud buildings called the 27th February Village, which cumbersome title commemorates the day on which the landless Saharawi Democratic Republic was founded, in 1976.

Thirty women are weaving brightly patterned rugs and carpets on the simplest of hand-looms. The carpets are made of thick, coarse sheep's wool, in bright, strong colours and improvised designs, and I'd buy a couple if we weren't on our way to Timbuktu.

The women run the camps, says Metou. They cook, build, administrate and raise the children. The young men leave at eighteen for military training.

I ask her if keeping a conscripted army isn't just a romantic gesture, bearing in mind there has been no fighting for years. Her response is quick and unapologetic.

'My people are tired of being ignored. If force has to be used to gain our birthright of independence, then that's the way it must be.'

Smara camp is so well run that it really doesn't resemble a camp at all. As I look out from a low hill, which is now the cemetery, the pale brown mud houses blending in with the desert around them could have been there for ever. The considerable size of the cemetery, a scattering of rocks and boulders just outside the town, suggests that life expectancy is low. Bachir shakes his head vigorously.

'It is seventy, eighty years.'

Sanitation is basic, he concedes, but the air is dry and there have been no epidemics here.

He smiles at my nannyish concern. 'People don't die in the desert, you know.'

In that case, the size of the cemetery merely emphasises how long the Saharawis have been away from home.

That night in the camp we tuck into camel kebab and pasta cooked with carrots and turnips, served, as ever, with tea. Tea is central to the nomadic life. In a land where alcohol is forbidden and most bottled drinks are beyond people's means, it offers welcome, gives comfort, stimulates conversation and provides a focus for social intercourse. Being a rare indulgence in a land of extreme scarcity, its preparation is taken very seriously. The water we splash on our faces in the morning is not good enough for the tea.

'Too salty,' says Bachir. 'The best water for tea comes from 50 miles away.'

Water this prized should not be heated on a gas ring, but on a brazier with charcoal from acacia wood, which heats the water more slowly and provides better flavour. Once heated, the tea is poured from one vessel to another before being tipped into small glass tumblers from ever-increasing height. Then it's tipped from tumbler to tumbler, until the required alchemy is deemed to have taken place, whereupon it is poured with one last grand flourish that leaves a foaming head on each individual glass. These are offered around on a tray and drunk swiftly. Then the glasses are washed and a second serving is prepared, tasting delicately different as the sharpness of leaf and sweetness of sugar continue to blend. The process is repeated a third time and that's it. I'm told that if you're offered a fourth glass it's a polite way of saying you've overstayed your welcome.

Tonight Bachir's brother-in-law and two other men are sat around the brazier taking tea with us. Their eyes sparkle and their faces crease easily into laughter. It seems a good time to ask Bachir about the future for the Polisario.

He plays down the military solution.

'We still have many friends,' he argues, reminding me that only a year ago the UN Secretary General, Kofi Annan, and US Secretary of State, James Baker, had been staying in this same camp. The Moroccans might be supported by other Arab monarchies, like Saudi Arabia and Jordan, but the Polisario have powerful European allies, especially the Spanish, their old colonial masters, who now seem to be falling over themselves to help. Assuaging guilt? Annoying the French? Whatever the reason, Bachir is a grateful man.

'Five...six thousand Saharawi children go to stay with Spanish families every summer, and the families come back to see us.' His eyes shine in the lamplight. 'Two thousand came last year to the camps – doctors, nurses, teachers.'

He pauses as if aware I'm not convinced.

'We are small, but sometimes the small guys win. Look at Kuwait...'

But he and I both know that the Saharawis are, in world terms, much smaller small guys than the oil-rich monarchies of the Gulf.

DAY SEVENTEEN SMARA CAMP

ABOVE

Sweet tea is the national drink of the Sahara. Everything stops for its preparation, which must never be hurried.

My request for a bin for the rubbish rapidly accumulating in our cramped quarters is met with a blank stare. Rubbish is a Western concept. What I wanted to throw away – paper, a spent packet of film, a mineral-water bottle – certainly wasn't rubbish to them, and as Krikiba and the children riffled through my pile of rejects, I felt embarrassingly over-stocked. What we see as basic necessities they see as complicated over-indulgences. Take toothpaste, for instance. Sidi and Khalia, the terrible twins, are fascinated by our teeth-cleaning rituals. Not just that we prefer to foam at the mouth rather than use acacia sticks like everyone else, but that once we've foamed we seem to have such trouble getting rid of it. At first light the streets of Smara are dotted with frothing Westerners looking for somewhere to spit out and little heads peering out of doorways to observe this quaint ritual.

Nor is toothpaste the only problem. There's a toilet paper crisis looming. All of us, family and crew, evacuate into the same hole in the ground. It's situated in a mud enclosure in the corner of the yard and is about the size and shape of a small slice of Hovis. There is a plastic jug of water beside it, which is considered sufficient for washing and cleaning. Those of us brought up to regard toilet paper as one of the essentials of civilised society are rapidly bunging up this delicate system and waste levels are rising alarmingly. There are reports that Krikiba has been seen coming out of the hut with a rubber glove on up to her elbow. I'm sure it's as well for everybody that we are moving on tomorrow.

DAY EIGHTEEN   SMARA CAMP TO TFARITI

The wind is rising. As it gusts it hisses against the tent and there's a grittier than usual texture to the freshly baked bread this morning. We've eaten most of the camel by now, but it appears at breakfast today in one last manifestation. Along with the usual offering of tea, coffee, bread and oranges is a dish of beans and diced camel liver. Out of a confusion of politeness, greed and a misplaced desire to experience all life has to offer, I pop a couple of cubes into my mouth. I know immediately that this is a mistake. The liver has a high, slightly gamey piquancy. But it's too late. One has already gone before I can retrieve it. I put up my hand to palm the other, only to meet Krikiba's eye. She beams at me expectantly. What can I do but grin and swallow.

In bright sun, sharp shadow and a cold wind the drivers Bachir has organised to take us several hundred miles down the West Saharan borderlands to the Mauritanian frontier are loading up. Our overnight bags are being squeezed into any available space left around the 200-litre fuel drums, which weigh down two small pick-up trucks. Ourselves and the rest of the baggage, as well as a cook, food and cooking materials, are divided between three four-wheel drive vehicles, which stand as tall as the house we're about to leave.

The children are going to miss us. We've been like a travelling funfair for them, and the extended family presses things upon us at the last moment, including a cassette of Saharawi music and a near-impregnable can of Spanish ham, which none of them is allowed to eat. As a parting gesture, eighteen-year-old Hadi, Bachir's pretty, coy niece, introduces me to her boyfriend. He's a young soldier and doesn't smile. The long-suffering Krikiba is persuaded into a hug and even, for Vanessa, a kiss.

Finally, away we go, up the hill from the house, sliding and swerving on the fine sand until we have a grip on the stony rubble at the top.

My last images of Smara camp are the small plots on the edge of town, fenced with anything from rice sacks to beaten-out oil cans, where people keep their livestock – goats, sheep, even camels. Two young girls are dragging a length of chicken wire across the sand to build another enclosure. That life goes on like this in these most straitened of circumstances is extraordinary. Smara is becoming less like a camp and more like a proper town every day. For everyone under twenty-five this is their only home. And that's not good news for the Polisario.

All morning we rumble across the *hammada,* stony, gravel-strewn desert, which appears featureless and forbidding, but is constantly changing. At one moment we'll be on the flat, at another cutting down a ravine or passing a small hill, both of which seem to come from out of nowhere. A scattering of acacia trees suddenly evaporates, leaving no cover at all. At moments like this, when there is no single piece of shade as far as the eye can see, the desert becomes quite frightening, and our vehicles seem small and pathetically vulnerable. It's like being on a rowing boat in the middle of the ocean.

Fifty-five miles later we stop at a Polisario checkpoint. A rough barrier made from lengths of piping, a few outbuildings, goats sheltering beneath the skeleton of a jacked-

ABOVE

In Western Sahara.

(LEFT) *Camel stew*
with the drivers.

(CENTRE)
Tyremarks on the
surface of a typical
reg, the flat gravel
or coarse sand
plains which are a
driver's delight.

(RIGHT) *Looking*
across to a section
of the 1000-mile
Moroccan wall,
and the minefield
in between.

up, wheel-less lorry. A couple of Toyota pick-up trucks stand side by side with a couple of anti-aircraft guns in the back. The Saharawi army, Bachir points out.

The only exception to the general air of lethargy is the presence of a single swallow, darting and swooping above us.

I assume this is the border between Algeria and Western Sahara, but no-one seems quite sure. Bachir, squinting into the wind and dust, says we must move on, we've many hours driving still ahead. Najim, who's driving me and Basil, has wandered off and ambles back as the engines are being re-started, bringing wild dates for everybody, straight off the tree.

There is no surfaced road of any kind, but we follow the piste, as they call it, and every now and then pass a black tyre half sunk into the sand. The sight of these markers, sometimes at 5- or 10-mile intervals, becomes immensely reassuring.

At least someone has been here before us.

For a while, the terrain turns viciously stony, as if all the sand cover had been sifted through, leaving only this underlay of sharp grey points, jabbing at our tyres and sabotaging our progress. Ironically, it's on a much less hostile surface of soft white shells that we have our first puncture. Bachir kneels, scrabbles in the dust and picks out a handful of stones. He straightens up.

'Look, you see. Shells, little fish. This was all sea bed once.'

The desert as ocean again.

A half-hour later we're hurtling across a hard-baked gritty plain, flat as an ironing board, with nary a bush or a boulder breaking the surface as far as the eye can see. The drivers can at last put their feet down, and we fly across the desert, each vehicle swathed in its own dust, a string of small clouds chasing each other.

It's well into the afternoon before we find anywhere suitable to stop for lunch. A scattering of smoothly rounded boulders offers shade and there are a few dry and whitened trees for fire wood. As the drivers gather wood, the cook, a middle-aged man with a broad, guileless face, thick moustache and greying hair, walks a little way off and falls to his knees in prayer. He picks up a handful of dust and rubs it up and down his forearms and on his brow, mimicking, I suppose, the act of purification in a waterless world.

The meal is, surprise, surprise, camel stew, cooked in a pot over the fire, and accompanied by good sticky rice and washed down with Coca-Cola, our main treat in this world without alcohol and wistfully referred to as Coke du Rhône. Now we are indisputably in Western Sahara, Bachir is a changed man. He looks around at the rocks and the desiccated trees with proprietorial satisfaction.

'Ours is the best desert!'

I laugh. But he doesn't.

'It is known to be the greenest, Michael.'

Greenest? I look around at the tawny undergrowth. This is chauvinism gone mad.

'All the great desert poets come from this part of Western Sahara.'

A woman laden down with possessions appears amongst the rocks, going apparently from nowhere to nowhere. When she comes closer the drivers shout a greeting. She nods amiably, comes over for a chat and carries on. It's certainly a friendly desert.

Hours later, the vehicles have stopped again. The sun has set and the horizon is a sand-stained yellowish rim. Our drivers have got out and are kneeling in a line in this desolate place, bowing to Mecca. Bachir, hands sunk deep in coat pockets, looks out ahead. He doesn't join them.

'I am not devout,' he says matter-of-factly.

An hour later, more mundane thoughts. Where are we going to eat and where are we going to sleep? We've been on the road twelve hours and Bachir has stopped the vehicles and is consulting with his driver. No-one appears to have a map, but there's much pointing into the darkness.

Then we're all urged to get in again. They've missed a turning.

Half an hour further on and out of the pitch blackness appears the outline of a long, low, grimly unwelcoming building on the crest of a hill. Built by the Spanish military, this decommissioned barracks is to be our home for the night. We're billeted in two rooms with seriously dodgy wiring. Turning the light off involves physically pulling apart two wires to deactivate the current. No-one dares turn it on again.

The cook is the only one who seems unconditionally happy to be here. With a real kitchen to work in, he sets to work on a vegetable stew, with just a little camel in it.

WESTERN SAHARA

Revenge of the camel. Plucked from deepest sleep, I just have time to stumble up from my mattress, grab torch and toilet paper, pull open the jarring metal door of our dormitory and race to the nearest lavatory. A strong wind has got up and I'm aware of how Gothic a scene this must be – white T-shirted figure with disordered shock of hair, sprinting along concrete passageways open to the sky, as the wind howls after him, setting doors and windows banging.

I know things are bad as I have to do this twice more, on each occasion reaching the hole in the ground only just in time and holding my breath against the stench emanating from it.

Five o'clock. Woken by the chimes of a grandfather clock. For a moment I believe myself to be safe and well in some ivy-covered country-house hotel, and then I remember that the sound is coming from John Pritchard's alarm clock and I'm actually recovering from diarrhoea in a barracks in Western Sahara.

Roger and Bachir try to cajole the reluctant, slumbering drivers into a six o'clock start, but they won't move until they've lit a fire and brewed some tea. It's nearer seven when we bounce and sway off down the hill, heading north and east for a privileged glimpse of the front line between Moroccans and Saharawis, one of the world's best-kept secrets.

In 1982, in an attempt to consolidate their military superiority over the Polisario, the Moroccan government began work on a system of fortifications stretching for over 1000 miles along the edge of occupied Western Sahara.

This mighty Moroccan wall, longer than the Great Wall Of China, reportedly costs $2 million a day to maintain. As we brake, turn, twist and sway for mile after mile across a carpet of fractured stone slabs I should be feeling intrepid and privileged, but to someone suffering from camel poisoning the ride is slow torture. By gulping mouthfuls of air and staring fixedly at the horizon, I manage to hold out for three hours before the desire to shed last night's stew becomes uncontrollable and I have to ask Najim to pull up.

I retch violently, spewing potatoes and carrots on the desert floor (probably the most moisture to have fallen in that spot for years). When it's over I feel a soothing hand on my brow. It's Khalihena, tall, grave, the oldest and quietest of the drivers, who gazes down at me with wise concern through a pair of thick tortoiseshell-rimmed glasses. He holds out a bottle of water and motions me to wash my face.

I feel too ill to be embarrassed, and ridiculously touched that he should be the one to take care of me like this.

Though the Moroccans and the Polisario have observed a ceasefire for the last eleven years, they have not become friends, and as both sides have troops in positions near to the wall, we have to approach with the utmost caution, accompanied now by two armed pick-up trucks. Then it's a scramble up a slope dazzlingly rich in fossilised fish, plants and other evidence of the old once-fertile Sahara. From a ridge at the top

we look down over a mile-wide no-man's-land that separates the two sides. There's no question of going any further, as the Moroccans have mined the border.

I realise that this wall, an abomination to the Polisario, keeping them, as it does, from their own land, also defines them and inspires them and, in their eyes, legitimises their struggle. There can be no question of a contest between equals. The Polisario army numbers around 20,000 men, but despite the ceasefire it's kept in readiness. To see them at work we are driven from the wall to the HQ of the Second Army District, in a cleverly camouflaged position protected by monumental rocks, strangely weathered and smoothed, like a hillside of Henry Moores.

In the lee of these boulders are mud-brick huts, with corrugated metal roofs, and the occasional Russian-built tank pulled in close for safety. On a parade ground, marked by small stones laid out in neat rows and painted white, the flag of the Saharawi Arab Democratic Republic flutters above three more tanks and four pick-ups fitted with anti-aircraft guns. A massive curved rock, resembling the head of a whale, juts out on a rise overlooking the parade ground, and beneath it a narrow

ABOVE

The whale-nose rock that houses one of the Polisario's military headquarters. One of their second-hand Russian tanks charges about on manoeuvres.

71

entrance leads into the belly of the whale, a deep cave lined with carpets and cushions which is the nerve centre of this particular army post.

I'm still in the grip of whatever microbe is ravaging my system, so I retreat to the coolest corner of the cave and sit out a lunch of salad, goat and oranges, thinking of the only two things that appeal in these circumstances, sleep and death.

Unfortunately, neither is an option, as the commander of the Second Army District has made himself available for interview. He's a man of dignified composure and stern, hawk-like eye, who gives nothing much away. How does he keep up morale when there has been no war to fight for thirteen years? No problem, he claims. They are all committed to the struggle for free expression for the Saharawi people. And they have sophisticated weaponry. When I press him for more details this seems to mean the ageing tanks from Eastern Europe and the fortified Toyota pick-ups drawn up below.

Later, he and I walk out to inspect the troops. They are a ragged band, small in number, an assortment of ages wearing an assortment of uniforms. One has green espadrilles instead of army boots. Unless the Polisario is hiding some crack force from us, their military potential, even for guerrilla fighting, seems negligible.

The heat rises and my system continues to reject whatever is in there that it doesn't like. Once outside the cave, there is no escape or comfort. The skies are cloudless. The heat and the constant dusty wind scour my skin and turn my throat to sandpaper. There is no toilet but the desert, and as I crouch behind boulders feeling utterly miserable I am filled with desperate admiration for the soldiers who have endured conditions like these for years and a formless anger at those who make it necessary for them to do it.

It's a two-hour drive back to the barracks in Tfariti. I have to ask them to stop once again but this time I'm bent double with nothing to show for it. Everyone else turns their back, but Khalihena comes over to me once again, pours me some water, motions to his mouth and repeats in his soft French, '*Mange, mange*'.

When I get back to the barracks, I take his advice, and thanks to a combination of Pepto Bismol, acupressure recommended by Basil and fresh bread and cheese, I steady the system and fall into a long deep sleep.

DAY TWENTY   TFARITI TO MEJIK

Though in my memory the fort on the hill will always be a sick room, I leave Tfariti with the optimism that always attends a departure and the prospect of a new destination.

BELOW

Inspecting Polisario troops near the wall. Their problem is partly lack of equipment, partly motivation after an eleven-year ceasefire. The flag of the Saharawi Arab Democratic Republic flies at the right.

Bachir aims to travel another 200 miles to the southwest, setting up camp for the night before moving on tomorrow to the rendezvous with our Mauritanian team at a place called Mejik.

Through the cracked glass of our windscreen we can see the relatively green landscape around Tfariti revert rapidly to stony desert. Despite the lack of cover, there always seems to be something out there, a solitary tree, a trotting herd of wild donkeys, even a skeletally thin dog that sniffs at us as we go by. And always the wind, sweeping across, sifting the sand, smoothing the rocks, leaching the rough ground and exposing the fossilised remains of a previous, very different Sahara, which, as recently as 10,000 years ago, was a grassland full of wild animals.

We stop for lunch in the shade and cover of a fallen acacia tree. Bachir rubs some resin off the bark and tells me to taste it. A sharp, cleansing, minty freshness.

'Arabic gum. Very good for all kinds of intoxication.'

I know the name well. Over the centuries, fortunes have been made from gum arabic, and it's still high on any list of West African exports. A preservative for food, it's also used for pharmaceuticals and making inks. It's rather satisfying to find something so precious in the wood the chef is gathering to make our fire.

The fire is started by rubbing twigs together, then larger branches are laid on. Mohammed Salim, one of the drivers, face old and weathered, cheekbones cantilevered out, skin pulled tight as a drum, is sifting through the sand for camel droppings. So good is the camel at absorbing and re-using what it eats that these come out as small, regular-sized, dark brown pellets, referred to by the experts as nuggets. Quickly hardened by the sun, they make ideal pieces for a board game. Mohammed marks out a grid of squares in the sand and lays the pellets out like draughts. Najim, who he's challenged to a game, breaks twigs to use as his men. So the game of *dhaemon*, a sort of desert draughts, begins. As it warms up, Mohammed Salim becomes more and more excited, emitting a string of cries, shrieks, theatrical screams, imprecations and histrionic submissions to Allah, occasionally catching our eye and cracking a conspiratorial smile. Najim plays the straight man, not that he has much option, and wins the game.

Lunch is far behind us when, amongst swirling dust, tussocky grass and severely decreasing visibility, Bachir brings his lead vehicle to a halt and consults, rather anxiously, with Haboub, the most dashing of the drivers. There's much kneeling and peering off into the soupy dust clouds. Are we lost? Bachir's reply, intended to be reassuring, rapidly becomes one of our favourite sayings, to be used often in times of deep crisis.

'No we are not lost. We just cannot find the place.'

He suggests that we drive on after dark and try to reach Mejik. No-one complains, but there is an unspoken anxiety amongst us. Given the combination of dust clouds, pitch darkness and lack of any identifiable road or track, how good is our chance of finding Mejik?

Haboub shrugs, flashes a big white-toothed grin, flicks open a leather pouch and fills his pipe.

We reach Mejik a little before nine. Though there is a well-lit UN compound

ABOVE LEFT
*Recording fond
farewells to Bachir
at Mejik, near the
Mauritanian border.*

ABOVE
*The team that
brought us safely
through our first test
in tough desert
travel. Mohammed
Salim is on my right,
and next to him
is the gentle
Khalihena, who
looked after me at
my lowest ebb.*

nearby, we are booked once again into a barracks, set in a crumbling concrete-walled enclosure. Someone has at least made a stab at brightening up the place. The narrow, unroofed strip of passageway outside our rooms has been laid with crazy paving, and along it runs a dried-up garden bed decorated with Russian shell-cases. The accommodation, consisting of two large unfurnished dormitories, a lavatory and washroom, is much the same as at Tfariti, except that, instead of a plastic jug, this lavatory has a luxury attachment, a flush.

I pull it. Nothing happens.

DAY TWENTY-ONE   MEJIK to ZOUERAT

Slept soundly and am now packing to make ready for the crossing into Mauritania.

The border is only 15 miles away. Bachir says that we will be the first foreigners ever to cross it at this point, after negotiations made possible because of the currently cordial relations between Mauritania and the Polisario.

Over a last meal of bread and coffee he expands on this.

'We have nothing in common with the Moroccans. We have everything in common with the Mauritanians – culture, language, songs, dance.'

The UN mission here, frustrated by both sides in its attempt to organise a referendum on the future of Western Sahara, has run up costs of $250 million and may well lose patience. Doesn't he think there will come a time when they will have to reach a compromise?

Bachir doesn't hesitate.

'There can be no compromise. We will be like a camel's thorn to the Moroccans.'

He is smiling, a little grimly perhaps, but not without some relish.

'The more a camel tries to get a thorn out of its foot, the deeper it goes in, and the harder it is to get rid of it.'

At eleven, a line of vehicles emerges from the swirling sand to the south and soon we're shaking hands with a new set of escorts. Compared with the Saharawis, the Mauritanians, marked out by their billowing pale blue robes, which they call *boubous*, carry with them a worldliness, a touch of confidence and panache, which comes, I suppose, from having a country of your own.

Cassa is dark, attractive, in his thirties, I should imagine, and seems to be in charge of the operation, alongside an Englishman, Bob Watt. Abdallahi, pale-skinned, more

Arab than Berber, is our official helper from the Mauritanian Ministry of Communications. Rumour has it that he's the Minister himself.

Mohammed Salim, so ebullient at desert draughts yesterday, is subdued. He has some problem with his eye and we've left him medicine from our filming kit. Nevertheless, he hugs me with surprising force as we begin our long farewells.

The fort at Mejik and the waving Saharawis are quickly obscured by a violent sandstorm. I still have my dry desert cough, which the sand hissing against the windows and squeezing in through the floor isn't doing anything to improve. Visibility drops to a hundred yards. It feels as if we are in limbo, and the lack of any point of reference increases the unreality of anything we glimpse outside. Did we really pass a new-born camel, still wet from its mother, lying on the sand? Or a UN border patrol in four immaculate white Land Cruisers, their aerials swinging and bending in the wind like fishing rods?

Then, three short, sharp shocks in rapid succession – a line of concrete houses, a railway line and a hard-top road. Never mind water in the desert; after days of being thumped and jolted and flung about, it's tarmac in the desert that sends the spirits soaring.

The controversial Mauritanian border is not marked, and there is nothing to indicate a change of country until we reach a checkpoint, a metal rondavel, clanging violently in the wind. Two tall, loose-limbed guards peruse our passports, with more bewilderment than suspicion, and then we are free to enter the town, nay veritable metropolis, of Zouérat, where there are bicycles and motorbikes and cars and garages and shops and sports grounds and, at last, a hotel, the Oasian. The Polisario camps were much cleaner than Zouérat, and young boys there did not flock round, hands out for money or presents, as they do here.

But, for now, the promise of cold beer and a hot shower makes up for everything.

There is no hot water, owing to a problem with the boiler, but the beer is awfully good and I'm able to get through to Helen on the satellite phone and tell her I was dying but survived. She tells me that last night she dreamt I was in bed beside her, sent back home by the BBC for being physically not up to it. I'm quite touched by the fact that we should be having the same anxiety dreams.

MAURITANIA

DAY TWENTY-TWO ZOUÉRAT

One significant change since we crossed the border is the appearance of baguettes and croissants at the breakfast table. For the first sixty years of the twentieth century, first as a protectorate and later as a colony, Mauritania, land of the Moors, was a neglected part of the French empire in Africa. La Mauritanie, as big as France and Spain put together, with a population barely that of Paris, became a place of exile, a dustbin for troublemakers, sidelined from the real French interests in Senegal and Morocco. But the French brought their *boulangeries* and the Mauritanians kept them when they became an independent Islamic republic in 1960.

It's interesting to see what survives of the colonial presence in these countries. In Western Sahara the Spanish legacy lives on in the Polisario, in their education and their political allegiances, and yes, I did have some *chorizo* with my camel one evening, but that's about it. Here in Zouérat, the French influence seems superficially stronger, extending beyond baguettes to *lycées* and *gendarmeries*, pastis in the bar and French news on the television.

After breakfast I walk outside to take a look at the town. Seeing me coming, a gauntlet of salesmen rise effortlessly from their haunches to enjoin me to buy this or that ornament, scarf, ring, necklace, leather pouch. I smile widely and appreciatively and do not stop. When I reach the gate, I pause for a split second, which is long enough for a young man to enquire solicitously about my health before showing me some postcards. I make for the street. Before I can reach it two young boys leap off a donkey cart stacked with charcoal and race towards me, all big smiles and outstretched hands.

'*Donnez-moi un cadeau. Donnez-moi un Bic!*'

When I decline they scamper off and leap back onto their cart, aiming a couple of wild blows at the donkey.

Zouérat is a frontier town, with all the mess and brutality that goes with the sniff of money. In the cluster of jagged peaks to the south of the town is enough iron ore to last 200 years, a resource that has transformed this corner of the desert into a multi-million-dollar asset, supplying 40 per cent of Mauritania's foreign earnings.

All the jobs, houses, public transport and associated support trades are in the domain of SNIM, Société Nationale Industrielle et Minière, the once French, now Mauritanian-owned company that mines the ore. Without SNIM Zouérat would be no more than a collection of tents.

Which, in the poorer parts, it already is.

The back streets of Zouérat are open rubbish tips, lined with low, shabby buildings, but when the doors are open, business spills out everywhere, like the desert after rain. Barbers, garages, telephone points and lots of *quincailleries* (ironmongers). Cutting, fabricating and panel beating seems to be going on in every corner. I watch a middle-aged, red-robed man, using only an axe, hammer and his own sandaled foot for purchase, transform a BP oil drum into a 6-foot length of fencing in less than five minutes.

The reason why ironmongery should be the growth industry here is all tied in with desertification and the influx of nomads. Three years of drought have brought thousands in from the desert, desperately in need of shelter. We go to meet a family living in 'tin city'. Their home is a tent within a compound fenced with recycled metal. The outside of the tent still bears the manufacturer's imprint, 'Mining Explosive. Product Of South Africa'. Inside, the sacks are lined with strips of patterned cloth, and the woman who has invited me in indicates a rug. Her mother fiddles nervously with a row of beads. I slip off my shoes and squat down. Both of the women are in black. Others of the family, all women or children, gather around and regard me curiously. Tea is prepared, as in Western Sahara, with much ritual. They speak in Arabic and Cassa translates their story.

They came in from the desert five years ago and still have no mains water, relying on the irregular visits of the water cart. Nor do they have electricity, though a neighbour has recently let them have a lead off their supply. She proudly points out

78

an uncovered cable snaking across the sand from the fence next door. They have a goat and live mainly off rice and couscous. A younger sister makes some money clearing sand from the railway line. One of her boys goes to school; the other doesn't, because he is mentally handicapped and there is no provision for him. There is, in all this, not a trace of self-pity. They simply hope the rains will come and turn the desert green again and enable them to return to the life they know best. Meanwhile, home is a tent of explosive sacks behind a fence made of oil drums.

'What makes you happy?' I ask.

Even mother, nervously twisting her beads, smiles as this is translated to them. They don't even have to think of the answer.

'Whatever God gives, makes us happy.'

Outside in the street, the gang of children following us down through the rubbish in which the goats graze doesn't look as if much makes them happy. In too many of their eyes is the flat, unresponsive blankness of poverty. In the livelier ones there is something more, a sullen resentment looking for an outlet.

An interesting incident on our way back to the hotel. Despite the present government's desire to keep it quiet, it's well known that Mauritania was one of Saddam Hussein's staunch allies, so much so that Saddam sent his wife and children to the town of Atâr, 100 miles south of here, for safekeeping during the Gulf War. Roger has noticed a painted sign portraying Saddam, looking dapper and suave in suit and tie, above a tyre shop. When he asks if we can film it, not only is the answer no, but Abdallahi, our man from the ministry, makes a personal visit to the shop and demands that the sign be taken down instantly.

DAY TWENTY-THREE   ZOUÉRAT to AZOUGUI

The iron ore that is the bedrock of the Mauritanian economy is shifted from the desert to the coast on a single-track railway line, which is as important to the country as the iron itself. The Polisario knew this, and their repeated attacks on the line are what eventually forced the Mauritanians to abandon plans to occupy Western Sahara back in 1979.

It's not surprising therefore that we have to negotiate two or three increasingly serious roadblocks as we drive 9 miles south and east from Zouérat to the Guelb mine.

With the storm still howling across the desert, sand-ploughs are out keeping the road clear, and our first sight of the boxy superstructure of the mine buildings is through a spectral cloud of rasping stinging dust.

At Guelb, the desert has been transformed into a dark satanic world of noise and movement. Caterpillar trucks grind up and down, bringing freshly mined material to the crushers. From there, conveyor belts carry the pulverised rock to a hopper, which

fills railway wagons at the rate of a 100 tonnes a minute. Today, the wind is catching the iron ore dust between hopper and wagon and sweeping most of it out across the desert in billowing black clouds. Through this mad screaming tempest of wind and dust, yellow and blue diesel locomotives, bells sounding dolefully, keep the wagons moving slowly forward.

Groups of maintenance workers pass by, faces muffled against the blackened sand, dark glasses covering their eyes, looking like mummified escapees from some experimental hospital. Everything about them is threadbare apart from their gleaming new shovels.

Three iron ore trains run every day, seven days a week, between the mines and the Atlantic port of Nouâdhibou. The good news for us is that one train a day also carries passengers.

Just after midday I find myself at a platform-less halt known cryptically as 'Arrêt TFM'. There must be a couple of hundred people gathered here as the monster of a train shuffles slowly towards us. For what seems an eternity, 163 wagons, piled high with rock and black dust, roll past before the two passenger coaches at the back reach the station.

When they do, and the train has shuddered to a halt, there is pandemonium. Passengers don't mount the train, they storm it, scrambling up the steep embankment aiming for two narrow doors, both of which are manned by railway officials whose sole duty seems to be to repel them. They shriek at the crowds and the crowds shriek back. Enormous women with enormous bundles leap onto the ladders and force their way past. A pair of arms emerges from a window and a baby is tossed up into them. A man with a roll of carpet on his shoulder turns, Laurel and Hardy-like, one way and then the other, thwacking people on either side. Human buttresses are formed, leading from the embankment to the train doors.

Casting all human decency aside, I elbow my way past old women, children and blind men and grasp the rail, shouting above the noise that I have a Première Classe ticket. The guard shakes his head and bars my way. I'm about to lose what little control I still have when I realise the guard is directing me to the last car on the train, a box-like wagon with circular holes in its side that looks suspiciously like a recycling container. This, it turns out, *is* Première Classe.

Once inside the container its appearance begins to make sense. It's essentially a guard's van, with a central raised section like a ship's bridge, from where company operatives can survey the length of the train, which today is roughly a mile. From up here I can see that those who were not able to get aboard the coaches have scrambled onto the goods wagons and are settling in on top of the iron ore. One wagon is entirely occupied by a herd of goats.

This ship of fools moves off southwards at a steady 25 miles per hour. Alongside us the

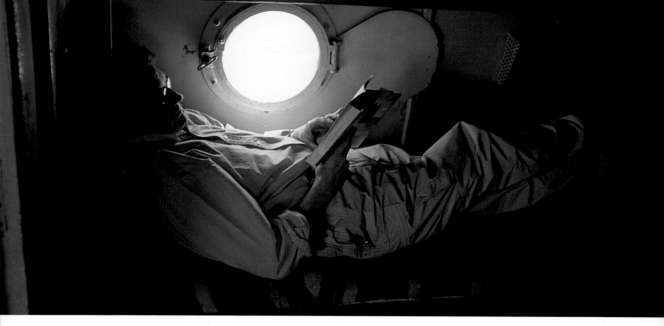

tarmac road falters and merges with the sand. This line is now the only man-made route across the desert.

It is not pretty desert. Grey dust blows over a scruffy plain of rocks and rubble, enlivened occasionally by the detritus of a derailed train or the bleached corpse of an abandoned pick-up truck. I lie down and try to read, but it's not easy, as the slightest change in speed convulses the train.

After several hours of extremely slow progress the train rumbles to a halt at a small town called Choûm. Scarcely has it done so than Choûm station is transformed into the scene of a major disaster. Passengers getting off the train claw at half-open doors as passengers getting on the train hurl themselves at the same half-open doors like soldiers entering a besieged city. Babies are thrown about, the carpet man is cutting his own swathe through the crowds and the low hum of diesel engines mingles with the pathetic falsetto of ore-stained goats.

This is where we get off. If we can.

From Choûm the train turns west to reach the Atlantic coast sometime tomorrow. We pick up the vehicles and head south and east, into the interior of Mauritania, away from the long arcing border of Western Sahara, which has held us like a magnet these past ten days.

As if reflecting the change of direction the landscape changes too. A long escarpment wall has risen up from nowhere and dominates the eastern horizon until the light goes down and it blends into the general darkness. Our convoy rattles on, twisting and turning until the track tackles the escarpment head-on. For the first time since crossing the Atlas Mountains we are climbing, steadily, if not spectacularly, following the thin dusty plume of the vehicle ahead.

We level out on a plateau of splintered rocks. It's a bare, dispiriting place.

Night falls, and with it comes that vague anxiousness I've felt many times since we left Morocco. A feeling that we could go on like this for days and nothing would ever change.

I wake from a bumpy back-seat slumber to find we've stopped. Ahead of us figures in veils flit away from our headlights into a large, crisply flapping tent. Cassa has got out and is striding off into a grove of trees. We disembark. Stretch legs, yawn, drink some water. It's nine o'clock by my watch when Cassa returns with furrowed brow and motions us into the vehicles.

Apparently, a friend of his, who was to put us all up tonight in his 'Typical Nomadic Tent', has disappeared into the desert, as nomads do, and not come back.

So, off we go again. Back into the night.

Half an hour later, dots of light flicker in the distance. They prove to belong to a small encampment outside the little town of Azougui, which bears unlikely signs of tourist facilities. As we turn into the compound our headlights pick out a painted board, the name of an *auberge* and the reassuring words beneath it, '*Près de la Ville. Loin du Son Stress*'.

It's not where we were meant to be, but no-one's complaining.

DAY TWENTY-FOUR   AZOUGUI TO ATAR

Pass the night in a thatched hut, shared with Basil, with barely room to stand up straight. Woken in the small hours by the sounds of a ferocious cat fight. The ensuing trip to the loo is quite tricky. The door of the hut is tiny. I crawl out like a bee leaving a hive, to be rewarded with a massive and magnificent night sky. In the absence of moonlight the definition and abundance of the heavens is overwhelming, and I find myself praising my Maker for giving me such a weak bladder.

The morning reveals a number of similar straw huts, shaped like igloos and set around a large tent, over 30 feet square, and two whitewashed stone buildings with gabled roofs which look incongruously like Welsh chapels. Looking beyond the camp, I see a much less inimical landscape than the rest of the western Sahara. Palm trees and long grass fill in the empty spaces between the acacia trees and dry-stone walls

LEFT

Camp-site accommodation at Azougui. At least we didn't have to put them up.

border the tracks that lead up to the quiet, laid-back little town. Over a breakfast of fresh-baked bread and bananas, Cassa tells me that Azougui was once a trading post on the edge of the desert, where gold and salt and slaves changed hands. It was from here that a particularly aggressive dynasty of Berber peoples known as the Almoravids set out on a quest for more land, which led them north, to found Marrakesh, before moving across the Strait of Gibraltar and into Europe.

Cassa, a youngish man, elegant and rather aristocratic, runs tours into this part of Mauritania, and I would not dream of questioning the validity of anything he says were it not for his playful but confusing habit of hopping from intense seriousness to hooting laughter in the same breath.

On our way south and east we pass through a remarkable landscape, where the constant, unblinking process of disintegration and decay that characterises the Sahara takes rich and varied forms, from spectacular, Rio Grande-like mesas to soft sand dunes, crumbling escarpments and moon-like rubble-strewn plains. In the midst of this austere beauty is the small town of Atâr, neither austere nor beautiful. But today and tomorrow Atâr will be in a world spotlight. The Paris-Dakar Rally is coming to town.

The Paris-Dakar arouses mixed emotions. For the organisers, it is the most gruelling event on the motorsport calendar, pitching man and machine against one of the harshest environments on the planet. For opponents, like the French Green party, it is 'colonialism that needs to be eradicated', costing sums 'equal to the annual health budget of some of the countries the race crosses'.

In 1999 it was held up by bandits whilst crossing Mauritania. In 2000 threats from Algerian fundamentalists forced the contestants into an air-lifted leapfrog over the country, and last year the driver of a back-up vehicle lost a leg after hitting a land mine near the Moroccan wall.

But the Paris-Dakar, now commonly known as The Dakar, as Paris is no longer its obligatory starting point, has, since its inception in 1978, survived wars and rumours of wars, fatalities and serious accidents, to grow and flourish, carried on by its own obstinate momentum and man's insatiable urge to do things the hard way.

Somewhat ironically for a town surrounded by desert, Atâr suffered from catastrophic floods in the 1980s and all buildings of character seemed to have been washed away and replaced with nondescript concrete and breeze block. One exception to the overall dusty brown of the narrow streets are the Total gas stations, which are a riot of liberally applied red and white paint. Total, it turns out, are the sponsors of the Dakar Rally.

We find accommodation, albeit modest, at the Auberge El Medina, on a corner where four sandy streets meet. An unattended donkey trots past as we push open the heavy metal doors into a courtyard bordered with pink oleander and yellow hibiscus. Mats are laid out for communal eating and two large tents stand at one end of the yard. Privacy is not a characteristic of desert life. The idea of a room of your own is alien to a country whose traditions are nomadic and gregarious, but the proprietors of the Auberge El Medina have judiciously spread their cultural options. On the other three sides of the courtyard are five rooms with locks on the doors. However, each room has at least six beds in it.

Auberge avrah El Medina
استراحــة أفـــراح المدينـة
Tourisme-Invitation-Locations de voitures
Prestation de Service
D.G : Sid Ahmed Ould Salek
Tel. : 002 222 764176 - Atar
002 222 59072 NKC
Fax : 002 222 764176 - Atar

Walking outside after we'd settled in, I had expected to see a town gripped by Rally fever, with banners, bunting and bars open all day. There are, of course, no bars in the non-alcoholic Islamic Republic of Mauritania, and the lack of bunting and banners is explained later in the afternoon when the Rally finally hits town.

It comes, not along the road, but down from the sky. A series of distant rumbles heralds a steady flow of cargo planes, amongst them a Hercules and three or four high-winged Russian Antonovs, descending to the south of the town. They bring in the Rally, keeping it as exclusive as any travelling circus, a self-sufficient unit effectively isolated from any reliance on, or interaction with, the local people.

Atâr airport is in very good condition. The Rally organisers have seen to that. It stands on the outskirts of town, an immaculate collection of domed and arcaded buildings standing out from the surrounding half-built houses and empty walled compounds like a Christmas present on a rubbish tip. A small city has sprung up on the tarmac, huddled around a dozen planes and half a dozen helicopters, all of which, apart from an elderly cream Dakota belonging to the Mauritanian air force, are only here for the Rally.

One Antonov freighter is fitted out as a hospital, another as a catering store. Still others belong to the big works teams, whose riders bivouac in matching tents pitched in the protective shade of the wings. Striped marquees have been erected for the

LEFT

The First World flies in for the day. Atâr airport becomes media city as the Dakar Rally hits town.

administration and the press, lap-tops cover trestle tables, mobiles are constantly in use (though it's impossible to get a mobile signal anywhere else in Mauritania), fridges full of cold drinks hum away in the desert sun.

But the plane that really matters is the Hercules. Without the Hercules, Atâr would not have got its gleaming new airport and freshly laid tarmac, for inside its ample flanks are the 22 tonnes of editing equipment, which provide the television coverage on whose revenue the Rally's survival depends.

Wires and cables spill like entrails from its belly, connecting up satellite dishes and generators and even a makeshift studio, complete with potted plants, set up on the tarmac for live interviews with the drivers, which will be pumped out to the four corners of the world.

Way beyond the bustling, hi-tech centre of this instant city, a suburban sprawl of less privileged competitors stretches to the far corners of the airstrip. At its shadeless limits, where the tarmac runs out and the rubble begins, a tent, a Union Jack and an old Range Rover, with a row of white socks drying on its bonnet, mark the headquarters of the only British interest left in the Rally. The tent is shared by Dave Hammond, a short and amiable motorbike rider, and his two mechanics. Dave is what's known as a privateer, someone who has entered the race 'for the romance of the event', without the backing of any of the big teams. Not for him the Mitsubishi millions. His fuel tank bears the name of Webb's Garages of Cirencester.

And bears it proudly. Fifty-two bikes have already dropped out and Dave is lying twenty-first of the 115 still left. He's optimistic. At this stage of the rally the pressure is on the big boys and they begin to make mistakes. Dave reckons that if he doesn't do anything silly he'll pick up places at the expense of those being forced to take risks.

I ask him if he has any sense of where he is. He shakes his head and laughs.

'I just know we're going south, because it's getting hotter and hotter.'

The Dakar Rally, it seems, is really nothing to do with seeing the world. It's about machines and drivers. Where you are is less important than how fast you got there and whether you still have a vehicle that can get you out. Someone tells me of a first-time American competitor, thrown off his bike five days ago in Morocco, who'd asked plaintively, 'Is there much more sand out there?'

DAY TWENTY-FIVE ATAR

You have to be up at sparrow-fart to catch the Rally. The first riders on this time-trial stage, a loop starting and ending in Atâr, have left the airport by eight o'clock, and it's been a long and tricky drive to find a position along the course ahead of them. Once again, the first sign of activity is aerial. A muttering and thudding fills the valley and seconds later a silver helicopter streaks in over sand and stone tracks it has taken us an hour to negotiate. It circles gracefully, picks a spot and swoops to earth, disgorging a camera crew at the point where the piste is marked by a low but nasty run of bumps. A few locals have gathered to watch. They crouch on their haunches, arms resting on knees, looking more bemused than expectant. A donkey watches impassively from a nearby clump of tamarisk trees. A few yards further on, a group of village women are

OPPOSITE

(TOP) *Breaking the silence. The first of 115 motorbikes slides and slithers through the sand dunes south of Atâr.*

(BOTTOM) *An extraordinary day in the village of Tougadh. A rally car heads up between the dry-stone houses. Three hundred vehicles of all sizes will go up their high street in one afternoon.*

87

standing up against a flimsy fence, holding a sign on which is written 'Go, Johnny Go!', believed to be a reference to the presence of the veteran Gallic rocker Johnny Hallyday in one of the cars.

More helicopters appear. Some land in a scatter of sand, others hover briefly before sweeping away in search of the next good vantage point. Then the first of the bikes comes into sight around the base of a sand dune, swaying and skidding past at speeds of around 60 miles per hour, sending up a fine plume of red sand as its rider, standing, arms and legs braced, works furiously at throttle and brake to get a grip on this treacherous surface.

One of the bikes hits a submerged stone and careers off course, flinging its rider to the ground. He remounts and roars by. We check the number. Somehow it had to be. 126. Dave Hammond, Great Britain.

Before the cars come through we move on to a better vantage point overlooking the village of Tougadh. Because it's up in the hills, the buildings of Tougadh are sturdier than most I've seen in the Mauritanian Sahara, a mix of rectangular houses and circular huts, most of them resting on a skilfully cut dry-stone base and topped with mud and thatch. The village lies across a rising slope, with the head of the valley at one end and a thick grove of date palms at the other. There is no movement amongst the huts. A figure lies asleep outside one of the houses, head resting in the crook of an arm.

Then comes a distant hum, like the sound of a swarm of bees. Moments later the sound changes from swarming bee to angry hornet and a thin line of dust can be seen snaking through the palms. Swinging wildly on the sandy track, the lead car bursts out of the trees and into the village. Compared with the motorbikes, whose riders could at least be seen grappling with their machines, it's disappointingly anonymous. A red box driven by two Lego men. Compelled by Rally regulations to observe a speed limit whilst passing through a village, it croaks and barks through the gears with rather bad grace as it climbs between the houses and over the hill. A young man from the village clambers up, waving vigorously at us. For a moment I think this must be the first Mauritanian to show any excitement about the race, but it turns out he wants to sell us some of his dates.

For the next two hours the sixty-five cars left in the race snarl by, hauling the message of McDonald's and Microsoft, PlayStation and Gauloises through the sleepy, unappreciative village. After the cars come the trucks and an armada of support vehicles, until all that's left is a Toyota Land Cruiser containing three journalists covering the rally. They seem in no great hurry and are opening up the daily ration kits issued to them by the organisers. David Park, from the *New York Times*, is impressed.

'What have we got today? *Pâté de volaille.* There's sausage, cheese, two biscuits, one for the pâté, one for the cheese. *Petit Napoléon.*' He shakes his head in awe and admiration. 'It's so...French!'

A line of village children stand watching Park and his friends as if they've come from Mars. They might as well have done. In almost every material respect they are different from the inhabitants of Tougadh. Well-fed, prosperous, highly mobile, technologically sophisticated, multinational. Everything this part of Africa is not. Park hands out most of the content of his ration bag to the children. His smile is broad, theirs are tentative. Then his Toyota fires into life, the palm thatch fence sways in the slipstream and the last of the Rally is gone, possibly until next year, probably for ever. A little way up the hill, a man still lies asleep with his head in the crook of an arm.

All the competitors, apart from a few stragglers, are back at the airport by mid-afternoon. Minor injuries are nursed, positions checked. Stories and rumours spread through the camp. One car somersaulted over a dune, but when the co-driver

BELOW

Tougadh village. Western wealth makes little impression on the locals. The adverts are all for the television coverage.

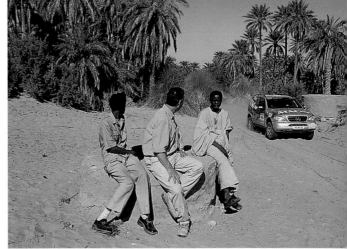

managed to struggle back to lay a helmet on the dune as a warning sign the next car flew right over him. Alfie Cox, one of the top bikers, won the stage, despite riding the last 200 miles without water after a fall had severed his supply. Leading the six trucks left in the race is the Russian team, admired by one English journalist less for their driving than their spectacular devotion to the hard stuff.

'Anything'll do. They finished off the windscreen washer fluid last night.'

And Dave Hammond is still in the race. Despite two falls, he completed the 250-mile course in just over four hours and has moved up to eighteenth place. He and his mechanics are cleaning the bike meticulously.

After they've finished they'll gather with other riders to watch video footage of their day's performance.

There's a strong family feeling at work here. At heart, the Dakar Rally is about fraternity – bands of brothers united by common language, enthusiasms and ambitions. I admire their mad bravery, but we don't have much in common. Mauritania excites me much more than motorsport.

DAY TWENTY-SIX ATAR TO CHINGUETTI

It's still dark when I wake at the Auberge. It takes a while to work out why the room appears to be shaking. Then the dull reverberation focusses into a familiar sound. The planes are leaving. The circus is moving on. The Dakar Rally is taking to the skies again.

Sure enough, as we pass out of Atâr later in the morning, the airport is empty, the tarmac cleared. Soldiers are no longer in position. The corrugated metal sheets of a '*Toilette Publique*' are being dismantled. A line of damaged bikes waits to be collected and flown home. A goat sniffs around the leftovers of the bivouac and somewhere out in the desert the strike force heads south. They'll be in Dakar long before us, that's for sure. But we'll have seen a lot more.

It's a good day to be on the move. Skies bright and clear, mellow winter temperatures peaking at around 30°C/86°F. We're climbing up between the sheer, brick-red walls of the Adrar Massif in scenery that could have come straight out of a John Ford Western. What's more, we're on that luxury of luxuries – a freshly tarmacked road, paid for and constructed by the Chinese in return for fishing concessions off Mauritania's Atlantic coast.

Having done its basic job of taking us through the pass and onto the escarpment, the tarmac ends abruptly. The road reverts to dirt track but soon the rubble gives way to softer, sandier terrain, and by the time we reach the outskirts of Chinguetti we are on the edge of a sand sea, classic date-box desert, for which the Arab word *erg* sounds awfully inadequate.

The fine golden sand looks soft and seductive, but it is the most difficult and dangerous surface and dune-driving requires great skills. Despite clever use of the four-wheel drive, we have to make three attempts to climb one towering dune. My heart is in my mouth each time, for we seem so close to tumbling over and crashing down the slope.

Once at the top I'm left gasping, not so much at the perilousness of the ascent, as by the revelation of the sand sea, stretching to the horizon. The sinuous outlines of the dunes, formed by the wind into hundreds of thousands of peaks and crests and troughs, is mesmerisingly beautiful. Though the sand is constantly in motion, being smoothed and reshaped by the wind, there is an illusion of complete stillness, the sculpted contours of the sandscape smooth as marble, not a grain out of place, everything in perfect equilibrium.

John studies it more philosophically.

'I suppose you could say it's the ultimate wasteland,' he observes. 'The world's surface reduced to fine dust.'

He's right of course.

DAY TWENTY-SEVEN CHINGUETTI

Looking over the battlements at Fort Saganne, our French Legion lookalike hotel, as another hot day gets underway, I can see below me a network of lanes and low stone and plaster houses that could have been there for months or years, it's hard to tell. Their walls are uneven, often broken and collapsed into piles of rubble. A woman who has been peeing unselfconsciously in the sand goes back into her house. The front door is of corrugated metal, hanging from one hinge. Beyond is an area of wide sandy spaces with shops and long, low, concrete civic buildings. To one side stands the tall shell of the electricity generating station, its walls punctured by Polisario mortars twenty-three years ago and still unrepaired. But a half-mile or so beyond all that, stretched across a low hill and bordered by palm trees, old Chinguetti, with its assortment of towers and red-gold stone walls, stands out handsomely, like a mediaeval hill town.

From the battlements of Fort Saganne, Chinguetti, seventh holiest city of Islam, looks a place of substance and civility.

When we drive into the old town, across the bone-dry football pitch that occupies the flat plain between old and new Chinguetti, the reality is rather different. For a start, the taller and more spectacular of the two minarets turns out to be a water tower.

Though the old mosque has been beautifully restored, the warren of streets around it is like a ghost town. Discarded sardine tins, batteries, padlocks, Pepsi cans and electric cables lie half-buried in the sand. Birds dart through the ruined houses, and occasionally a veiled figure will call out from a doorway, indicating that their house is not abandoned and pointing out the word '*boutique*' scrawled beside it on the wall and the small collection of local artefacts dimly visible inside. In other streets the stone walls are all that remains. Behind solid carved doorways, once prosperous houses lie open to the sky and the sand.

The desert is taking over Chinguetti.

There are surprises. I'm trudging up a side street when I hear the sound of voices chanting. It comes from the other side of a low wall, in which a green door stands ajar. I peer round it and find myself in a white-walled courtyard. A dozen children, all clutching wooden boards covered with Arabic writing, are sat in a row facing the wall, reciting texts in high sing-song voices. Standing above them, occasionally stooping to correct some misreading is a tall, elderly man, veiled in black and white, with hollow cheeks and a straggly grey beard, as long and pointed as his face. He is the imam of the mosque whose minaret, shaped like a Gothic church tower, we passed earlier. This is his house and also the *medersa*, the Koranic school, where the children learn the holy texts, and where some of the better students will be able, one day, to recite the entire Koran from memory. They don't seem to be learning anything else.

He shakes hands with Cassa but not with any of us, I notice, but when he answers our questions his fierce countenance cracks easily into a twinkling smile, revealing two prominent, immaculately white teeth.

BELOW

Writing was a work of art for Islamic scholars. The calligraphy in the books in Chinguetti's libraries is up to 1000 years old.

Beckoning us into the shade, he orders two of the senior boys, clearly his favourites, to offer round a wooden bowl of *zrig*, a thick mixture of goat milk, water, millet and sugar.

In a voice thin and husky from a lifetime of summoning the faithful he tells us that the minaret is the second oldest in continuous use anywhere in the Muslim world. Until very recently, he says, he used to climb up and make the call to prayer from the top of the tower; now he's not strong enough and has to rely on a microphone down below.

Along a side street nearby, the word '*Bibliothèque*' is scrawled in white paint on the stone lintel of an otherwise inconspicuous doorway. Stepping inside, I find myself in a room, no more than 15 feet square, with bamboo mats on the floor and rough-plastered walls. An old man rises to greet me.

Behind him, stacked on shelves, are bundles of papers wrapped in leather bindings or manila folders. They are books and documents of extraordinary beauty, many of them 600 or 700 years old. In some cases the pages have come loose from their bindings, but in all of them the quality of the work is exquisite. They have been in his family for centuries and he treats the texts like old friends, moving his finger from right to left, as the Chinese and Japanese do, across the delicate, spidery calligraphy.

There is a commentary on the Koran, with notes around the margins, and a book of Islamic law, still clearly readable, detailing legal procedures – numbers of witnesses, rights of the accused – all dating back to the golden days when Chinguetti was one of the great centres of Islamic scholarship.

'This land,' he says, head inclined towards mine but eyes fixed somewhere in the distance, 'was called Chinguetti before it was called Mauritania.'

I ask him if there might be a price at which he'd part with a book like this, but he shakes his head. These are his life, and part of the life of his fathers and forefathers. He cannot let them down by selling them.

In the main square of Old Chinguetti is a more organised collection of the city's treasures. The Bibliothèque Al Halott can be found off the courtyard of a fine old house, behind ancient acacia wood doors. Beneath weathered black beams are bulky modern filing cabinets containing 1400 manuscripts. A father-and-son team looks after them, and so valuable are the works that they only allow visitors in one or two at a time. Their pride and joy – '*le plus ancien ouvrage*' – is a Koran, brought here from Mecca in 1000 AD. They have a book on astronomy dating from the fourteenth century, clearly showing the planets of our solar system circling the sun, proving that Arab scholars knew something that the authorities in Europe refused to acknowledge for a further 200 years.

Six o'clock. The best time of day. People are out in the streets again, shops are open, children, rolling old tyres, race after each other. The big heat is off, the setting sun turns the desert a rosy purple and the sounds of the city soften to a murmur.

Walking in the new town, I find myself first watching, then participating in a game of *dhaemon*, as taught me by Mohammed Salim of the Polisario. An erect, bare-headed man, who clearly fancies himself as the local Grand Master, is taking on all comers and thrashing them. He barely raises his eyes from the sand as I'm sat down opposite him and given my quota of *crottes de chameau,* camel droppings. Then something goes wrong with his strategy. Soon I have at least a dozen friends and advisers ready to manage my every move, shouting, debating and arguing with increasing hysteria as they scent a rare victory in the air.

Sure enough the sticks are uprooted with increasing regularity and the all-conquering camel turds are sweeping across the sand, until, with sharp cries of delight, the foreigner steals a victory.

LEFT

Yes! The turds have it! England 1, Mauritania 0.

95

I seem to have had all Chinguetti on my side, for as I walk back to the hotel later I keep getting waves of acknowledgement, broad grins and cheery shouts of 'Champion!'

My stock with the owners of the Hôtel Fort Saganne is already pretty high.

'Vous êtes le deuxième star ici!' they enthuse, 'le premier star' being Gerard Depardieu, who stayed and worked here whilst making what was by all accounts a very bad film called *Fort Saganne* in 1984. I only wish their facilities matched their view of my status. Though I am in Depardieu's room, the generator provides light and electricity only fitfully, the bedside light is operated from a switch 20 feet away from the bed, the pillow is made from some form of granite and the painting and decoration seem to have been completed by someone with a serious grudge against society.

It all becomes a bit clearer when they reveal that Depardieu didn't stay in this room at all, but in a Winnebago parked outside. They even show me the spot.

'It was parked over there!'

My room was the one used in the film itself.

As Fort Saganne was all about the terrible privations endured by members of the French Foreign Legion, this explains a lot.

DAY TWENTY-EIGHT   CHINGUETTI TO NOUAKCHOTT

Around a quarter to seven the generator coughs into life, which means electricity and hot water will be available until half past nine, when they turn it off again. Up onto the battlements for a last reminder of the panorama of Chinguetti, this quintessential image of the desert. It requires a vivid imagination to evoke the glory days of the thirteenth and fourteenth centuries, when Ibn Battuta came down here from Tangiers, when there were seventy-six libraries in the town and when the constant coming and going of camel trains between Morocco and the fabulous kingdom of Mali made Chinguetti one of the centres of the civilised world.

Now the desert is quiet. The trade has gone elsewhere, by ship around the coast, on overland trucks that can't cope with the fine sand seas that enclose Chinguetti.

But, splendidly isolated as it may feel, Chinguetti is only 1200 miles from the coast of Europe, and if not trucks and boats, then aeroplanes may yet be its saviour. There is a growing curiosity about the desert, and as more tourists brave the Sahara south of Morocco this particular combination of landscape and history could well bring some money back to this historic city.

These tourist-board thoughts come to me as I wait at the small airstrip outside Chinguetti. I'm cadging a ride to Nouakchott, the Mauritanian capital, aboard a Cessna, from which Nigel has been filming the desert sands.

We peel off the baking tarmac and into the air, spreading panic amongst the camels careering below us. Soon the ancient crust of the old Saharan plateau pushes through the desert sands, exposing fault lines that reveal shiny, fractured, black rock and reminding me more than anything of the world's second largest desert, Antarctica.

After two hours in the air the colours begin to change. The charred blacks and browns of the escarpment give way to a green and white landscape as we slowly descend towards Nouakchott. The green is from stands of trees and fields of crops, a reminder of what irrigation can do in the fiercest of deserts, but it's the white that predominates, a great spreading undercloth of limestone and salt, as if the desert had been bleached as it reached the sea.

Our plane banks and turns and as it begins its final approach to the Mauritanian capital I can just about make out the Atlantic Ocean, away to the west.

Below us, streets and cars and palaces and office blocks and other visions of a way of life I'd half forgotten race up towards the plane. After where we've been, the thought of descending into the midst of a million people seems a great anticlimax, and the more I look forward to the creature comforts of a big city hotel the more I feel that I'm betraying the desert.

DAY TWENTY-NINE NOUAKCHOTT

After one night at the Monotel Bar-El-Barka I realise that my appreciation of the simple life is a cracked and broken vessel. Maybe it's a question of age, but the delight I have taken in switching the air-con on and off, flushing and re-flushing the lavatory, caressing the bedside light and reading the laundry list from start to finish, including the women's section, suggests to me that I am not cut out for deprivation.

If twelve days of desert travel can reduce me to gibbering delight at the sight of one of the world's shortest room-service menus, what is to become of me when we turn east again, back to the sands?

There is water outside my room that is just for swimming in. It's surprisingly cold and refreshing. The only other occupants are two Mauritanian children, who seem amazed by the whiteness of my body, which, fresh from a long English winter, is very white indeed. They stare open-mouthed, as if seeing a ghost.

Thirteen years ago, whilst filming *Around the World in 80 Days*, I was stuck on a Yugoslav freighter moving agonisingly slowly across the Bay Of Bengal. The tiny mess room was dominated by a map of the world. To help pass the time, my cameraman, Nigel Meakin, and I competed with each other to memorise every African country and, for extra points, the name of its capital. Mauritania was a tough one, but Nouakchott was a match winner. Nouakchott was the Holy Grail of obscurity.

Which is why I experienced more than the usual frisson of first-timer's excitement when I saw the name on the airport building, and why I immediately bought up all three postcards in the hotel shop. And why I'm rather ashamed to learn that this city we could never remember is the biggest in the Sahara.

I take some comfort from the fact that this is a recent development. Nouakchott, whose name, my guidebook tells me helpfully, may mean 'Place of Wind' or 'Place of Floating Seashells', was only created in the late 1950s, and even by 1980 had less than 150,000 inhabitants. Then came fourteen years of drought and an influx of refugees, which has pushed the population beyond the million mark.

Located at the collision point of Sahara Desert and Atlantic Ocean, the city of Nouakchott feels a bit like a lifeboat, tossed between two seas – one sand, one salt –

with new people scrambling on board all the time. It has had neither the time nor the resources to create an identity or shape a character. It is just a place full of people.

There are some grandiose government buildings and a quarter where diplomats and foreign businessmen live in well-fenced comfort, but the heart of the city, down by the Grand Marché is a steaming, jostling mass of on-street commerce. The buildings that line the Avenue Abdul El Nasser lack any distinction, but in a sense that's not the point. They are just spaces to be filled, emptied, leaned against and sheltered beneath by the throng of buyers, sellers, hawkers, beggars and all the other players on this congested stage: smooth young men in dark glasses, exuding unspecified threat, blind old men being led about by young companions, venerable, bearded figures swathed in veils, and poised young girls in deep blue robes balancing on their heads trays of soft drinks the colour of dentist's mouthwash. Around them a ragged army of street sweepers, with faces wrapped like mummies, carry out the Sisyphean task of keeping the capital clean.

The crowd is fed by a cruising stream of green and yellow minibuses, setting down and picking up constantly. Weaving amongst them are all shades of the transport spectrum, from donkey-drawn carts to Mercedes 200s, with missing fenders, sightless headlamps and window-cracks like spider's webs.

The children beg blatantly and cheerfully.

'*Donnez-moi quelque chose!*'

I see no-one buying, selling or reading a newspaper.

The Atlantic shore, a mile or so from the centre of the city, offers the prospect of space and sea breezes, somewhere to cool off away from the clamour. I make for it at sunset, following the road across a desolate wasteland of broken shells and crusted sand dunes (the white blanket I'd seen from the air yesterday). The road does not, in fact, lead to a place of peace and quiet contemplation (they don't build roads in Africa for that sort of thing); it leads to a great heaving fish market, the Plage des Pêcheurs, Fishermen's Beach.

Dominated at one end by the curved concrete roof of the market building and at the other by the ghostly hulks of two wrecked freighters, this half-mile stretch of beach seethes with human activity. Donkeys pull carts through the sand, exhorted with sharp blows from their drivers. A man passes through the crowd with a plank on his head, carrying a dozen loaves of fresh-baked bread. Salesmen offer football shirts and trainers, combs, brushes, even a set of gleaming new spanners. Women in bold patterned veils or turbans gossip together, breaking off every now and then to call to their children. It's a family affair, part Billingsgate, part Blackpool, part B&Q. The majority of those here are black Africans. The Arabs, with their nomadic traditions, don't eat much fish, preferring the desert staples of camel, mutton or goat meat.

Long low boats with crescent-shaped hulls painted bright primary colours are everywhere, some drawn up on the beach, others out on the viscous Atlantic swell, bringing in their catch from the cool and fertile offshore currents. When full, the boats come to within a few yards of the shore and a score of porters plunge into the water. Mostly teenage boys, they compete with each other, racing with trays of swordfish, barracuda, sea bass and red mullet balanced on their heads, up through the crowds to

OPPOSITE

(TOP) *Nouakchott beach, where the Sahara meets the Atlantic. A mile of fish market with a backdrop of wrecked freighters.*

(BOTTOM) *Never a shortage of helpers to bring the boats in. A boy (right) waits with his plastic tray to carry fish up to be weighed. The best of the catch never reaches local waters; it's trawled by foreign factory ships out beyond the horizon.*

the market. Their sense of urgency and the accompanying din of shouts, protests, yelps and laughter indicate the sense of elation that such an abundant food source can bring to a small country, but one of the market traders puts it in perspective. Many of the boats here, he says, are from neighbouring Senegal, and what does come in is only what has been rejected by the Japanese, Korean and Chinese factory ships lurking out beyond the horizon.

DAY THIRTY NOUAKCHOTT

Strange weather. A warm wind blows from a brooding, hazy sky. The air is heavy, as if it might rain, which in a city that receives only 4 inches a year (London has nearer 30) would be quite an occasion. I feel a little disoriented by Mauritania. Having passed through an enormous country, I find myself in this wide, flat, shapeless capital feeling that I could be anywhere. I remember my colleague Graham Chapman on a Python tour of Canada being asked by a local tourist guide what he thought of Regina, Saskatchewan. Graham looked around at the flat expanse of prairie stretching away in every direction and then enquired, with winning politeness, 'Why didn't they put it over there?'

Guidebook information is scarce, only fifty pages in my *Rough Guide*, half that for neighbouring and much smaller Senegal, so for on-the-spot information I seek out the honorary British consul, Nancy Abeiderrahmane MBE, or Nancy Jones from Essex, as she was before she married a Mauritanian in the late 1960s. I found her at work in a spotlessly clean compound off an unmade, sand-strewn road, from which she runs the highly successful Tiviski dairy business. Beneath the shade of two spreading neem trees and between an unloading tanker and a refrigerated delivery van, I'm welcomed by a small, vivacious, middle-aged woman in a white sari, obviously treated with respect by her workforce. The yard and the unloading bays, where milk is brought in from farms and from hundreds of small producers, many of them desert nomads, is constantly being hosed down. '*Portez Le Turban SVP*' (Please Wear a Turban), says the sign on the door of the plant, and Nancy calls someone over to help me tie a length of black cotton into a *howli*, the Moorish head-wrap. It isn't easy. My nose keeps getting in the way. The man is dismissed and another more senior member of Nancy's 180-strong workforce takes over. He doesn't fare much better. It's a bit like tying a bow tie, easier to do for yourself than someone else. Nancy notices I have some hair showing, which is hygienically impermissible, and yet another man, who for all I know could be the chairman of the board, is summonsed. He does the trick, and, looking like a passable imitation of Lawrence of Arabia, I step, not into the desert, but into the bottling plant. It's the coldest place in Africa; a gleaming world of stainless steel and streamlined automation. Milk from cows, goats and camels is poured into cartons at the rate of 2000 an hour. The plant works seven days a week and sells product to over 2000 shops. The water they use is recycled to irrigate a garden on a nearby roundabout.

In the office, flanked by computers and a sign on the wall, 'Don't EVER Give Up', I'm treated to a tasting of Tiviski's products, including conventional cow's milk,

sweeter than its English counterpart, and less conventional but quite delicious ranges like date yoghurt, camel cheese and, the pride of her production, camel milk. Camel milk, Nancy assures me, is the answer to all our prayers.

'It has half the fat of cow's milk, and less sugar, so good for diabetics. It has a lot of vitamin C. It's good for vascular problems, women take it to have a clear complexion and they say it's a tonic for men.' Nancy smiles, and takes a breather before adding, unconvincingly, 'whatever that means'.

'One protein in it is similar to human insulin, and as camels are pretty close to humans in the evolutionary tree, so the proteins are closer to humans, and it's less allergenic than cow's milk.'

I want it and I want it every day from now on. But I can't, because I live in Europe, and the European regulations don't cover camel products. The EU won't even acknowledge that camels have products.

'But we're getting there,' says Nancy, and I believe her. She's not the sort of person to start out unless she intends getting there.

I ask her about Mauritania.

Life is hard for most people here – 'Everybody makes do with very little' – but she points to rapid change. Forty years ago there was not one mile of tarred road in the entire country. Now there is water and electricity supply to most homes in the city. It is a tolerant country; women do not have to cover their faces or accept polygamy. If a man wants a new wife he must divorce the old one first. This makes divorced women much sought after in Mauritania. They do not have any ties and they generally will have benefited from a divorce settlement. She feels quite comfortable as a female entrepreneur in a country that has women in the cabinet, law, medicine and even in the army. 'People,' she says with a touch of a smile, 'are very nice to women.'

ABOVE LEFT

The southern Saharan look. A woman, more Negro than Arab, chews on an acacia stick, the Saharan equivalent of toothbrush and toothpaste combined.

ABOVE

Fabrics for sale in Nouakchott market. Bold colours and patterns are one of the great delights of the southern Sahara.

101

She nimbly sidesteps the knotty question of slavery, which was only formally abolished here in 1981, but acknowledges that the Moorish social system is complex and tribal, with warrior and scholar tribes.

There are two national sports. One is *dhaemon*, the desert draughts I played in Chinguetti, and the other poetry.

'In a decent gathering like a wedding party the young men are expected to improvise four verses of poetry and others to compose a reply. Everybody can recite lots and lots of poetry.'

She sees similarities between Mauritanians and the British.

'They love wit and they're always ready to say something funny. And you'll have noticed the country runs on tea. The cooking is, likewise, not terribly noteworthy.'

DAY THIRTY-ONE   NOUAKCHOTT to ST-LOUIS

It's 127 miles from the capital of Mauritania to the border with Senegal. Both countries were once part of Afrique Occidentale Française, a huge slab of the French colonial empire. As we drive out of Nouakchott this morning, we are reminded of the new world order.

The American embassy is a fortress, bristling with razor wire, sprung with alarms and guarded by armed men. The Presidential Palace, a drab grey mass, of considerable size and very little beauty, was built by the Chinese.

However, the French influence lives on. As we pull up in the town of Tiguent we're ambushed by half a dozen children, heavily armed with baguettes, who crowd around the doors, shouting and jabbing loaves through the window until we submit and reach in our pockets for our last few *ouguiya*. The bread tastes good; a richer, stickier consistency than French baguette and with the added ingredient that marks it out as fresh – Saharan sand.

The French language remains the lingua franca and the one in which we're interrogated at a series of army roadblocks.

At one of these enforced halts, a tall, thin, young soldier in camouflaged fatigues approaches our vehicle and examines the contents carefully. His eyes flick towards us.

'*Parti à Rosso*?' he asks.

Yes, we reply cautiously. We are going to Rosso.

He looks us up and down, slowly, then appears to come to a decision. We hold our breath.

'*Vous avez une place?*'

He wants a lift.

As we near the Sénégal river, the bleached white shell-fields of Nouakchott give way to terracotta dunes dotted with spiky grass scrub and acacia trees just tall enough to provide shelter for the Fulani herders. As the sands of the Sahara blow in from the north and east, they're forced progressively closer to the Sénégal river. Only ten years, earlier the issue of land ownership along the border brought Mauritania and Senegal

to the brink of war. Senegal kicked out Mauritanian traders and Mauritania allowed equally violent reprisals against 'southerners'. Today relations are better, but the security presence is strong enough to make filming a delicate task.

By midday we are passing a network of irrigation ditches and the first glimpse of grassland for two and a half weeks. The fields contain sugar cane, rice and grazing land, grown under a scheme which I see from a billboard is financed by the government of the Emirates, 3000 miles across the other side of the desert. An example of pan-Islamic co-operation, which could prove a much bigger influence on West Africa than anything French, American or Chinese.

At Rosso we reach the river and the next frontier, and take our place in a shuffling line of vehicles, most of which look like survivors of a stock car race, weighed down to the floor with goods, wires hanging out of empty headlamp sockets. We're a captive audience and vendors gather at the windows. It's very hot and hard to be patient in the face of endless demands for *cadeaux* and *bonbons*. We are not allowed to film and the ferry gates are shut.

Repair to the Pâtisserie El Belediya, which serves food on metal tables beneath walls of peeling paint. We are the only Westerners. A television set high on the wall is showing women being interviewed in houses reduced to rubble. It's hard to tell if it's the West Bank or the suburbs of Baghdad, recently hit by air strikes ordered by America's new president, George W. Bush, but none of those watching shows any hostility towards us.

After eating a skeletal chicken in casserole, I buy a carton of Nancy's Tiviski brand camel's milk from the freezer behind the counter and drink it outside on a porch where there is, at least, some breeze. Basil is doing his flowing t'ai chi routine, which a couple of locals watch with amused curiosity.

'Kung fu?' asks one of them.

I nod. 'Sort of.'

After three journeys round the world with him, I'm used to Basil being mistaken for Bruce Lee.

Three hours later we are aboard the 80-foot floating platform that will take us into Senegal. It runs on African time, leaving only when it is full to bursting point.

The river, about a half-mile wide, curves languidly towards us through what might almost pass for meadows, which dip down to tall reed beds. Occasionally, the slim,

103

wooden canoes they call pirogues will put out from either shore, precariously packed with foot passengers, all standing.

On the far side are low buildings, a single palm tree, a water tower and a small crowd watching us as keenly as we're watching them. The fact that the town on both sides is called Rosso seems to misleadingly minimise the difference between the two banks. In fact, the Sénégal river, rising over 1000 miles away in the mountains of Guinea, is an important boundary. It separates not only Mauritania from Senegal, but also Sahara from Sahel, the transitional land, half desert and half savannah, whose name means 'shore' in Arabic. More significantly, the Sénégal river divides Arab Africa to the north from Black Africa to the south.

The last few passengers hurry aboard, urged into a sprint by the long-awaited rumble of the diesel engine. We move stiffly out into the stream. I want to stare into the dark brown tide and think romantic thoughts of Saharan rivers, but it's impossible. I've been trapped by a cheerfully persistent ten-year-old boy called Lallala who wants something, anything, from me.

I try to shut him up by giving him a tin of Smith and Kendon travel sweets I have with me. It doesn't work. He wants me to translate all the words on the lid.

'Ken-don? What is Ken-don?'

On Senegalese soil just before four o'clock. Our minders engage in a long negotiation over equipment and visas at the handsome customs shed, built like a small French town hall. It bears not only the inscription '*Directeur Général des Douanes de Republique de Sénégal*', but also a motto, '*Devenir Meilleur Pour Mieux Servir*' (Become Better to Serve Better). Very un-African.

104

Another long wait. Buses and trucks squeeze out of the narrow car park. Currency changers move amongst the recently arrived, offering deals on the Mauritanian *ouguiya*, which, on account of the foreign aid propping up Mauritania, is stronger than the CFA franc used by Senegal.

A tall man in a white robe wanders around calling out 'Me bank!' and waving a wad of notes.

To begin with, the roads this side of the border are much rougher. Tarred but severely pot-holed, they ensure a jolting, punishing ride towards St-Louis. Then, quite suddenly, we appear to have time-travelled to provincial France. The road surface becomes smooth and white-lined. Every village leading into St-Louis has speed restrictions and signs warning us to belt up, back and front. And there are cyclists everywhere, turning out of leafy lanes and emerging from the university campus on drop-handlebar bikes, wearing Tour de France T-shirts. I can't remember seeing bicycles at all in Mauritania. Basil agrees.

'Beat-up old cars and donkey carts and nothing in between.'

Shortly before six we cross a wide estuary onto a narrow island with a cathedral and cinemas and draw up beside the clipped hedges, shady balconies and colourful awnings of the Hôtel De La Poste, where a long line of Monsieur Hulots is waiting to sign in ahead of us. I can even use my mobile to phone home. This is more than culture shock. It's cultural convulsion.

BELOW

At the end of the island on which St-Louis, first French foothold in Africa, was founded, a museum and cultural centre rises beside the waters of the Sénégal. A school visit is in progress.

SENEGAL

DAY THIRTY-THREE ST-LOUIS

I've spent the last twenty-four hours in France. It was unadventurous, but it was easy, pottering around the hotel from bar to restaurant to the Piscine Jardin with its wrought-iron flamingos, or just sitting on my hibiscus-clad balcony watching the majestic Sénégal river sweep beneath the majestic seven-span girder bridge built by Louis Faidherbe, Governor of Senegal, in the 1860s. After a bit, the Frenchness became almost suffocating, from the check tablecloths to the endless pictures and models of the *colon*, the caricature of the Frenchman in Africa, complete with pipe and pith helmet.

The overriding obsession of the Hôtel de la Poste is with the 1920s, when St-Louis was the most important town in French colonial Africa and a company called Aeropostale launched a regular mail service from Toulouse to Dakar. The pilots flew their fragile planes alone, often through the night, without radio or radar, in all weathers. They became national heroes, with one of them, Antoine de Saint-Exupéry, writing bestselling books about his experiences. On 12 May 1930, a young man called Jean Mermoz took off from St-Louis and headed out across the Atlantic Ocean to make the first successful airmail connection with South America. The sky was no limit. Soon they were flying as far as Buenos Aires and even over the Andes to Santiago, Chile. Then, in December 1936, Mermoz left St-Louis in his sea-plane 'Croix du Sud' to make his twenty-fourth crossing of the Atlantic. He was never seen again.

Mermoz-mania still grips the hotel. Paintings of the planes and the epic route they covered are spread across the walls and even on the ceiling of the restaurant. In reception there are framed press clippings and evocative posters, and in a mural halfway up the stairs the head and shoulders of Mermoz rise from the cold grey waters of the Atlantic, as if gasping for one last breath.

Before flying he always stayed at the Hôtel de la Poste, and always in room 219, on the corner, with the river on one side and the Art Deco post office on the other. It's the room I'm in now.

Today I venture out of this tempting haven and take a longer look at St-Louis. No sooner have I stepped out into the street than a score of voices compete for my attention, crutches and wheelchairs race towards me and arms beckon me towards the pony and traps that wait listlessly by. I hire one for the morning and we set out across Faidherbe's bridge, which clangs and rumbles beneath a constant stream of foot, car, bicycle and hoof traffic.

One book I'm reading describes its builder as 'a visionary', a man who more than anyone embodied the ideal of a West African empire built upon the virtues of French culture and the French way of life. Faidherbe believed unquestioningly that *la mission civilisatrice*, if decisively and compassionately applied, would benefit the indigenous people, enabling them to set aside their ancient superstitions and divisive tribal loyalties and share in the Gallic enlightenment. They would become *les évolués*, the evolved.

BELOW

Fishwives in St-Louis. The fires burn all day long at this massive smokery on the banks of the River Sénégal.

It was already too late. The mixing of French and African cultures had been going on long before Faidherbe. Soldiers and traders from Bordeaux settled the town in the mid-seventeenth century and many married the local Fula women, creating an aristocratic class of mulattos, or *métis*, as the French called them. Many of these women became powerful and successful matriarchs, known as *signares*, and they wielded great influence in St-Louis.

My thin and straining horse, his coat worn black by the harness, seems happier when we are off the bridge, on which he slithered awkwardly. As we explore the quieter backside of the island, along by the wharves where the warehouses for the rich trade in gum arabic were located, it becomes clear that the French dream of urban orderliness is not shared by the majority of the Senegalese. The roofs of the old, red-tiled, balconied colonial buildings are full of holes. Their once neat shutters are missing and the rutted dirt streets beneath are full of people, talk, small-scale enterprise, food and rubbish.

Another, shorter bridge takes us onto a long thin finger of land between the river and the ocean. Having water around is such an unfamiliar experience that I hire a pirogue to take me back to the hotel. On the way, we pass an extraordinary Dickensian scene. Stretching along the banks of the river is a great concourse of fish smokeries. Long racks of darkening fish stretch across a fuggy landscape of makeshift ovens, tended by fierce and grimy women. They scream abuse and wave their arms at us when the camera turns towards them.

Eat a late lunch at the house of Jacob Yakouba, one of the best-known Senegalese artists. His house is surrounded by a pink-washed wall covered in bougainvillea and there is a large tent in the garden, where friends, fellow artists, writers and politicians can hang out. Here Jacob, like a cultural Godfather, dispenses advice, encouragement and artistic protection to a considerably extended family.

He's a stocky bear of a man, a Senegalese Picasso, with a massive head and thick calves emerging from capacious navy-blue shorts. He's been painting since he was seven. Despite his bull-like size, his gaze is gentle and his speech unexpectedly soft. I watch him working in his studio on a disappointingly

conventional portrait of a pretty, loosely clad woman. The walls of the studio are thick with similar paintings, all quite joyfully sexy.

'I prefer to paint women, first because of my mother, who helped me to become an artist. Then, because of my wife Marie-Madeleine. When I meet her it give me strength to focus my work on women.'

He admits that painting women so explicitly in a Muslim country could be a problem, but he has an international reputation and, anyway, fanaticism doesn't exist so much in Senegal.

'In St-Louis all the big families are Catholic or Muslim. We have always lived side by side. At Christmas the Muslims celebrate with the Catholics and during *Tabaski*, the sheep festival, the Catholics celebrate with the Muslims.'

He completes a last, long brush-stroke, caressing the outline of neck and shoulder, and stands back, head cocked.

'Anyway, women are beautiful. I was born from a woman so I don't see why there should be any taboos.'

At that moment there is a swirl of pink at the door and the aforementioned Marie-Madeleine makes a modestly grand entrance, to see if we are ready to eat. I realise that not only is she a formidable presence, but also her formidable figure is the subject of many of the paintings.

We sit round the table and all dip in to a single dish containing a powerfully delicious concoction called *domoda*. Fish balls, made with green onions, parsley, garlic and spices, are served in a rich stew with sweet potatoes. When I ask how long it must have taken someone to prepare all this Jacob beams at the womenfolk.

'They did it all,' he says generously, before adding, 'in the Moulinex.'

Much laughter.

Marie-Madeleine is probably better known in Senegal than Jacob, as she appears regularly in a TV soap opera, in which she plays a tough woman refusing to be traded between husbands. All of which makes for an interesting insight into marriage *à la Sénégal*.

Jacob explains that Islam gives the man the right to have up to four wives, but legally, under the Family Code, he must choose monogamy or polygamy. Once chosen the option cannot be reversed.

ABOVE

Life in St-Louis.
(LEFT) *Outside a shop with a tall, dashing salesman and short plaster figures of the* colon, *the caricature of the French colonialist in Africa.*
(CENTRE) *Women return from the market, heads full.*
(RIGHT) *At lunch with artist Jacob Yakouba and his soap-star wife, Marie-Madeleine. Beside her is either next week's script or a BBC contract. Either way, she doesn't look happy.*

109

Marie-Madeleine remembers the day she and Jacob went to the tribunal to get married.

'They asked Jacob, "Do you want to be monogamous or polygamous?"'

Jacob goes on. 'When I said monogamy, the judge just looked at me and said, "Hold on. Are you crazy, man?" I said why. He said, "You're a man, you'll regret this."'

Marie-Madeleine heaves with laughter.

'And how long have you been married?' I ask.

'Thirty years.'

As I leave I tell them we have to be in Dakar next morning. Jacob grimaces.

Has he ever thought of moving to the capital?

He shakes his head dismissively.

'Never!'

'Why is that?'

'Dakar has no soul, no life! *Pas d'âme!*'

DAY THIRTY-FOUR DAKAR

I peer desperately through the window of our vehicle looking for the soul of Dakar, but all I can see is a 30-foot-high Coca-Cola bottle and a lot of sheep. Then we plunge down beneath a flyover and onto a thickly clogged four-lane highway leading to the centre of the city.

Six hours after leaving St-Louis, we're picking our way slowly through suburban neighbourhoods sporting parking meters, traffic lights, health clubs, even a cyber café, and more sheep.

BELOW
All needs catered for on the streets of Dakar.

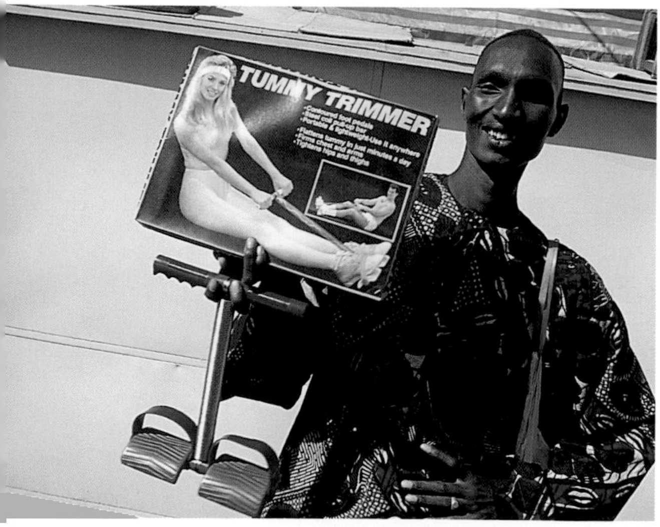

I'm bewildered by all this ovine activity, until I learn that we are a week away from *Tabaski*, the day on which Muslims commemorate the story they share with Jews and Christians of Abraham being commanded by God to sacrifice his son Isaac, only to spare him at the last minute and allow a sheep to be substituted. At *Tabaski* the head of every Muslim household must kill a sheep and cook it for his family. The deed must be done personally and the sheep must be alive on *Tabaski* morning, so a frozen supermarket sheep will not do. Which must account for the enormous number of fluffy white creatures massed in the city of Dakar this afternoon. Wherever a few blades of grass can be found they're nibbling away – on traffic islands, motorway verges and football pitches. Jarga, a sheep-fattening product, is advertised on billboards, and a banner spread across the street proclaims '*Promotion Tabaski*! *Gagnez des Moutons*!' – 'Win A Sheep!'

It's not only sheep they're selling. Every traffic jam is a retail opportunity in Dakar. Salesmen come tapping at the glass, offering up a formidable array of carved heads, sunglasses, hi-fi equipment, shirts, cutlery sets and carving knives (presumably for doing the deed on *Tabaski* morning). So slow is our progress that at one point salesman's enthusiasm successfully coincides with occupant's boredom, and Peter, our camera assistant, purchases some irresistible electronic bargain. The goods are handed over and Peter is sifting uncertainly through his CFAs when the lights change and we move unexpectedly rapidly across a busy intersection. The salesman plunges into the traffic and races suicidally after us. Just as he catches up, another bottleneck clears and we accelerate down a main road. All of us inside are now rooting for the waving figure behind, who, with total disregard for personal safety, leaps, vaults, twists and turns his way through the traffic to reach us just as the lights flick to green. Like a relay runner stretching for the baton, he grasps the money, and a great cheer goes up as we pull away.

Evening at our hotel overlooking the sea. Yellow weaver birds are busy in the trees, which swing and bend in a pushy westerly breeze. A couple of miles offshore is the low rocky outline of Goree Island, dark as its history. Goree was a trading depot for the rich produce of the African interior, gold, skins, gum arabic, but above all the several million slaves bought from Arab and African traders and shipped to the plantations of America by Portuguese, English, Dutch and French. Not that it was a business for which Westerners were originally responsible, for it had been going on long before they arrived. It's estimated that between ten and fourteen million slaves were transported across the desert between 650 and 1900. Goree has become the symbol of this most cruel of all Saharan trades, and is now a World Heritage Site, with many black Americans coming over to remember ancestors for whom Goree Island had been their last view of Africa.

I order a Gazelle beer and open up my map. I'm at the most westerly point of the African continent. However, there is a train that leaves this city twice a week for Bamako, the capital of Mali. It will take us back into the interior and to within striking distance of Timbuktu. That, I remind myself, is why we are here.

Dakar has a reputation as a lively, liberal, cosmopolitan town with a thriving music scene, which is why we find ourselves, late on this first evening, in a thatched shed down by the Fish Market. One side is open to the sea and the Atlantic slurps gently against a jetty, causing soft breezes to waft in and aerate the sticky atmosphere inside. Unfortunately, these cooling breezes also carry a pungent aroma of sewage and rotting fish. This seems to make absolutely no difference to the enthusiasm with which everyone throws themselves into dancing, foot-tapping and drinking to a six-man band called Nakodje. The sound is a fusion of Western and West African, with saxophone, clarinet and guitar lining up alongside Fula flute from Guinea and a *balaphon* (like a xylophone) from Mali. The audience embraces white and black, men and women in equal numbers. I find myself sitting next to a group of staid-looking Senegalese men in suits. They show a surprising interest in our filming and are keen to know if my programmes sell in Senegal. When I shake my head apologetically their eyes light up with relief, and they explain that they are Muslim and if it had been on Senegalese TV their wives would have seen them drinking beer.

The manager, a rangy black man with rubbery legs and red eyes, has taken a shine to me and announces my presence here to a bemused audience.

Towards the end of the evening, I'm at the bar drinking a last Flag beer and talking to Malek, the young Senegalese bass guitarist, who's halfway through a business management course, and Tom Vahle, an American member of the band, who has taught himself to play the Fula flute.

'It only has three holes in it. It's a combination of singing and blowing at the same time.'

An arm snakes round my shoulder and the face of the club manager looms close to mine. He's seriously unsteady now and I'm not altogether sure what he's on about.

'I'm Lebou,' he says with a flourish. 'We are fishermen, right. Dakar belongs to us.'

He's also an ex-basketball player, now sixty years old. I'm impressed and ask him how he stays in shape. He leers, wobbles, grabs my head and whispers loudly in my ear.

'Making love. Every single night.'

This boast completely convulses him and induces a brief coughing fit. My recollections of the ensuing conversation are hazy, to say the least, but I do remember a nicely surreal exchange when he was expanding on his previous experience.

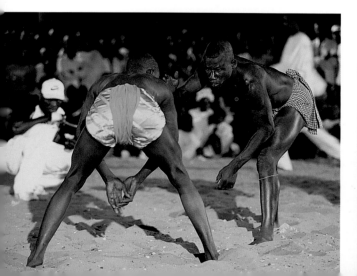

'Is this different from the other clubs you've managed?'

'Oh...yeah.'

'Why?'

'The other clubs were,' he pauses for quite a while, searching for the right word, 'rectangular.'

DAY THIRTY-FIVE DAKAR

The national sport of Senegal is *la lutte*, wrestling, and there is a competition tonight out in Pikine, one of the poorer suburbs of Dakar, which will be attended by Mor Fadan Wade, the great hero of Senegalese fighting, and one of the president's bodyguards. Though we have an early start to catch the Bamako train tomorrow, this sounds like an unmissable opportunity.

It's a long drive across town and the paved roads have turned to sand by the time we pull up beside a collection of low, dimly lit buildings. We're warned to watch our belongings, but the young men who crowd around the bus offering to carry our gear are exuberant rather than threatening, and I feel more secure out here than in the centre of town.

A circle of white plastic chairs marks the ring where the wrestling will take place. The sandy arena is illuminated by floodlights on tall poles and a PA system is already in operation blasting out exhortations to the slowly gathering crowd.

I'm taken through an entrance behind the floodlights to meet the man himself. A passageway opens onto a small courtyard, which resembles a scene from my first illustrated Bible. Mor Fadan, a huge man with shaved head and wearing a light blue robe, dominates the space, and around him are gathered, in various attitudes of deference, men, women, children and, of course, sheep. A steady stream of people come in to shake his mighty hand. Someone calls me over and the fawners and grovellers are pushed to one side as I'm led before him.

His sheer bulk could bring out the fawner and groveller in anyone, but it's the only thing about him that's intimidating. His handshake is soft as putty and his voice is deep and measured. He answers my damn fool questions with extraordinary patience. Yes, this is his house. Yes, he has two wives, but bashfully adds that he can't remember how many children, and, yes, he is the African Olympic Wrestling Champion.

BELOW
Wrestling is the second biggest sport in Senegal.
(FAR LEFT)
At a local contest in a Dakar suburb, the boys show how it should be done.
(CENTRE AND RIGHT)
My failed attempt to leave without the cheerleader noticing. Ah well, something else to add to the CV.

He talks of the popularity of the sport, which is second only to football in Senegal, and it's clear that this man who can fill stadiums is only here tonight to encourage the young local boys. The entourage closes in again, someone finds me a Coke and I escape outside for a breather.

The ringside is filling up and the ring is full of leaping, strutting, chasing and grappling children mimicking their heroes. The night-time chill reminds me of the desert. It must have been around 35°C/95°F on the streets of Dakar this afternoon. Now it's cool enough to pull on a sweater.

Mor Fadan asks me to sit beside him during the fights. This is quite a moment for a shy boy from Sheffield, entering the ring and being introduced to the local mafia as Mor's new bosom buddy, but there's still no sign of any serious grappling taking place.

The contestants are parading around the ring in a rhythmic dance, all linked together and kicking their feet out in a sort of macho hokey-kokey. Then, one after the other, they approach the thudding drums and dance up against them, rhythm fighting rhythm, as they strut their aggressive poses, kicking the sand like angry elephants. The drummers, stripped to the waist and glistening like contestants themselves, keep up a relentless, brain-scouring beat.

A couple of comperes work the crowd, screaming themselves hoarse, urging, exhorting, praising, joking. It's after midnight when the local politicians, bigwigs and worthies make their appearance, all anxious to clutch, and be seen to be clutching, the champion's hand.

By now, the contestants, uniformly lean, wiry and young, are stripped down to single elaborately tied loincloths, like underfed sumo wrestlers, raising the level of excitement amongst the women in the crowd. (There is none of the public segregation we saw in the Arab countries). Their cries and shouts of encouragement merge with the throbbing of the drums and the relentless yelling of the comperes as the bouts, at last, begin.

Starting with a curiously fey stance, like cats on their back legs, the wrestlers flap at each other's hands, before grasping each other in a shoulder lock. A flick of the legs from this position can send an opponent off balance and onto the floor, and once a shoulder hits the sand the bout is over. Some contests last a few seconds and others can go on for minutes, as bodies freeze in perfect equilibrium, each one waiting for a moment of weakness to send his opponent tumbling. It lacks the theatrical flamboyance of Western wrestling but makes up for it in a fascinating contest of balance, co-ordination and sheer physical strength.

By one o'clock the crowd has grown to several thousand and I'm told this will last long into the night. Mindful of the fact that we start a thirty-six-hour train journey tomorrow, I'm going to have to go. A discreet exit is not possible. As I get up to leave one of the comperes spars up to me and draws me into the ring, dancing before me and grasping me in mock combat until he releases me with an enormous beam on his face. The crowd laughs and applauds. As we drive out of the dusty run-down suburbs and head for the sea, I'll not easily forget my night in Pikine.

DAY THIRTY-SIX   DAKAR TO BAMAKO

The railway line that runs for 760 miles from Dakar on the Atlantic Ocean to Bamako on the River Niger was built long before the countries it connects came into being. When work began in Bamako in 1907, Mali was called French Sudan, and when the railway reached Dakar in 1923, Senegal was an anonymous part of French West Africa.

Not surprisingly, the station from which we are due to leave at ten o'clock this morning is a confident example of the colonial style. It consists of three arched bays, framed by red and brown brickwork, with wrought-iron canopies, pilasters supporting decorated tile friezes, separate entrances marked 'Départ' and 'Arrivée', and a big working clock in the central tower. On either side of the central façade are louvered galleries, which look to be occupied. Laundry lines swing in the breeze and I think I can see sheep up there.

We've been warned that Dakar is the pickpocket capital of the world, and exploratory arms have already stretched through the minibus windows. An opportunist salesman tries to interest us in a range of 'Titanic' sports bags, which, as the volume of our luggage is already proving a problem for the porters, is an act of mindless optimism.

As the Bamako express only runs twice a week, there's a certain amount of nervous tension as we walk ourselves and our procession of porters through 'Départ' to the platform where our train, twelve coaches and four freight wagons long, sits waiting in the sun. The coaches, old French railway stock painted light and dark green with a red stripe, bear the barely legible name Chemins de Fer de Mali. A General Motors diesel is panting heavily at the front.

We pull out of Dakar twenty-one minutes late and run for a while past red-brick, red-tiled sheds. These soon give way to a depressing run of goat-attended rubbish dumps and people squatting down beneath fading signs that read 'Défense d'Uriner et Déposer ses Ordures' (No Urinating or Dumping of Rubbish).

The train is a huge consumer unit, a small town on wheels, and wherever we stop we attract crowds of suppliers. As we crawl through the suburbs of Dakar it's like taking a train through the middle of a department store. On both sides of us are piles of handbags, underwear, men's fashion, ladies fashion, shoes, scarves, robes and hats. All within inches of our rumbling steel wheels.

The restaurant car is going to be a vital part of our survival strategy. First signs are encouraging. It's comfortable enough, with a mural painted at one end, and not too busy, as most of the passengers bring their own food or buy at the window.

ABOVE

Pensive moment in the buffet car of the Dakar-Bamako express, when the shirt was still clean and the delay only three hours. It grew to eight.

RIGHT

Like driving through a department store. The train narrowly misses a market outside Dakar.

An American woman and her companion, a man from Guinea, are at one of the tables. She's a New Yorker living in Dakar. She has silver earrings and a thick pair of Ray-Bans. I ask her what she misses about Dakar when she goes back to the States.

'Oh, just about everything,' she says, drawing out the words with relish. 'The way people say hello to each other, take time to greet each other.'

Greeting is important in Africa. I've noticed that. It's not something that should ever be hurried.

We fall to talking about countries and boundaries. Her friend Barik regrets the failure of an attempt to set up a West African federation after independence.

'The countries shouldn't have been isolated. Historically, there were huge states that covered large portions of the Sahara.'

The Mali Empire and the Ghana Empire were two such states. Rich and sophisticated civilisations of the fifteenth and sixteenth centuries when, according to Barik, people travelled in perfect safety across vast areas. The modern states, he thinks, have created arbitrary and unworkable boundaries. He cites the River Sénégal border between Mauritania and Senegal.

'The same people live on both sides of the river, but they can no longer cross freely.'

We're now away from the crowded Dakar corridor and passing through flat countryside studded with the curious battleship-grey baobab trees. With their thick metallic trunks and stubby branches, they look like some prehistoric arboreal throwback, gnarled and twisted like old prize-fighters.

The baobab is not like other trees. It gets smaller as it grows older. It stores copious amounts of water in its trunk and can survive for hundreds of years, because it won't burn. Its bark provides rope and packing material, its sweet-smelling flowers provide food and decoration and a medicine called *alo*, its pulp is good for blood circulation and its seeds for fertiliser. Scarcely surprising, therefore, that this ugly duckling is a source of considerable superstition, revered in every community and often used as a burial place. Looking at them as they pass by the window, they look friendless and faintly absurd, and it isn't hard to see why people believe the story that the devil planted them upside down.

In a nearby couchette is an English teacher, an impressive Fulani woman in a pale purple robe and headdress and a striking silver necklace. With her confident English and her forthright, expressive delivery, she seems to epitomise the strength and presence that I've seen in many black West African women. Rather disconcertingly, for such an embodiment of the matriarchal virtues, her name is Daddy. Well, that's how it's pronounced. It's spelt D-h-a-d-i.

I ask her about the role of women in West Africa.

'She is the protector, you know, the keeper of, let's say, a culture, a civilisation. It's the role of a woman to take care of children, you know. She can give advice, she retains a lot of secrets.'

When I ask her what sort of secrets, she uses the example of female circumcision, or excision, which is still carried out here when girls are ten or eleven.

'It is said that a girl must be excised. If she's not excised she's like a male.'

I've heard this justification for circumcision before. The belief that the foreskin is something female in the male and the clitoris something male in the female.

'There is a woman who is going to be in charge of their education during that time of excision. She's going to teach them how to take care of their husband when they get married. She's going to teach them to be submissive to their in-laws, their husband, for a good wife is the one who is submissive. So, that's why I was telling you that the woman holds the secret of African society.'

BELOW

A sweet potato changes hands at Kayes station. The mud-stained coach bears the logo of Chemins de Fer de Mali.

ABOVE

At Kidira station on
the border between
Senegal and Mali. To
the left of my green
train is the Bamako-
Dakar express going
the other way. It
consists of the
smarter silver stock
of Senegalese
Railways.

'Is it changing? I mean all this being taught to be submissive.'

She spreads her hands helplessly.

'This is something crazy. I'm not going to be submissive to my husband, you know. Maybe to respect my husband, but he's going to respect me too.'

As for female circumcision, she thinks it will begin to die out. The National Assembly in Senegal has brought in a law against it, but the women who were practising it, the ones who held the secrets, are having to be given financial incentives to end their vested interest in this particular ritual.

Dhadi is a Muslim, but stoutly against the prevailing custom of polygamy.

'First of all, I'm jealous. I don't want to share my husband. And then second,' she wags her finger to formidable effect, 'in every polygamist house there is trouble. Because co-wives, you know, are jealous. Sometimes one of the wives will go to the marabout...'

'The marabout?'

'Well, he's the kind of priest...he's a seer. He can see into the future and also he can, you know, make some juju. And for example, if one of the kids fails his exam, she says to the marabout, "It's my co-wife. She's a witch. That's why my kid can't succeed."'

She doesn't hold out much hope that polygamy will go the way of circumcision. She reckons only 3 or 4 per cent of Senegalese feel as she does.

'These are hard times. I believe it will change, but it will be hard, very hard.'

It's not just what she says but how she says it that makes Dhadi exceptional. Or maybe not. Maybe African women are by nature more direct, more open, more honest and considerably less submissive than their menfolk expect them to be.

Night falls and we are still some way short of the Malian border. To the bar, where three or four customers are gathered in the gloom, drinking Cokes from the bottle. I'm the only one ordering beer, until the crew finish filming of course. The barman is a big man with a tartan cap and shades. A radio is crackling out. Highlights of a football game. Last night Senegal were playing a vital World Cup qualifying match with Morocco. I ask the result. It was a draw. Senegal are through to the finals.

Chicken for supper. It's fine, but the bench I sit on collapses.

DAY THIRTY-SEVEN DAKAR TO BAMAKO

After a night of slow jolting progress, during which I dreamt of baobab trees and disorder, we've reached Kidira, on the Senegal-Mali border. It's been daylight for almost an hour and the train has been firmly stationary since then.

This is up-country rural Africa, with none of the shouting and hysteria of the city we left twenty-one hours ago. Because of the great heat, people move slowly, if they move at all. Employees of the railway unload packages without urgency, breaking off at the slightest excuse to slap hands, exchange jovial greetings and embark on long, animated conversations punctuated by inexplicably hysterical laughter.

When we finally depart Kidira at half past nine, we've slipped four hours behind schedule. Five minutes later we cross the Falémé, a tributary of the Sénégal, cutting north to south with a red earth escarpment rising on its eastern bank. We're now in Mali. By midday we're alongside the Sénégal itself, flowing strong and substantial, through the arid bush country, known by its French name, *la brousse*.

A long halt at Kayes, which has the reputation of being the hottest town in Africa, set in a bowl surrounded by hills full of iron-bearing rock. Check my thermometer. It's 39°C in the shade, 102°F, not bad for February. The barman and restaurant car staff are out on the platform, seeking relief beneath an umbrageous mimosa. Opposite is a big handsome run-down colonial building, an uncommon mix of Franco-Moorish styles, red brick combined with horseshoe arches and elaborate balconies. It appears to be occupied by dozens of families. By the side of the railway track the words '*Défense d'Uriner, 3000 Fr.*' are fading slowly from the wall.

Just when it seems we might be destined to spend the rest of our lives in Kayes, a

LEFT

At Mehani in Mali, the local train we've waited two hours for pulls in, and becomes an instant shopping mall.

119

shudder runs through the train and we jerk into motion. Our endlessly cheery guard reckons we'll be in Bamako at ten o'clock tonight and slaps his hand in mine to seal the prediction.

The scenery changes now, as we cross the land of the Malinke people, from whom Mali took its name. This is more like the heat-cracked plateau of Mauritania than the flat bush country of Senegal. Escarpments and weirdly sculpted rocks rise around us. We stop at stations without platforms, surrounded by thatch-roofed rondavels and mud huts, where women with charcoal braziers in one hand and corn-cobs in the other ply the train, selling bananas, roast goat, loaves of bread, tea, smoked fish, yams, bags of nuts.

At a place called Mehani we are becalmed again, waiting for a train from Bamako to come through on the single-track line ahead of us.

I feel tired, unwashed and greasy, but I keep my spirits up by reading Sanche de Gramont's *The Strong Brown God*, and imagining how immeasurably more awful it was for the British explorer Mungo Park, as he made his way through this same territory in 1796, intent on becoming the first Westerner to set eyes on the fabled River Niger.

Dusk is falling as the Bamako-Kayes train comes in. It pulls up opposite us, each window crammed with faces.

The last sight I remember before night falls is crossing the Sénégal for the very last time, at the point where, fed by the Bafing and Bakoye rivers, it is a majestic half-mile wide, its banks turning a deep ruddy brown in the dying light.

It's ten o'clock and we are still so far from Bamako that I cannot even make light of it with our friendly guard. Faced with the realisation that we shall have to spend another night on the train, the spirit seems to have gone out of everyone. They just want to be home, not on this hot and sticky train, full of people but empty of almost everything else. There is an air of resigned listlessness as we swing once more into the darkness.

MALI

DAY THIRTY-EIGHT   BAMAKO

As if this second, unscheduled night is not wretched enough, my bowels, so well-disciplined since Western Sahara, suddenly demand attention. It's as if they know that it's hot, the train is unstable, there's no water left in any of the lavatories and there's someone sleeping in the corridor who I have to step over each time.

As my internal convulsions match those of the train, I look in vain for any sign of city lights, but it's not until five o'clock that I hear J-P outside my door.

'Breakfast in Bamako,' he announces cheerfully.

Forty-three hours after leaving Dakar, eight hours later than schedule, having covered the distance at an average speed of 28 miles per hour, we creak to a halt at Bamako station at 5.40 on a Monday morning. For a moment all is quiet. The first streaks of dawn light pierce the clouds in the eastern sky, the smell of a new day edges out the smell of an over-used train, and though we can see only the darkened outlines of station buildings, there is an air of expectation.

Then the doors swing open and for the first time I realise just how many people have been aboard the Dakar-Bamako express. And how much they've brought with them. The narrow platform is soon submerged beneath people and their stuff. Chairs, sofas, lengths of carpet, great bulging sacks, cooking stoves, lengths of piping. All become weapons in the fight for the exit.

We are trying our best to film this, which only adds to the chaos. Two men offering us taxis and cheap hotels follow us everywhere. Somewhere further up the platform there are cries and shouts and people fall back as a scuffle begins. A man suspected of stealing has been dragged off the train and is being savagely beaten by his fellow passengers.

I make a scrawled note in my diary: 'Bamako Station, 5.40 am. The Heart of Darkness'.

Breakfast in Bamako. Part Two. A couple of hours ago I felt like a piece of litter ready to be swept up and thrown away. Now I'm sitting by the banks of the River Niger with a cup of coffee and a plate of bacon and eggs in front of me. I'm washed and freshly dressed and have just seen a sunrise as beautiful as any since this journey began. Deepest gloom has given way, suspiciously quickly, to pure, uncritical ecstasy, as we sit on this terrace on stilts built out over the river that will lead us to Timbuktu. A golden sun grows in confidence. There is a swimming pool, fresh fruit, and a day off to rest, relax and generally wallow in the delights of not having to move.

DAY FORTY   BAMAKO

At first light this morning the surface of the River Niger shone like silver, and as I watched, a boy in a dug-out canoe slowly poled himself through the water hyacinth, a slim black silhouette against the lightening sky, as spare and sharp as a character in Chinese calligraphy.

An hour later the sun is up and the banks of the river are lined with children

BELOW

Bamako, Mali. First sight of the River Niger. The terrace of the Hotel Mande, on which I eat the best breakfast of the entire trip, pokes into view from behind the bougainvillea.

bathing and men and women washing. This is where the hotel laundry is done and it's deeply satisfying to watch my travel-worn jeans being pounded against the rock whilst I drink a cup of coffee on the terrace.

We drive into Bamako. The road surface is like a Mohican haircut. A thin strip of tarmac, worn down to hard-baked earth on either side. Like Nouakchott in Mauritania, Bamako is a city that has grown fast since independence, and for the same reasons – drought and the southward march of the Sahara Desert. Forty years ago, 160,000 people lived here; now there are more than a million, one tenth of the population of this huge country, and enough of them have old, poorly maintained cars to fill the air with a pervasive soup of pollution.

We pass buildings that date Bamako's history like rings on a tree trunk. First, and nearest the hotel, the gorgeously named Bobolibougou market, a forest of stalls stretching way back from the roadside and disappearing into Stygian gloom. Their knobbly wood frames and thatched roofs cannot have changed much since Mungo Park came here. Further into town, the road leads us past the heart-sinking bulk of the Hôtel l'Amitié, ten storeys of grey concrete with grass sprouting from the cracks. This unlovely landmark is a reminder of the days after independence, when Mali took the hardline socialist route, bankrolled by China and the Soviet Union. A later stage of development is represented by the Saudi-financed road bridge across the Niger, and one later still by the unmissable BCEAO tower, a bank headquarters which looks from a distance like a skyscraper made of mud. This could be said to represent the latest phase of Mali's development – African capitalism.

The everyday commercial life of Bamako is not to be found in air-conditioned office blocks, but out in the open, on the hot, busy streets. This is where we find the fetish stalls, stocked with animal skins, shrunken monkey heads, dried ears and hearts, bird's feet, crocodile parts and all the other charms and potions for the *gri-gri* – black magic or traditional healing – which is still such a powerful force in the country.

This is where we find the windowless huts of businesses with names like 'Coiffure, Harrods style' and 'M. Yattara, Boutique', the latter, consisting of a table, a bench and a kettle, located outside the gates of the station we arrived at two mornings ago. So low were my spirits then that I hardly noticed the station itself, which is another French colonial gem, faced in local red sandstone, roofed in terracotta tiles and dominated by a clock tower with the proud inscription 'Chemin de Fer de Dakar en Niger' picked out in gold leaf. Sadly, the original clock has gone missing and been inadequately replaced by one out of somebody's kitchen. Less grand, but equally purposeful inscriptions adorn the walls of the forecourt, including two *'Défense d'Uriner'* signs and a third which warns: *'Défense* Absolut *d'Uriner'*, under pain of arrest by Special Police. The mind boggles at what sort of highly honed skills these special police must require.

Order a coffee, which is made in a tall glass with about eight grains of Nescafé and half a tin of evaporated milk. It tastes disgusting. Mr Yatarra is a character though. He speaks good English and eyes us with lofty amusement. When J-P asks him if he is happy for us to film, he pats the side of his voluminous *djellaba*.

'I am happy in my pocket,' he says beadily, demonstrating a shrewd feel for First-World guilt.

'This is Africa. You must give me something. We are many.'

A beggar approaches, holding his tin with the stump of a severed arm. Mr Yatarra ignores him.

Watching people coming and going, I'm impressed once again by how much in Africa travels by head. A woman strides by, carrying a riot of carrots that seem to sprout from her like orange dreadlocks, another bears two large clay pots, each at least a foot across, one on top of the other and both on top of her head. A very lean, tall man in a 'Giggs 11' T-shirt, a pile of sports bags on his head, reluctantly breaks step to avoid an older man, head bent beneath the weight of two double mattresses.

In an attempt to make sense of such an exhilarating but unfamiliar world, I hope to meet up with Toumani Diabate, one of a group of local poets and musicians which is building a growing following for Malian music in Europe and America, and whose album, *Djelika*, I've been listening to constantly for the last three months.

Everyone seems to know Toumani. As soon as I mention his name Mr Yatarra nods and points out the way to his house.

'Another coffee?'

'Not right now, thanks.'

It turns out that Toumani has seven houses and no-one is quite sure which one he's in. We're told to await him at the most likely, a tall rambling complex off a baked-earth street. It's a modest enough area, but lines of broken glass and razor wire on top of the 15-foot walls of the courtyard are a bit of a giveaway. The rock star-style elusiveness and eventual arrival in dazzling white open-topped Mercedes lead me to suspect ego trouble. I could not have been more wrong.

The expedition that finally solved the riddle was inspired not so much by religion or commerce as scientific curiosity. The African Association, founded in London in 1788, charged the young Scotsman Mungo Park with the task of discovering, once and for all, 'the rise, the course, and the termination of the Niger'.

Park and his expedition started inland from Gambia in June 1795. After extraordinary misadventures, terrible hardships and considerable dangers, they reached the town of Ségou over a year later.

Mid-afternoon, 204 years later, *I*'ve reached Ségou, after a four-hour drive from Bamako, and I'm standing on a soft sand beach with a copy of Mungo Park's journal, *Travels into the Interior of Africa*, open at his entry for 20 July 1796.

'As I was anxiously looking around for the river, one of them called out, *geo affili* (see the water), and looking forwards, I saw with infinite pleasure the great object of my mission – the long-sought-for, majestic Niger, glittering to the morning sun, as broad as the Thames at Westminster, and flowing *slowly to the eastward.*'

With this single observation, Mungo Park saw off 2000 years of error. It was one of the great geographical discoveries. Encouraged, Park set himself the greater task of tracing the course of the entire river. He was brave, but also obtuse and severely inept at man management, and ten years later he died in a hail of spears and arrows as his boat raced through a gorge at Jebba, in what is now Nigeria. He never succeeded in following the river to the sea.

Looking out now across a broad, placid, unexpectedly blue stream, with kingfishers hovering and sweeping down into the reed-beds, it's hard to believe that this river could have been the cause of so much pain and grief before the riddle of its course was finally solved, forty years after Mungo Park stood here. We now know it to be the third longest river in Africa, flowing for 2600 miles from the mountain rainforests of Guinea, making a long slow horseshoe bend through the Sahara, then turning south to reach the sea in a wide marshy delta near Port Harcourt in Nigeria.

Ségou is one of a string of towns sustained by the Niger, and despite having busy streets and one or two company headquarters, its mood seems to reflect the pace of the river, calm and pleasantly unruffled. Lorries rumble ponderously up from the riverbank, laden with freshly made mud bricks that have been hardening in the sun. Out on the stream, fishermen in pirogues as slender as driftwood pole themselves in and out of a lazy current, so sluggish that, to be honest, I wouldn't be able to tell which way it was flowing. A sandy road has become a temporary football pitch and misdirected passes bounce off cars without anybody seeming to care very much.

Between the high walls of old colonial villas, a track leads through to a riverside street, on which is a haven called L'Auberge. A small terrace with white tables and red chairs leads into a cool dark room with a long polished wood bar, which doubles as reception. The only occupant is a tall, ascetic, white man with an untended beard and a backpack that rises above his head like some portable throne. The walls are decorated with masks, drums, necklaces of cowrie shells and some richly carved wooden doors, which, I'm told, are made by the Dogon people who live, almost hidden away, in the mountains north and east of the river. The special of the day is chalked up on a board. Rabbit with baked apple. The prospect of anything without chicken in it reduces me to near-slobbering hysteria.

The owner appears from behind the bar. He's soft-spoken and welcoming and his name is Abi Haila. He's Lebanese. His countrymen, he says, are like the Irish, scattered all over the world. His father's family came here in 1914 on a boat full of emigrants, who got off in Dakar thinking it was Brazil, or so he says. Anyway they stayed and prospered and now run a number of hotels and businesses. This appealing, hospitable, unpretentious place seems a tempting alternative to the drive to Djenné, but it's fatal to blur the distinction between holiday and filming, and after a couple of chilled Castel beers it's back to the schedule.

We eat on the move. Goat roasted at a stall on the outskirts of Ségou and served in brown paper. Once past the aromatic taste of the charcoal, it's a long, long chew. I'm still finding bits of it in my teeth when we turn off the main road and into Djenné five hours later. The overhead lights of a gas station illuminate an enigmatic scene; a donkey and cart drawn up beside a petrol pump.

Djenné is surrounded by the waters of the Bani river for most of the year, and even now, when the river is low, we have to wait for a ferry to take us across. Alongside us is a pick-up, whose cargo seems to defy all the laws of physics. Boxes, bags, plastic sacks, rolls of carpet and car tyres rise above it, layer perched on swaying layer, and on top of it all are a half dozen trussed sheep.

LEFT
Riverbank life at Ségou. Livestock sniffs around the brickyard.

DAY FORTY-TWO DJENNE

ABOVE

*Architectural star
of the Sahara. The
Great Mosque at
Djenné, the largest
mud-brick
building in the
world. The
projecting wooden
posts are for the
masons to stand on
during the yearly
re-mudding of the
mosque.*

Of all the cities on the edge of the Sahara Djenné is the one I'm most excited about. Ever since I first saw pictures of the mud-made Great Mosque with its distinctive conical towers, pierced by wooden beams which jut out of the walls as if the building were undergoing acupuncture, I've had it marked down as somewhere unique and exotic.

Obviously others have too, for my night's sleep at the tourist *campement* is constantly interrupted by sounds of flushing, washing, coughing, farting and footsteps. This journey has been so far off the beaten track that I'd forgotten about tour groups. These are the first we've come across since Marrakesh. One group is British. I know I shouldn't feel this way, but when I'm asked if I've ever been to Stoke-on-Trent all my romantic illusions of desert travel begin to wilt.

Watch brilliantly coloured geckoes darting about the garden until our guide arrives. He's an energetic, eloquent, persuasive local man called Amadou Cissé but known to all as Pigmy, because by Malian standards he is compact. I instinctively feel I shall be all right with Pigmy. He's steeped in local life and has a twitchily restless urge to show me the town. He wears a loose brown robe, one of the wide-brimmed, triangular Fulani hats with a bobble on top that remind me of Moroccan tagines, dark glasses and a big silver Rolex. It's going to be hot he says (what's new?), so we should get out early. It's also market day, so the town will be full, and what's more, it's the market day before the festival of *Tabaski*, so it will be full of sheep. As head of a household he is expected to make a sacrifice and a decent-looking ram is top of his shopping list. We launch into the crowd, most of whom Pigmy seems to know intimately. Barely breaking his stride, he networks his way forward, grabbing hands, kissing cheeks (of men only) and tossing tantalising morsels of information over his shoulder.

'That's my cousin, he's crazy!...Her brother knows my sister...He is my friend, he owes me money.'

There is no sheep shop as such. Pigmy merely pushes through until he finds a man standing on a corner with a few animals around him. He is a lot older than Pigmy with a pinched face, shrewd moustache and white skullcap. After handshakes and banter he indicates his best beast and Pigmy squats down and begins to feel around.

'It should be a really good and complete sheep, you see.' His voice drifts up from somewhere down by its backside. 'Not with one eye or one leg.' He examines its balls closely. 'Should be like a very nice sheep.'

Pigmy straightens up and turns to the sheep merchant, pointing out a tiny contusion on its nose. 'You have some problem here.' He shakes his head and ostentatiously starts to look elsewhere.

The sheep seller knows that with less than twenty-four hours to go before *Tabaski* he may well get left with surplus animals. Numbers are discussed. Pigmy haggles him down from 40,000 to 37,500 francs, about £37.50. A lot of money, but as Pigmy says it is an important festival and a man in his position is expected to buy the best he can. Two boys are summonsed and sent to deliver the beast to Pigmy's house. We plough on into the crowd.

Many of these people are not from Djenné, but from surrounding villages, too small to have markets of their own. The men fish and herd the animals, the women prepare them for market, making yoghurt, smoking fish. He shows me the different sections of the market: the Bambara people with their millet and rice, the Fulani with their milk and butter, and the smoked and cured produce of the Niger fishermen, disconcertingly called Bozos.

He gives me advice on how to tell Fulani women. Swiftly raking the crowd, he picks out a strikingly tall woman in a dress and headscarf of busy matching patterns.

'She is one.'

Pigmy points at her face.

'You see the tattooing here, round her mouth and this here,' he says, indicating a small mark below her right eye. 'This shows the family she is from.'

I'm impressed by his diagnosis, until he rather spoils it by adding, 'I know her. She is my sister's cousin.'

After the two of them have exchanged a brief and apparently contentious piece of family gossip, we move on.

'They are the most beautiful women in Africa,' he enthuses, breaking off to draw my attention to someone who looks more gorgeous than any we've seen today.

'She is not Fulani,' he says dismissively, 'she is Songhai.'

He comes up to a girl with a round face, doe-like eyes and large breasts.

'She is Fulani,' says Pigmy with a big smile. 'This is Aya. My family wanted me to marry her.'

I think I'm beginning to get the hang of this. If Pigmy fancies them, they're Fulani.

Making the most of the shade, we walk through a low building onto a factory floor of women at sewing machines, maybe forty or fifty of them, every one clacking away at full tilt to satisfy the crowd waiting to collect repaired clothes, re-stitched sheets, finished dresses, robes, headdresses. Then we're out of this dark and tumultuously noisy room and into a light and tumultuously noisy square, at the far end of which, bathed in dusty sunlight, is the building I feel I know so well, the Grande Mosquée, the largest mud-built structure in Africa.

'In the world,' Pigmy corrects me.

To Western steel, glass and concrete tastes, the mud-walled mosque seems to obey none of the normal rules of construction. It's organic, fairy-tale architecture, the ultimate winner of any beach building competition. Instead of the columns, capitals and cornices we've been brought up to think of as architectural basics, it features tall conical shapes reminiscent of termite mounds. Three 40-foot towers, each one crowned with an ostrich egg, face onto the square, linked by a wall of slim, pointed buttresses.

The mud walls are renewed every year in one great communal enterprise. Women carry the water to mix the mortar, which the men then carry and apply to the walls, using the projecting beams like scaffolding. During the work, anyone who needs refreshment is invited in and given tea by the old ladies of the town, but anyone seen to be avoiding work is hooted at by the women.

Pigmy waxes lyrical about the hundred pillars inside and the hundred windows in the roof, but when I ask if I can go and see them he is apologetic. Apparently, some Americans recently used the interior for a fashion shoot and so offended local sensibilities that non-Muslims are no longer allowed in.

We walk back together to Pigmy's house, through quieter streets, where all the houses seem miniatures of the mosque, walls modelled with plaster laid over mud brick, one organic outer-skin, buttressed and rounded off. Outside one house, a group of children are mixing fresh mortar with their feet, imitating the tradition of the *barey*, the master masons of Djenné. The mortar looks grey and lifeless until it dries on the walls and soaks up the sunlight and turns a soft brown. At sunrise and sunset it is golden.

At Pigmy's house I meet his wife of eight months. She sits in a doorway of the courtyard, having her ankles hennaed for the big day tomorrow. She's placid and pretty, with an aura of quiet ease that contrasts sharply with Pigmy's restless energy. I ask how they met. Apparently, she sold milkshakes in the market and Pigmy flirted with her (as I'd seen him do with cousins and sisters of friends that he encountered earlier today). Milkshakes, however, grew into true love. His parents were not keen, because she was a country girl and he was a relatively affluent city boy. Pigmy is strong-willed and insisted on marrying her, even though the price he paid for not having a wife found for him by the family was to forfeit gifts from his parents' friends.

He speaks earnestly of her many virtues, but she says nothing, just turns her big brown eyes towards him. The woman who is preparing her feet for the henna is, by contrast, an older woman, with a canniness that reflects a much deeper knowledge of life. Occasionally she will break into Pigmy's romantic banter with muttered asides that send him into fits of laughter. He turns to me.

'She is like a *griot*,' he explains. 'She is free to say anything she wants.'

This sounds interesting.

'Can you ask her to tell me the real story, Pigmy?'

He translates. She replies with a wicked smile. He rocks back with laughter.

'She say, if she were English, she would tell you a lot of things, but she don't speak English.'

He throws a sidelong glance at his adoring wife.

'I think it's good she don't speak English.'

DAY FORTY-THREE DJENNE

Tabaski morning in Djenné. The dust is rising in the streets. Pigmy, resplendent in a billowing robe of crisp white cotton trimmed with silver and grey embroidery, is walking with me and many hundreds of others to hear the imam's address and witness the ritual sacrifice that will be the signal for the day's festivities to begin. I feel conspicuously dull in my chinos and Gap Oxford, for all around me people are in their traditional finery. Malians dress splendidly anyway, but today they pull the stops out. No two people in this vast throng seem to be dressed alike.

This celebration of the sparing of Abraham's son from sacrifice is one of the most important days in the Muslim calendar. It's not so much the sparing itself they celebrate, but Abraham's act of obedience, his willingness to sacrifice his own son if that was what his God ordered him to do. Submission to the will of Allah is the cornerstone of Islam. It is what the word Islam means.

There are so many people expected at these special prayers that the mosque is too small to hold them, so the ceremony takes place in an open area at the edge of town. Getting there is like being in a football crowd on its way to the stadium. We're swept along by a generally good-natured, expectant, ever-growing tide. It's going to be a very hot day, and many are carrying prayer mats in one hand and big, colourful umbrellas in the other. At the site, worshippers assemble in long rows, those with the biggest umbrellas and the finest prayer mats in the front and the least privileged in an overspill yard with only strips of paper to kneel on.

Women are conspicuous by their absence. When I ask where they are Pigmy shifts a little uncomfortably.

'The women will be at the back,' he says vaguely.

The truth of which I can't check, as the back of the crowd is now so far away.

Pigmy estimates today's attendance at around 8000. All over the Arab world there will be similar gatherings, and by the end of the day several million sheep will have disappeared off the face of the earth.

The imam steps up to a microphone set up beneath the sort of garish orange umbrella you might find at a beach bar. A few feet away, tethered in the shade of a neem tree, is the beast he will soon slaughter. It paces about, bleating every now and then and eyeing the growing crowd nervously, like an actor on opening night.

At half past nine silence falls over this vast congregation and prayers begin. A light breeze stirs the young trees. The long rows of worshippers chant their prayers and

kneel and rise, kneel and rise, in unison. I check my thermometer. It's 35°C/95°F
in the shade.

After the prayers, a collection is taken and the impressive discipline of the
worshippers breaks up. Some of the older men are helped away, the younger ones are
allowed to move up to get a better view of the proceedings and everyone starts chattering,
even though the imam is still delivering benedictions and demanding responses.

I hear Pigmy mutter 'Enough benedictions', but it's another five minutes before
the imam concludes the blessing and two of his assistants move forward and release
the sheep from the tree.

This is accompanied by a great surge forward to the area where the sacrifice will
take place, completely obscuring the view of Nigel and Basil, who have been at
carefully chosen camera positions for an hour or more. Everyone is turning to each
other and shaking hands and exchanging greetings. My hand is pumped as
enthusiastically as anyone else's.

'*Sambe, sambe. Amina,*' Pygmy teaches me to say. I presume it's the equivalent of
'Happy Tabaski'.

Somewhere in all this mass of humanity, the first sheep of the day dies in Djenné.

Pigmy now has to emulate the imam's sacrifice and he is unusually preoccupied
as we trudge back through the winding streets of the town. A cloud of dust raised by
the feet of 8000 celebrants hangs thick and unavoidable in the hot and motionless
air. By the time we reach his house I feel as if I've swallowed a small desert.

Pigmy makes a traditional round of the neighbours, briskly darting in and out of
doorways exchanging greetings.

'*Sambe, sambe. Amina.*'

Trickles of blood, running out of waste pipes and into the open drains that run
down the centre of the streets, indicate that for some houses, the sacrifices have
already begun. At Pigmy's house, grand by Djenné standards, with upstairs rooms for

BELOW

Thousands at prayer
on Tabaski *morning,*
in their best outfits.
Dress code: be
different from the
person next to you.

relatives, we are welcomed by his father, who sits in half-darkness by the door, greeting everyone with a handshake and a broad smile. Through in the courtyard, Pigmy's wife, together with his mother and aunts, all gorgeously attired, sit on upturned plastic buckets, slicing vegetables.

They remain profoundly unimpressed, as a knife is put into Pigmy's quivering hand and he and the £37.50 sheep make their fateful tryst in a corner of the yard. Pigmy, not yet an expert, is, thankfully, assisted by a butcher, who instructs him in the art of swift throat-cutting. The deed is done in accordance with the ancient law, and the sheep is lifted over a drain. The blood pumps from its neck and runs away beneath the wall and into the street.

Pigmy looks much relieved as the knife is taken from him. It's carefully washed by the butchers, who immediately set to work skinning the carcass. With temperatures in Djenné creeping up to 40°C/104°F, their speed and skill is, as they say, of the essence.

Should you ever have to do this at home, here's a hot tip from the professionals. Slit the skin around one leg, then blow through the incision until the skin inflates and breaks clear of the flesh beneath. It takes time and considerable lung-power, but if all goes well the hide should slip off like a banana skin.

Half an hour later the sheep is reduced to the sort of anonymous chunks we Westerners are more comfortable with and Pigmy's majestic mother is dropping them one by one into the pot. All that remains of yesterday's purchase is the head and a pile of feet stacked neatly in one corner of the yard.

Nothing, I'm told, is wasted. The head will be boiled for soup, which Pigmy raves about, and the testicles will be distributed to the young boys of the neighbourhood.

'It helps to make them clever,' explains Pigmy. A theory which, if proven, could change school dinner menus forever.

The festive meal, to which I'm invited, is a considerable anticlimax. It's cooked beautifully but consumed rapidly and in silence, apart from a few laughs when I commit the dreadful faux pas of using my left, or washing, hand to scoop up the food. We squat or sit cross-legged round one large dish, men separate from the women, who eat in the corner where they cook. Family and friends arrive and dig in, as if they've been on hunger strike. I could do with a much more leisurely, discursive pace, if only because I still have great trouble rolling rice into balls with three fingers of one hand, then dipping this into the fresh bubbling stew without scalding myself.

I find my gaze straying over to the women. Pigmy's mother, dressed in vibrant red like a pillar box, chews away on a huge bone whilst his wife, a freshly hennaed vision in lilac gown and hat, munches contentedly, and doesn't catch my eye.

Then all at once it's over, and the traditional three glasses of powerful mint tea are prepared.

'Always drink after the meal, not before. It is too strong for the taste,' counsels Pigmy.

Then fond farewells. They seem genuinely sorry to see us go, but I can't help feeling there'll be much more fun when the camera's gone.

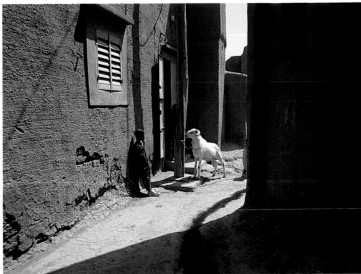

We work our way back to the *campement* along streets stained with blood and strewn with sheep's feet, dodging across the cracked and broken remains of a covered French drainage system. It seems a shame that this attractive and ancient city, older than Timbuktu, once proud possessor of great libraries and over sixty Koranic schools, should have left such a system to rot.

From my conversations with Pigmy, the decline seems to have set in many years ago. In 1591 to be precise, when the glorious Songhai Empire, which succeeded the equally rich and civilised Mali Empire, unsuccessfully faced an invasion from Morocco. Though numerically superior, the Songhai army's bows and arrows were of little use against Moroccan muskets. A dark age followed. The Empire collapsed, the gold trade passed out of their hands and the Touareg nomads moved in to control the trade routes.

The French tried to improve public services and more recently UNESCO has raised funds to preserve the old mud buildings, but Djenné, like Chinguetti in Mauritania, remains a casualty of history, a shadow of what it must once have been.

Still, *Tabaski* has brought the town to life. No longer confined to courtyards and back-rooms, the women who have prepared the feasts are now out on the streets, meeting, strolling and confidently flaunting their freshly plaited hair and freshly hennaed heels and exultantly extrovert outfits.

I borrow a *mobylette* and drive into the centre of town for one last look at the biggest mud building in the world. In front of the mosque, children are prodding charcoal fires on which they will cook the sheep's head soup. A trio of schoolboys, giggling with delight, show me the ancient art of making whoopee cushions out of sheep's scrotums.

We leave Djenné through the brick archway with its pointed oval battlements, down to the ferry where Brahmin cattle graze, seemingly oblivious to the white egrets on their heads. It's sunset by the time we board the ferry and the flies are out.

Tabaski *snapshots.*

ABOVE LEFT
Young boys, given the sheep's testicles after Tabaski, *use the scrotums as whoopee cushions. A gap in the market here, surely.*

ABOVE
The first sacrifices stain the streets of Djenné.

DAY FORTY-FOUR   MOPTI TO DOGON COUNTRY

Whereas Djenné felt trapped by the river, Mopti, only 65 miles northeast, thrives on it. Its natural advantages are obvious. A hundred yards from the hotel's Soudan-style mud portals, the Bani flows in close parallel with the wider and grander Niger. These two great rivers come together less than a mile away.

Not surprisingly, Mopti has become the riverine trading centre Djenné once was, and if we want a boat to take us to Timbuktu this is the place to find it.

But it's the day after *Tabaski*, and this normally busy port seems to be suffering from a hangover. Not an alcohol hangover, obviously; more of a sheep hangover. As they used to be everywhere, in courtyards and on street corners, on lorries and boats and motorbikes, on the tops of buses and the back of pick-up trucks, their disappearance leaves a bit of a gap, physically and perhaps psychologically as well.

The normal babble of commerce is stilled and though the occasional pirogue slips out across the Bani, white sail raised to catch the breeze, Mopti seems gripped by torpor.

It's not difficult to find the Niger ferry boats. They look like floating apartment blocks. Three blue and white, triple-decked, steel-hulled monsters drawn up alongside one another. There's no way to get to them that doesn't involve slithering down the effluent-strewn bank of the river, and I have to pick my way over discarded tins, dismembered animals, twisted clothing, motor car parts, a petrified cat with rictus grin and string pulled tight around its neck, and other things I dare not even look at. I reach a wooden gangplank, which leads onto a barge, from which it's a step over the deck-rail and onto the ferry.

Silence, broken only by the hollow ring of my footsteps on sheet-steel plates. The Niger ferries seem completely abandoned. Then I become aware that on the next ferry, moored up against this one and sporting the name 'Tombouctou', there is a small group of people, lounging in chairs around a charcoal brazier, from which a wisp of smoke rises.

I make my way across, half expecting to be ordered off, but instead I'm met with smiles and offered a cup of tea by a trimly bearded man in a violent orange and blue floral robe and green headdress. He turns out to be the captain of the *Tombouctou*. His

wife is scrubbing down a whiskered fish, which normally lives in the river mud. It wriggles angrily and appears to continue to do so until, and a little bit after, she slits it down the middle. She slices it deftly and lays the fillets on the fire. Another man sits on a plastic strip chair, one leg drawn up, picking at his toes. There are two others, one in T-shirt and trousers, the other in a bulbous pale blue robe. I ask if they're passengers. The captain laughs and shakes his head. They're his brothers come for tea.

The *Tombouctou* is clearly not going anywhere. The captain points at the stinking mud banks I've just crossed.

'The water is too low.'

We could wait a day or two. I ask him when he will be operating again.

'July.'

'*July?*'

Now that's another matter. July is over three months away. The fish begins to sizzle nicely and one of the captain's brothers has made some tea.

I knock back the first glass and stare out at the river. I'm feeling rather foolish, but the captain could not be more understanding as I explain the purpose of our journey, and he nods with wide-eyed interest when I tell him where we've already been. He's a travelling man. I learn from him that for big ferries like his the Niger is only navigable for six months of the year, and with the river this low our best bet is to try the smaller local boats down in the port.

Thanking him for his help and his tea I retrace my steps back across the foul-smelling ooze. I'm rewarded by a chance encounter with a man who knows a man who knows a man who has a *pinasse*, a stouter, bigger version of a pirogue, which, if we make it worth his while, could be encouraged to take us up river. Because of the *Tabaski* holiday, this would not be for a few days.

He indicates the boat, a gawky, gaudily painted vessel, drawn up on the mud and leaning slightly to one side. An upper deck and engine house, bearing the words 'Pagou Manpagu' and decorated with playing-card symbols and the crescent moon of Islam, have been grafted, ruthlessly, onto a long, curved hull.

The delay is frustrating. We were all subconsciously prepared for a return to the

ABOVE

(LEFT) *Going nowhere. One of the big Niger ferry boats becalmed at Mopti.*

(CENTRE) *Carpet salesmen at the Mopti dockside, picking their way through indescribable things left behind by the receding river.*

(RIGHT) *Mural of Dogon Country. A sneak preview of my next destination on a hotel wall.*

heart of the Sahara. Decide to apply the boy scout motto 'adopt, adapt and improve' and head out to the Bandiagara escarpment to spend the next few days camping amongst the Dogon, a unique tribe, neither Muslim nor Christian, who, for 600 years, have virtually cut themselves off from the rest of the world.

Late afternoon. It's becoming abundantly clear that, as far as the Dogon are concerned, their 600 years of privacy are up. A new highway is being built between Mopti and Bandiagara. Graders and rollers are at work and dust clouds hang in the air. Occasionally, a minibus emerges from the haze and rattles past us, carrying an exhausted tour group back from what they call Dogon Country.

Then the new road curves away to the south and I realise that it's not a conveyor belt for tourists after all, but the first stage of a trunk road across the border to Ouagadougou, the thriving capital of neighbouring Burkina Faso. This leaves us stuck at a barrier on the outskirts of Bandiagara, arguing with two or three surly men who, with no apparent authority, are demanding 500 CFAs per person and 250 per vehicle before we can proceed.

Having settled for 250 francs from each vehicle and nothing extra for the occupants, these self-appointed toll collectors roll a red and white striped oil drum out of our path with bad grace. Maybe they put a curse on us. After a mile or so, the springs crack on one of the vehicles.

We refresh ourselves with slices of mango bought from children on the street, whilst our drivers bind up the fractured leaf springs with an inner tube from a bicycle tyre. This piece of improvisation is immediately and searchingly put to the test as we proceed on progressively stonier, more unstable tracks up onto the escarpment. We seem to go on for ever. Dusk falls. I begin to see things in the half-light. Ghostly figures with enormous gleaming foreheads turn out to be women with aluminium water pots on their heads, and giant likenesses of Edward Scissorhands turn out to be baobab trees racing towards our headlights.

The road begins to drop down in a series of hairpin bends, bouncing us up and down and side to side at the same time. Despite this, I fall into a brief doze as we reach the valley floor.

I'm woken by a ferocious revving of engines. Our four-wheel drive is sliding about, out of control, rushing forwards then slipping back. Our driver brakes, reverses, revs up again and charges forward. By the light of our crazily swinging headlights I can see what the problem is. We're halfway up a sand dune and the wheels are unable to grip.

A voice shouts out of the darkness. One of the other vehicles has come back to lead us up. This time we make it, up over the rise, and our driver sweeps alongside his colleagues as if he'd just won a Grand Prix rather than nearly killed us.

In a shallow bowl of sand, ringed with low bushes, stands a semicircle of small tents. To one side, beneath one of the few trees of any size, a fire is burning. I've lost count of the hours since we left the banks of the Bani river, but it doesn't matter now. We're in Dogon Country, and this is our new home.

DAY FORTY-FIVE TIRELLI

The Sahara is officially said to begin north of latitude 16. The Pays de Dogon (it sounds so much better in French) is around 14 degrees north, but the cool night, which had me scrambling into my sleeping bag around 4 am, and the sand that has already found its way into the most private parts of me and my luggage, take me right back to our days in Western Sahara. As if the insidious sand isn't enough, there is the added refinement of *krim-krim,* thorny burrs camouflaged in sand, which attach themselves to skin and clothing like fishhooks. Those of us who have already used the bushes as our bathroom have been particularly affected, and in quite sensitive places too.

There are bonuses of course, one of which is the spectacular sight of the escarpment wall, rising about a mile to the west of the camp, its long straight brow glowing red and gold in the early sunlight.

Little is known about the first people to inhabit the 125-mile escarpment other than that they were little and were called the Tellem. They fled to safety here 1000 years ago. They were planters and crop growers and no match for the Dogon hunters, originally believed to have come from the Nile Valley, who took over their land 400 years later, in their turn fleeing, this time from the spread of Islam.

The Tellem built houses in and amongst the caves halfway up the cliff wall, some of which can still be seen. The Dogon use them as burial grounds, often hauling bodies up on the end of ropes.

I learn all this from Amadou, an urbane English-speaking Dogon, who lives in Bandiagara. There is no shortage of esoteric information about the Dogon. In fact, there is a joke that runs 'how many people are there in a Dogon family?', the answer to which is five. Two parents, two children and one French anthropologist.

BELOW

The Dogon village of Tirelli, almost camouflaged, huddles against the escarpment. Up in the rock face to the left are the cave dwellings of the Tellem, previous occupiers of these cliffs.

With Amadou as my guide, we drive over the ridge and down through scattered trees to Tirelli, one of a string of villages set at intervals into the base of the cliff. At first it's hard to tell if there's a village there at all. In the morning shadow its sandy-grey stone buildings merge with the rock in perfect camouflage. The effect is clearly intended.

The houses that rise steeply up the cliff-side are skilfully integrated with the massive boulders around them. They are built of dry-stone walls, capped with a smooth, chamfered layer of the clay, rice husks and straw mix known as *banco*. Water spouts project from the corners. Among the houses are the eye-catching granaries, with *banco* walls and pointed, overlapping mops of thatch, like witches' hats. There are men's and women's granaries. The women's are divided into four compartments: north, east, south and west. A representation of the world. Each one contains a different food: peanuts, millet, beans, rice. But in the middle of all these is a small circular hole, the centre of the world, and it is here that the women keep their most valuable belongings, money, jewellery, precious stones, gold and silver. There are no such fripperies in the men's granaries, which are used purely as stores for the staple diet of millet.

We wind our way up to the village, which is crisscrossed by narrow tracks. There is no room for vehicles here, and the heaviest loads, in particular water from the well below, are carried up in calabash gourds on the women's heads.

Amadou leads. He's wearing a Dogon hat, white and pointed, with tassels (to keep the flies off when eating), and a cool, loose, white cotton jacket over a black T-shirt, a combination which occasionally makes him look like a mad vicar. Almost everything he tells me about the Dogon confirms that, though modern influences are creeping in, this ancient inbred way of life bears no relation to any of the other cultures and religions that have shaped this part of Africa. The Dogon world is a one-off.

He introduces me to the headman of the village, Dogolu Say, a tall, impressive, serious man, in a pointed hat and an indigo robe. (This he casts aside in the heat of the day to reveal a Copacabana Beach T-shirt.) He, in turn, takes me first to see the *forgeron,* the blacksmith, a formidably powerful man in the Dogon world, taught by God (who they call Ama) how to bring fire up from the earth.

Progress round the village is slow, partly because of the heat and partly because of the endless greetings. African greeting is fulsome at the best of times, but a Dogon 'Good Morning' can last several minutes. Dogolu cannot pass anyone without initiating a ritual of questions and responses, delivered in sing-song rhythm and designed to ascertain the health of not just wife, sons, brothers, sisters, daughters, cousins, in-laws and anyone else you might have met in your life, but also house, onion patch, rice supplies, bicycle, dog, donkey and so on. Try it, with rhythm.

aga po (How are you?)

sèwa (Fine)

oumana sèwa (How's the family?)

sèwa (Fine)

ounou sèwa (How are the kids?)

sèwa (Fine)

yahana go sèwa (How's the wife?)

sèwa (Fine)

deh sèwa (How's your father?)

sèwa (Fine)

nah sèwa (How's your mother?)

sèwa (Fine)

And so on, and on. Once the list is completed the roles are reversed and the whole process starts again. It's a happy sound, with a style and bounce to it like good rap.

For the most important man in the Dogon cosmology, the blacksmith looks like any other short, harassed, middle-aged tradesman as he goes about his business in a low-roofed forge built up against the side of a great boulder, whose cracks and crevices provide shelf space for his tools. The fire is kept alive by his daughter, a girl of seven or eight, who sits at the fire busily working a pair of bellows made from goatskin and date-palm wood.

ABOVE

A carved door on a granary records the Dogon version of how the world began.

Apart from making things like clasps and locks for the granaries, the blacksmith makes knives for, and performs, male circumcision. His wife, and presumably one day the apprentice daughter who is working the bellows, performs the female circumcision. The explanation for this procedure in Dogon mythology is that Ama, who created the universe, made Earth to be his mate. Earth had male and female organs, characterised by ant hills and termite mounds. When Ama attempted congress with his beloved Earth, his entry was barred by the termite mound, which he had to remove before copulation could begin. So the termite mound represented the clitoris,

141

RIGHT

As Tirelli is built
high on the rocks,
everything has to
be carried up from
the valley below.
Usually by the
women.

and the world could not have been created until it was removed. Which is why, to this day, all the women in Tirelli will be, or have been, circumcised.

On the way back through the village we come across the hunter, another important figure in Dogon tradition. He's a slight, nervous man with a fur hat and a flintlock rifle, which may look quaint but is an important status symbol for the Dogon. I ask what there is to hunt in this hot, stony landscape. He talks of wild rats and monkeys, and produces a shrunken monkey head to prove it. The flintlock looks so ancient that I can't see it being a serious threat to life. We run the camera expectantly, but the first time the hunter fills his rifle with powder and demonstrates, nothing happens. He refills, fires again. Another click. Amadou and others offer advice, and the third time he virtually empties an entire goat-horn full of saltpetre into the breech.

This time there is a loud report. Ignited powder flies out of the side of the gun and I feel a series of sharp stings across my face. The hunter looks exultant. Amadou and the headman rush up to me. There are specks of blood across my forehead, some only millimetres away from my eyes, and sharp stabs in my forehead.

A happy side of the whole experience is that the hunter and I become firm friends. I accuse him of trying to kill me and make elaborate hiding movements whenever I see him. Whenever he sees me, he dissolves into helpless laughter.

By midday we surrender to the ferocious heat burning off the rocks and take a break on the terrace that acts as the village's reception area. Beneath a palm-thatch roof is a table, benches, a couple of hammocks and an array of carved artefacts. There are single figures, women with prominent eyes, long stylised faces and breasts projecting forward like rockets, and doors and panels with the ancestors kneeling in long rows, interwoven with lizards, tortoises and the most important creature in Dogon tradition, the serpent, credited with leading the Dogon people to the escarpment.

I'm drowsing fitfully when I become aware of other white faces on the terrace. A tall Dutchman is poking around amongst the carvings. He introduces himself as a former guide now looking for African art to sell to galleries in Europe. He doesn't think much of the collection here. The problem, he says, is that 95 per cent of the stuff is made for tourists. What he's looking for is the 5 per cent of original work that makes it all worthwhile.

He's friendly and knowledgeable and I find myself nodding sympathetically, but when he's gone I'm left with a considerable feeling of indignation. Africa is being looted once again, this time by someone of impeccable taste, who should know better. And it's pretty much defenceless, lacking the resources and the organisation to prevent its treasures ending up, like its animals once did, on rich men's walls, thousands of miles away.

Later, back at camp, our resourceful director, Mr Davidson has investigated the culinary situation and decided that the licence-payers' money is best spent on a freshly roasted goat. We're also working on a theory that wine can be chilled by burying the bottle in the sand an hour or so before drinking.

Despite the threat of *krim-krim*, most of the evening is spent crawling around in the darkness, trying to find where we've put it.

DAY FORTY-SIX TIRELLI

This morning I'm invited to lunch with Dogolu, the headman. He lives, with two wives and thirty dependents, in a labyrinth of buildings surrounding a precipitous, rocky courtyard. Such is the verticality of Tirelli that one side of their house is about 20 feet higher than the other. Dogolu squats on a rock and talks as the women prepare the meal. Life is not as confined here as it appears to be. Of his nine children, some are studying in Bamako, while others are married and living separately.

The ingredients for lunch are certainly fresh. Most of them are still running around the yard when we arrive. Calabashes full of water are being brought up from

BELOW

With Amadou, my guide, and assorted family members in the headman's compound. Thatched-roofed granaries in the background.

the well and millet is being pounded by three girls working pestles taller than themselves. It can take an hour or more of backbreaking work before the millet grain is sufficiently pulverised and the girls ease the laborious process by working in time to a soft, rhythmic chant.

Because the shadow cast by the midday sun is so deep, and because my dinner with Dogolu is to be filmed, J-P asks if the meal can be served on the sunny side of the courtyard. The headman looks at us pityingly, and I soon know why.

What follows is the hottest, and one of the least comfortable, sequences I've ever filmed. John Pritchard clocks the temperature in the unshaded overhead sun at 55°C/131°F. Dogolu has managed to coerce an assortment of male relatives to crouch round the communal bowl with me. Fortunately, there's only one course. It's a millet porridge, in the centre of which is a bright green sauce made from the baobab leaf, and, mixed in with this, a mutton, aubergine and onion stew. They urge me to eat but every time I pick up a glob of the millet paste it is so hot that I have to release it almost immediately. Desperate not to offend my hosts' hospitality, I try transferring smaller amounts, but it's still an ordeal. Passing the food from fingers to lips to tongue to throat is like walking over hot coals.

Amadou grins broadly at my discomfort and points out that among the Dogon the ability to eat hot food is a sign of manly prowess. Giggles from the circle around the pot. I laugh too, slightly hysterically.

Later, at siesta, my dreams are a heady mix of fire and flame and vaguely erotic termite mounds.

In late afternoon, when the day is beginning to cool from its earlier rock-cracking heat, the men of Tirelli assemble on the only flat area in the village for a ceremonial

BELOW

The hottest meal of my life. Temperatures of 55°C/131°F roast my head, whilst my fingers are scalded by a red-hot mixture of millet and baobab sauce. The tasselled hats are typically Dogon; the straw and leather wide-brim, worn by the headman, is Fulani.

LEFT

Watching the tingetange, *stilt dancers, at a celebration of the dead. Four or five feet off the ground, with masks, cowrie shell bodices and horsetails, the dancers require exceptional skills and long training.*

dance that is to herald a week of funeral celebrations. Amadou says that celebrations on this scale only follow animist funerals. Animism, which attributes a living soul to all natural objects – trees, boulders, clouds, thunderstorms – remains the religion of the vast majority of Dogon.

BELOW

A Dogon boy's drawing of a dancer's mask, which can be anything up to 18 feet long.

Before proceedings begin, men with fly-whisks clear children from the dancing ground. Women can watch, but only from a distance. The masked dancers enter. Two drummers start the beat. Then others join in, striking curved hand-bells, and a piper adds the sound of a whistle to set up a persistent, repetitive rhythm. A chorus, of whom Amadou is one, urges on the dancers, who leap into the ring, dressed in raffia headdresses and skirts in bright yellow, pink and orange over baggy Dogon trousers. The most spectacular dance is performed by half a dozen men on painted stilts, wearing girl masks decorated with cowrie shells and false breasts made of baobab fruit. All the other dancers have elaborately decorated headdresses, which vary from horned antelope heads to likenesses of birds and the huge wooden mask called *tiu* that can be up to 18 feet long.

It is dazzling in its colour and energy, but I'm frustrated at not being able to comprehend more than the surface of this complex, expressive ritual.

The end of the dance does not mean the end of celebrations in Tirelli. The dancers are rewarded with a special brew of *kojo,* millet beer, and things really get going after we've gone.

As I lie in my tent, exhausted, as we all are, by another hot day of hard labour, the sound of partying carries across on the night air and, not for the first time in West Africa, I'm lulled to sleep by the distant sound of people having a much better time than me. And they're at a funeral.

Made my own minor anthropological discovery this morning. I was behind a bush having a pee in the usual way when I noticed two of the Malian cooks also relieving themselves close by. I was standing. They were kneeling, rendering themselves at once less conspicuous and less affected by the brisk morning breeze. Is this just a desert thing, I wonder? Answers on a postcard please.

Today we strike camp and return to Mopti. Which is probably just as well, as food and water are both running out. I'd been getting quite skilful at washing my entire body in one mug of water, but that's the trouble with camping. Just as you're getting used to it, it's time to go home.

We drive down to Tirelli for the last time. Life goes on and there seems to be no evidence of a wild night. A man is stripping the bark of a baobab tree and slicing it into strips for binding thatch and tying wood. Others are at work on the onion field, vivid green in this bleached landscape. As the village's only cash crop, it's allowed precious supplies of extra water. A small market is set up among the trees.

Above these Thomas Hardyesque scenes rise the red-brown walls of the escarpment, protective and uncompromising at the same time.

As we clamber up into the village one last time I'm reminded of the severe beauty of the place. The proportions of the houses, the materials that match the surrounding rocks, the harmony of the village with its environment. The cliff is still, as it has been for 1000 years, a sanctuary, lacking cars and satellite dishes and overhead wires and things that seem to be everywhere in the world but here.

But it's no use getting sentimental. As we load our gear, women climb slowly past us, carrying the never-ending shuttle of water up to the village. They ignore our awkward smiles. As our car finally pulls away, I reach for the outstretched hand of a boy who rushes up to the window.

But he doesn't want to shake my hand. He just wants a pen or a sweet or a coin.

We remain us. They remain them. For how long, I'm not sure.

One of the small pleasures of hard travel is the way basics can be transformed into luxuries. Tonight, back at the Kanaga Hotel in Mopti, the finest champagne in the world would be no match for the forbidden delights of running water.

The heat and dust of the Pays de Dogon have taken their toll. The plastic cap on my tube of travel wash has melted, my urine is the colour of mustard and it takes so long to strip away the layers of dust that I feel as if my body might have turned to mud.

Tomorrow we face the Niger, so it's an early night. Lean over to switch off my light when a power cut kills it for me.

DAY FORTY-EIGHT ON THE NIGER

ABOVE

(LEFT) *Waiting to board our Niger river transport, the* Pagou Manpagu. (CENTRE) *Tablets of salt, brought by camel out of the desert to Timbuktu, await onward shipment at Mopti.* (RIGHT) *Cheer up! Presenter unhappy at lack of creature comforts on the long river journey ahead.*

Mopti is a changed place this morning as we head down to the waterfront in search of our transport to Timbuktu. The river is busy again. Slender pirogues, so weighed down with people that the boats themselves are hardly visible, are punted to and from the network of fuzzy green islands that lie revealed between the Bani and the Niger. The riverbank heaves with activity. A group of women in scarves and long saris are bent over vegetable beds hastily planted to take advantage of the newly exposed mud, and nearer the port itself rows of earthenware pots wait to be loaded. Beside them, to my surprise, for I thought such things never existed outside of Bible stories, are tablets of salt. They're slim, rectangular blocks, like large paving stones, bound with lengths of cloth, their grey crystalline surfaces glittering in the sunlight.

Salt was once so valuable to the people who lived south of the Sahara that it was traded weight for weight with gold. The forty or fifty tablets stacked here show that the Sahara's chief export is still in demand. I try to lift one and it's not easy. I'm told they weigh 40 kilograms each.

In the midst of all this organised confusion is the brightly coloured hull of our *pinasse*, but getting to it is not so easy. The market is in full swing and every salesman in Mopti seems determined to give us a send-off. Sunglasses, batteries, water, hats, fruit and fish are pressed on us from one side, and *bics, cadeaux, bonbons* are demanded on the other. A gauntlet of commerce. Death by a thousand offers. I suppose I should be used to it by now, but, today, the combination of heat, smell, weight of my bags and the scramble through the sewerish sediments is truly nightmarish.

Throwing my bags ahead of me, I reach for the helping hand of a crew member, who pulls me away from the nightmare and onto the deck of the *Pagou Manpagu.*

It takes me only a moment to realise that the *Pagou Manpagu* has no deck. One moment I'm poised on the side of the hull and the next I'm down in the bilges with everyone else. Squeeze myself into a corner beside one of the bridge supports and take stock. Makeshift bamboo-strip floorboards run along the line of the keel and already most of the space is occupied, mainly by women and children. Fires are being lit and food prepared. There is a shout from a boat alongside and I look up just in time to see a goat suspended in mid-air. It disappears heavenwards to be followed by another

three, wriggling and squirming as they're hauled past me onto the roof.

A few last arrivals jump aboard as the heat, trapped by the riverbank above us, grows from intense to suffocating. Then, with a long, sucking sigh, the hand-hauled anchor pulls free of the mud and we move slowly out into the stream. My feet slip momentarily and I look down to see that I've dislodged a floorboard and sent a line of cockroaches scuttling for cover. With flies fussing at my face, cockroaches retreating back to the dark recesses beneath my feet and a small circle of children staring curiously, I realise I've stepped out of a nightmare and into some Dantesque punishment.

And what's worse, I know it's going to look so damn picturesque on camera.

The babble of Mopti slips away on our port side and we make our way gingerly through the maze of small islands, not much more than sandbanks really, which lie at the confluence of the Niger and the Bani. Some are barren, others are covered with a thin frizz of green grass, on which ewes and lambs, goats and cattle graze.

Navigation is tricky. The pilot stands astride the bows like an Old Testament prophet, his pole rising and falling as he shouts soundings up to the helmsman, cross-legged at the wheel on the bridge above me.

Once out onto the main stream of the Niger, we run into a brisk, refreshing headwind, and, with navigation a little easier, the crew busy themselves with other problems, chief of which is stemming a number of leaks that appear to have sprung in the gnarled cedar timbers of the hull.

Young boys are despatched to scour the hold for pieces of old rag, which are then prodded into the leaks with sticks and nails. With the wind whipping up sizeable waves, it looks like a losing battle, but the crew seems unfazed, assuring me that now we're out on the open water the timbers will soon expand and close the gaps.

Later. I've made myself a nest in the bows, found some boxes on which to perch and watch the world go by. Above my head I hear the squeak of the greasy chain cable, which snakes its way, quite unprotected, along the length of the ship, between wheel and rudder. I've thought of travelling up on top, but though the upper deck is marginally cleaner, it's more exposed and, anyway, it's busy. The covered area is occupied by the crew, who lounge around and drink tea, and the rest of it is occupied by goats.

In the confusion of departure I've failed to register quite where we are. As often happens in the world's iconic places (viz. North and South Poles) the romantic loses out to the practical. Survival comes before reflection. Here I am on the Niger, a river whose exploration cost so many lives and whose exact course was not known to any European 150 years ago, and all I can worry about is a cockroach or two. I stare out across the choppy grey waters and try to think important thoughts.

To be honest, the scenery doesn't help. The river is about a quarter of a mile wide at this point and flows through an arid, sandy landscape, broken by occasional stands of mango and eucalyptus, planted I assume as windbreaks. There is a surprisingly abundant bird life along the riverbank – egrets and herons, waders, kingfishers, even an eagle – but the scattered villages of the Bozo fishermen are dispiriting skylines of low mud huts and flat, straw-thatch roofs.

The one delightful surprise comes as we round one of the few bends in the river. I spy something over on the southern shore which I first take to be a mirage. Indistinct in the dusty haze and rising out of nowhere is the pinnacled outline of a building of shimmering beauty, as if King's College Chapel at Cambridge had been transported from the banks of the Cam to the banks of the Niger. It's a mosque to rival that of Djenné, with a pale gold minaret, four-tiered like a pagoda, rising above a cluster of orange-tipped towers. Amongst these drab villages it is sensationally incongruous, as well as light, majestic and timeless.

It passes out of sight behind a grove of trees and we see nothing like it again.

Late lunch of couscous and vegetables specially prepared for the film crew. We watch with some envy as the rest of the steerage class passengers prepare themselves a goat stew, flames crackling away on the floor of the hold, only a couple of feet from where people are bailing out water. Soon afterwards, we put in at a small town. Amongst the newly embarking passengers is a white woman. Very white, in fact. The paleness of her skin is emphasised by a simple long black dress with red and gold trim around the neckline. She's as incongruous as the mosque we've just passed. A Viking on the Niger. She does, indeed, turn out to be Norwegian, and though she looks as if she had stepped off the plane from Oslo this morning, she has lived in Mali for six years as a Christian missionary, learning the Fulani language and writing a book on Fulani women. Her name is Kristin.

We sit and talk up in the bows, making the most of the cooling headwinds.

To understand Mali, she thinks, you have first to understand the differences between its peoples. There are the Bozos, who are the river people, and the Bobos, who live up in the inland Delta and have dogs and whose villages are not recommended for overnight stays. There are the ungovernable Touareg nomads of the north, who were in open rebellion against Bamako until four years ago and who remain very much a law unto themselves, with less than one per cent of their children in school. At the other extreme are the Bambara, more progressive and urbanised, and the Fulani, who see themselves as the aristocrats of Mali, with a sharply defined moral code which Kristin says is best described by the English word 'chivalry'.

I ask her what she makes of the apparent segregation of men and women in almost every area of African social life. Kristin thinks this is all about ways of seeing.

'Publicly they live a very separate life, but in private they're very attentive to each other.'

She thinks the image of the marginalised, oppressed African woman is wrong.
'They're very strong, very proud of who they are.'

Then how does she account for the continuing practice of female circumcision?

'What is sexual pleasure here and in Europe is quite different. We have a tendency
of thinking that sexual pleasure is impossible for a woman that has been circumcised.
I don't share that opinion.'

The waves are hitting hard now, rocking the boat and slapping at the hull as they
ripple beneath us.

Kristin is adamant that Western solutions cannot be applied to African
relationships. 'What men find attractive in Africa doesn't necessarily correspond to
what is attracting a man in Europe. You know, in Europe a woman should be skinny,
but here a woman should be fat. And the women are very concerned how to be
attractive and how to attract a man...'

At this vital moment we're suddenly thrown forward. With a shuddering
rumble the *Pagou Manpagu* lurches to a halt. We've run aground. Kristin seems
unperturbed.

'Isn't it serious?'

She shakes her head. 'I travel the river a lot.'

At that moment the pilot grabs his pole and leaps into the river, which seems a
suicidal thing to do, until I see him stride off into the middle of the Niger with the
water barely above his knees. He's joined by others, until the whole river is full of men
walking about. After much discussion they assemble at the back and push, but to no
avail. The *Pagou Manpagu* is stuck fast.

As darkness falls we're all taken off in a small boat and put ashore on a wide sandy
beach not far from the town of Konna. Kristin has had enough by now and decides to
carry on by road. The rest of us make camp as best we can and settle down to another
night under the stars. The good news is that we don't have to sleep on board the *Pagou
Manpagu*. The bad news is that after this positively Homeric journey we have
advanced precisely thirty-four and a half miles towards Timbuktu.

DAY FORTY-NINE ON THE NIGER

Out of the tent just after six. We are in a very bleak spot, a flat coverless expanse of mud and sand with a cordon of local Bozos, or possibly Bobos, already gathered and regarding us with unemotional interest.

Flat, coverless expanses present problems for the morning toilet. A nonchalant reconnaissance turns into a quarter of a mile hike, before I find anything resembling a dip in the ground.

Back at the camp I find a bowl of warm water outside the tent and coffee, tea, bread and fruit laid out on a table. Our little knot of spectators – old women, children, a couple of lean and mean dogs and an old man with prayer beads – waits patiently. They are not trying to sell us anything, for they have nothing to sell. They're waiting for anything we don't want. Mineral water bottles and film cartons are popular. Nigel donates a pair of his shorts, which, after a day in the bowels of the *Pagou Manpagu*, look beyond redemption to me, but are eagerly accepted.

Most of us are now convinced that the boat we were on yesterday was actually for carrying goods rather than people, which would account for the lack of most of the basics, including a deck.

Our spirits are immeasurably lifted, therefore, by the news that the crew of the *Pagou Manpagu* are refusing to take their boat any higher up the river, and if we want to get to Timbuktu we shall have to make alternative plans. With a huge sigh of relief we transfer to a local pirogue. It's 25 feet long, with a curved rattan canopy offering protection from the sun, and an upright rattan screen marked 'WC' offering privacy and a hole in the stern. The boat is lighter and much more agile than the *pinasse* and its shallow draught should see us safely over the sandbanks. And it has that rare and almost unimaginable luxury, seats.

The surface of the river is a mill pond this morning. A stand of tamarind trees is reflected serenely in the water. A line of cows, silhouetted against the eastern horizon, and the occasional sight of low, wood-hulled barges under sail add to the cosy impression that this corner of the Niger could be a seventeenth-century Dutch landscape.

As the day wears on, the alternation of trees, pasture and small fishing villages on one side of the river and exposed and featureless stretches of sand on the other becomes relentlessly monotonous. Occasionally, there will be something to divert the attention; the plunge of a kingfisher or a shiny orange-eyed hippo head breaking the surface, spluttering indignantly. 'Dear Sir, I wish to complain in the strongest possible terms...'

We put ashore every now and then at sad, impoverished little villages, where flies gather round the running noses of little children and their mothers' eyes look blankly back at us.

Then the river course widens out into a series of small lakes and there is nothing to see but water and sky. To keep moving is essential, not just to get us there, but also because it is the only way to alleviate the great heat of the day in this vast and shelterless landscape.

DAY FIFTY-ONE TIMBUKTU

In 1806, Mungo Park, ten years after becoming the first white man to see the River Niger, was within a whisker of adding to his reputation by reaching the legendary, remote and fabulous city of Timbuktu.

Unfortunately, the tranquil approach we're making tonight is markedly different from the conditions in which he came here. Everything had gone wrong for Park on his second visit to Africa, and Sanche de Gramont, in *The Strong Brown God*, sums up his problem succinctly: 'He was taking a makeshift boat pieced together from two rotten Bambara canoes down an uncharted river whose banks were occupied by Christian-hating Tuaregs and rapacious blacks.'

Not surprisingly, Park didn't stop to look around, and it was another twenty years before a fellow Scot, Alexander Gordon Laing, approaching from the desert to the north, became the first European to reach Timbuktu for nearly 300 years.

Neither survived to tell their tales.

Timbuktu remains well off any beaten track. There is an airstrip from which tourists are flown in and out, but it remains a city at the end of the road, centre of an administrative region but not much else. Yet its appeal remains almost as potent as it was for Laing and those who risked their lives to follow him. To the almost certain puzzlement of the locals, Westerners remain drawn to Timbuktu like moths to a candle. No other city remains as synonymous with the fabulous, the lonely and the remote. Timbuktu, *la mystérieuse*, they call it in the tourist brochures – a Holy Grail for the adventurous traveller.

It's hard to remain unexcited as we glide slowly in to the little inlet at Kabara, the port for Timbuktu itself.

Our arrival coincides with one of the very finest African sunsets, perhaps the best I've witnessed on this journey. In a huge sky, day and night are for a moment perfectly balanced. The sun going down on one side, as a full moon rises on the other. Colours change slowly and majestically. Light blue becomes pink-tinged grey and minutes later, as we grate against the gravel bank, half the sky is lemon and the other half is violet.

A hippo burps in the distance and above us a stream of bats swerves out across the sky. This is why I leave home. Moonlight bathes the groves of trees beside the good metalled road that runs the 14 miles from Kabara into Timbuktu. At the city limits the tarmac gives out and leaves us to the sand. I crane my head around to see if I can see anything fabulous, but all I see is a roundabout with a lumpy concrete monument and battered sign welcoming us to 'Timbuktu, City of Three Hundred and Thirty-Three Saints'.

First impressions – interiors lit by bare bulbs, donkeys swaying down the street with bales of hay ballooning around them, tall figures in indigo robes caught in the glare of our headlights.

Our hotel, the Relais Azalai, is on a low rise on the western edge of town, overlooking what until recently was a river. We unload and carry our bags in through a now familiar line of salesmen, only this time they are Touareg, lean, olive-skinned faces swathed in black and indigo headdresses. And they're not just outside the hotel; the staff at reception are also swathed in black or blue headdresses. This is the first sign that Timbuktu is not like other places. Up to now, nomads have always been on the fringes of urban life. In Timbuktu they run the place.

Enjoy a few luxuries – a shower, cold beers, a hot meal and a bed. My air-conditioning sounds like an overladen truck on a very steep hill. But what the hell, I'm in Timbuktu.

DAY FIFTY-TWO TIMBUKTU

Walk out of the hotel to look around, but it's quite impossible. The only reason a foreigner would walk out of his hotel unescorted is clearly to buy something, and the Touareg know nothing of the soft sell.

By the time I'm driven back in by the rattling of silver rings and the cries of 'I give you good price', I have time to take in a pretty depressing landscape. The walls of

Timbuktu look fine, but in front of them is another Timbuktu, a city of semicircular huts set in thorn bush stockades and covered in sheeting of rattan or plastic. Its trees and bushes are hung with plastic bags and children and animals share the sand.

It seems the Touareg, who founded Timbuktu 900 years ago, are still coming in from the desert.

My spirits rise when we're driven into town. A city that seems almost determined to be decrepit still has some beautiful buildings. One of the finest is the catchily named Djingareiber Mosque. It's also one of the very few buildings that would have been here in the golden age of the fifteenth and sixteenth centuries, when Leo Africanus described Timbuktu as a city where the king 'kept a magnificent and well-furnished court', with 'a great store of doctors, judges, priests and other learned men, that are bountifully maintained at the king's expense'. Irregular walls run round the mosque, curved and crenellated with rounded Sudanese outlines and supported with well-cut buttresses. The *banco* plaster that covers the walls is so recent that it's patterned with the handprints of those who applied it.

We are allowed inside. At the main door two boys offer their help.

'We will guard your shoes,' they promise solemnly, laying my travel-stained sneakers one beside the other with great tenderness, as if they were new-born children.

What strikes me immediately is how cool it is inside the walls, and how dark. Narrow arcades run through a forest of rough-plastered columns, 130 of them, receding into the gloom.

It has an ancient, unostentatious feel to it, enclosed and protective, intimate and impressive at the same time. There is little decoration. Long timber beams, said to be

ABOVE

*A Touareg cross.
One thing I did buy
outside the hotel.*

cut from Dom palms 60 miles away from the city, support the ceiling. The walls and columns are a mixture of local limestone, mud bricks and plaster. The extra strength of the stonework probably accounts for why this mosque has proved more durable than its counterpart in Djenné. It has stood here since 1327, when it was built by a man called El Saheli, credited as the inventor of the process by which mud bricks are made to this day.

I stroll amongst the columns, savouring the silence. Every now and then a shaft of sunlight breaks through, piercing the darkness like a silver blade, or a door opens, briefly silhouetting a figure against a shining wall of heat.

The imam of the Djingareiber Mosque is coolness itself. He arrives for Friday prayers decked out in a swirl of airy, white, cotton robes and a matching turban. A neatly trimmed white beard contrasts sharply with the deep ebony of his skin. After prayers he invites us to his house nearby. It's odd to walk in off the street and find yourself in a house carpeted with sand, albeit of much finer quality than the public sand outside. Also odd that in such a substantial property the interior doors should be faced with corrugated tin.

We sit in the sand and take tea together, whilst in clear and careful French he explains the history of Timbuktu. He's at great pains to emphasise the intellectual and scholarly achievements of the Middle Ages and the sharp and sudden decline that followed the Moroccan invasion at the end of the sixteenth century. Scholars were deported and killed he says, with grave concern, as if it had happened yesterday.

Talking to this wise and educated man, it's difficult to avoid the conclusion that Timbuktu has been in steady decline since the time of William Shakespeare.

Even when Europeans finally braved the hostility of the desert to reach it, there was a definite hint of anticlimax. René Caillié, who came here in 1828, found 'this capital of the Soudan, which had for so long been the goal of all my ambitions' to be little more than 'a jumble of badly built houses, ruled over by a heavy silence'. On the other hand, Alexander Laing, the Scot who beat him to it by two years, wrote that 'in every respect except in size...it has completely met my expectations'.

Laing's achievement in reaching Timbuktu at all becomes the more admirable, or insanely foolhardy, when you consider that in the 250 years following the Moroccan invasion, forty-three Europeans set out to reach the city and only four succeeded, of which he was the first. He crossed the Sahara from Tripoli in Libya, a 2000-mile journey during which he was brutally attacked and severely wounded by tribesmen on the way and murdered by them, for refusing to renounce his Christianity, on the way back. He was thirty-three.

During his five-week stay in the city, though, Laing was well looked after by the trading community and the house in which he stayed still stands.

On the wall above the door is a plaque to his memory, whilst in front of the house, stuck in the sand, a less discreet signboard announces in loud stencil that this is 'Mission Culturelle, Site No. 2. Gordon Laing'.

By the standard of the time, this slim two-storey corner house must have been quite substantial. Inside, the rooms are clean and empty. I'm told it's up for rent and consider putting down a deposit for the address alone.

An 8- by 5-foot downstairs room with yellow washed walls leads, via a flight of narrow stairs, up to another low room with delicately carved arabesque shutters, and from there onto a flat roof.

I stand out here for as long as I can bear the scorching midday heat, taking in the view.

Stretched out beneath me is a pale, dusty city with the colour bleached out of it. There are few modern buildings, and, apart from the pyramid-shaped minarets of the mosques, the overall feel is of flat roofs and iron-grilled windows, broken up by the occasional colonial touch: a stone arch, an attempted balustrade. There are satellite dishes on the walls but open sewers down the centre of the streets. Many buildings are either crumbling or derelict and the tents, families and livestock of the nomads have taken over the corpses of abandoned houses.

I shade my eyes and stare out beyond the walls to the desert, which has the city in an ever-tightening grip. Due north, the direction that both Laing and Caillié took when they left Timbuktu, there is no accommodation for the traveller before the town of Taoudenni, more than 400 miles into the desert. And you would not be welcome there. Taoudenni is a Saharan Siberia, an unimaginably hostile place, where Mali sends her criminals and troublemakers to work the salt mines, out of the sight of foreigners.

Back down amongst its narrow streets, Timbuktu feels tired, as if the effort of just being here at all is using up all her energies. There is none of the brash bounce of Mopti or the fragile charm of Djenné. The shops have little to sell, and though the Mission Culturelle does its best to direct you to interesting places, it does so without much conviction.

The best time to wander comes later, when the great disabling heat of the day is over. Then I happily potter in a warren of back streets, stepping over an open latrine to look more closely at a plaque announcing the house of one of the greatest Saharan explorers of all.

'Heinrich Barth 1853–1854.' Barth travelled thousands of miles across the desert and *did* live to tell the tale, becoming professor of geography at Berlin University. I buy bread straight out of one of the cone-like ovens that dot the city. The bread is good – light, and with just a hint of that familiar gritty texture which tells you, as if you didn't know by now, that you are back in the Sahara.

The local people are not the extroverts of Dakar or Bamako, but though they're wary of us, they're curious at the same time. I fall to wondering if I've been too hard on the city. Maybe, after eight weeks on the road, it's me that's knackered, not Timbuktu.

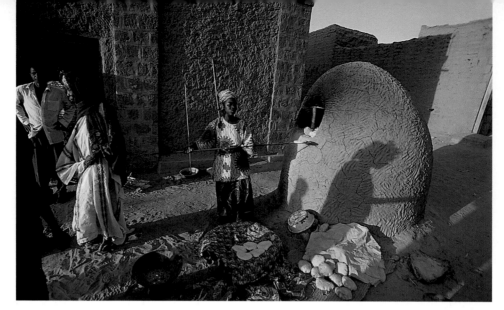

RIGHT
Fresh bread from the street ovens is one of the pleasures of Timbuktu.

OPPOSITE
The roads end at Timbuktu, so I'm getting in some camel practice, and making my first acquaintance with the Touareg, the 'veiled men' of the desert who founded Timbuktu 800 years ago. My Lawrence of Arabia pose slightly spoiled by suspicious mess to the right of my camel.

DAY FIFTY-THREE TIMBUKTU

Up at seven. In the courtyard of the Relais Azalaï a little bird, crown and breast dusted red, skitters amongst the lacework of bougainvillea bushes, tired and dry in the already intense heat. A boy is watering the mottled garden, valiantly but hopelessly, with a thin, trickling hose.

Reception is quiet. The beady-eyed salesmen who patrolled it last night, robes full of unmissable bargains, are gone. A solitary figure in crumpled blue and white robe lies curled up on one of the chairs, eyes shut, breathing deeply. Suddenly, without warning, his hands shoot out and with a resounding crack he clamps them either side of a mosquito. He examines his victim briefly and settles back to sleep.

It turns out that this is Mohammed, a camel owner who is taking us out into the desert to meet a caravan returning from the north and to help us find one with whom we can travel on from here.

He pulls himself wearily off the chair and greets us all with a handshake, though he says nothing.

It's only later, when I hear him talking with a friend, that I realise his voice has almost gone. The words squeeze out in a husky croak, and I wonder if this is a price he's paying for a life lived in the scouring sands of the Sahara.

A few miles out of town, past the nomad encampments, where the sand is dark with sheep and goat droppings, I climb to the top of a dune for my first sight of a camel train. A long, elegant procession breaks the perfect symmetry of blue sky and brown sand as it picks its way towards us. There are thirty or forty animals, all single-humped Arabian camels, properly called dromedaries, roped together in single file. I try to imagine what a sight it would have been in the heyday of trans-Saharan caravans, when 20,000 camels crossed the desert at a time. Today's modest column is led by a wiry Touareg with his black headdress unwound and draped around his neck. A sprawling herd of goats crosses their path. Industrious dung beetles scuttle about in the sand beneath my feet. A man in a vivid yellow robe appears on the crest of a nearby dune, accompanied by a young boy. He watches us watching him, and yawns. This must be the nearest the Sahara gets to a rush hour.

The camels draw closer, moving with a careful gait, noses upturned, as if finding

the whole thing intensely distasteful. On every one of their backs are slung two glittering silver-grey slabs of salt. I half expect to find commandments written on their sides. In fact, the only inscription on the tablets is the name of the owner, marked in red dye.

Mohammed greets the leader of the caravan, and whilst they talk the camels fold themselves gratefully down onto the sand, like collapsible tables, front legs first, back legs folded in neatly beneath their behinds. In motion and in repose these are graceful animals; it's just the bit in between that's a mess.

The blocks of salt they carry each weigh around 50 kilograms, over 100 pounds, so those camels with four on their backs would have been hauling almost a quarter of a ton of salt across the desert, fourteen hours a day, for the past three weeks. No wonder they are so happily sighing, gurgling, chomping and farting their appreciation at having arrived in Timbuktu. I wonder if they instinctively knew that the end was in sight, could perhaps sniff the waters of the Niger, onto which their burdens would soon be transferred and shipped downstream to the markets of sub-Saharan Africa.

The bad news is that, after talking to the leader of the caravan, Mohammed establishes that, with high summer and infernal temperatures just beginning, no more salt caravans will be entering or leaving Timbuktu for several months. If we really want to travel with a camel train, we will do better to head east, where there is still a regular salt run across the Ténéré Desert between Agadez and Bilma. I have read about the Ténéré. Set almost at the centre of the Sahara, it has a reputation for stark beauty and fierce heat.

Back at the hotel, my resolve falters. No-one, I'm firmly assured, will be in the heart of the desert in high summer. The nomads move south and will not return until after the rains, which will render much of the route impassable until they end in August and September.

So we decide to follow the ancient desert ritual of migration and return home. We shall use an English summer to cool off until the Saharan summer has burnt itself out.

NIGER

DAY FIFTY-FOUR   NEAR INGAL

There are, at a rough estimate, one and three-quarter million nomads in the Sahara, of whom about a million are Arab and half a million are descended from pre-Arab inhabitants, like the Berbers of Algeria and Morocco and the Touareg, Toubou and Fulani of the central and southern Sahara. Every year a substantial number of these transient populations converge on the town of Ingal, 70 miles west of Agadez, in the Republic of Niger, for a grand get-together called *Cure Salée*. It means, literally, 'salt cure', a celebration of the fattening of the cattle after the summer migration.

It's the beginning of September when we return to the Sahara and though the sun is still powerful, something is different. The desert air is humid. The hard brown earth is covered in a thin fuzz of green grass. The rains have come and transformed a desert that is always ready to blossom. Where there was only sand a few weeks ago there are now small ponds and trees waist high in standing water. And the Sahara is no longer a bug-free zone. At dawn and dusk the mosquitoes are out, malarial and dangerous.

The bush is busy with people, moving, like us, towards Ingal; but unlike us they are walking and have walked several hundred miles with their families and their animals to the summer grazing in the south and back again. We fall in with a group of Wodaabe, a pastoral and nomadic branch of the Fulani people, who are found right across the southern Sahara from Senegal to Chad.

They carry their goods on donkeys or on their backs. Most of them are barefoot or wearing flip-flop sandals. Their legs and feet must be immune to the sharp burrs that lurk in the tussocky grass, attaching themselves to skin and clothing, stabbing and pricking and defying all but the most delicate attempts to remove them.

Mothers carry the smallest children on their backs, but any child above the age of six or seven is at work, leading a donkey, carrying a lamb or keeping an eye on the sheep and goats. The older boys and the men are preoccupied with the cattle, the wealth of these families and virtually their only tradeable asset. Survival of the cattle is the reason they have made this long march and, now, when their beasts are fattening and their assets are so close to being realised, their protection has never been as important.

There are anxious faces. The group is heading towards a creek, where there is water and a place to spend the night, but as soon as the cattle smell the water they stampede forward and have to be restrained with shouts and sticks.

The donkeys have little option but to trudge doggedly through the bush, weighed down as they are with baskets, blankets, bed-rolls, braziers, babies, cooking pots and goatskin water bags.

Standing out from the tall, dark Africans is a short, ruddy European. Her name is Céline, and she's from Montauban in southwest France. For the last few weeks she's been travelling with the Wodaabe. Doulla Makao, her friend, is one of the leaders of this group. He's tall and slim and looks inconsolably sad, though I sense that much of this is down to sheer physical exhaustion. His manner is gentle and unhurried. He

ABOVE LEFT

Wodaabe on the move. As they spend only six or seven days at each site, everything must be portable. Triangular supports for the bed hang off the side of the donkey.

ABOVE

At camp. The bed, a Wodaabe status symbol, is the first thing to be set up.

161

speaks English and French and has travelled to Europe. He seems an unlikely figure to be tramping across the bush, but when I suggest this he doesn't seem to understand what I mean. These are his people, where else would he be?

His people consist of a group of families, his own and those of four or five blood relatives. Given that Doulla alone has three wives and, as he puts it, 'another on the way', as well as six children, the total adds up to that of a small village. They're on their way to *Cure Salée* but have decided against setting up camp too close to Ingal, as there is a rumour that the water there is tainted. Water seems to be the only thing these people fight over.

'Arabs control most of the wells,' says Doulla, 'and sometimes they don't want anyone else to have them.'

I ask him what they fight with. Knives, guns?

He smiles, indeed almost laughs out loud at the thought.

'No, no, with these,' he says, raising his fists like a boxer.

The thought of this frail ascetic figure trading blows with anyone defies the imagination.

They are trying to raise money to buy a well of their own, which, as Doulla says, would change their lives. They could leave some of their people here throughout the summer, especially the old and infirm, and the children, who remain uneducated because they're never in one place long enough.

They make camp close to a line of trees which rise above the scrubby bushes, denoting the presence of a water course. I ask Doulla how long they will stay here.

It depends on the amount of grazing land, he says.

'When there's enough, we stay for four to seven days.'

They have no huts or tents, but they do have impressively large beds, which the

women raise up on four funnel-shaped supports, a foot or so off the ground. They spread them with rugs and kilims in vivid, showy colours. Sticks are cut and stuck in the ground at the corners of the bed and thin cotton cloth slung over them to create some privacy. The sun goes down over a huddle of four-posters, making the bush look like a bedding department.

We pitch our more modest collection of lightweight, bed-less tents on a patch of bare sand nearby.

Night falls. As we sit down to a bowl of soup and a plate of something and rice, the sound of celebrations carries across from the Wodaabe camp, and soon Doulla emerges from the gloom, along with Perri, the head of the well-buying association who, at all times of day or night, wears a huge pair of Austrian dark glasses.

Doulla invites me to join their dance. It is the Wodaabe way of welcoming us into their group. I'm pretty exhausted, and was looking forward to climbing into my tent and crashing out, but to refuse would clearly be a serious breach of etiquette.

I'm led into the centre of a circle of Wodaabe men, clapping and chanting responses and moving round in a slow, rhythmic shuffle. Then the circle closes in, moving tight around me. I can smell sweat and the sweet earth smell of their clothes, but the smiles and the sound of the voices are reassuring. It may look like a war dance, but it's more like a ritual embrace, a binding together against a hostile world. Not for the first time, I sense that the Wodaabe are decent, tolerant people, inclined to peacefulness and probably easily exploited. Doulla translates their song for me:

> 'Oh lovely girl with eyes like gazelle,
> White teeth and face like the moon,
> Which shines like the sun,
> You are as beautiful as milk.'

They're not the only ones out dancing tonight. Nigel has rigged up a powerful lamp to shoot the sequence and in its beam is a huge swarm of insects, turning, twisting, cavorting and careering around each other. Decide against sleeping under the stars.

ABOVE
The beam from our filming lamp reveals that the air is alive, and not just with the sound of music.

DAY FIFTY-FIVE   NEAR INGAL

Because of the great heat of the day, the comparatively cool hours around dawn are valuable and much gets done. We are up at first light, just before six, but the Wodaabe women have been at work for an hour or more. The thorn bushes are hung with washing. The children are up and dressed and their mothers are out finding wood for the fire. After this they still have to prepare the food, milk the cows and fetch water from the creek.

As the bed forms the centrepiece of each family's living area, it doesn't surprise me to hear that the Wodaabe can't marry until they can afford one of their own. If they had mortgages, young Wodaabe couples would put them down on a bed. Another much-respected sign of wealth and status is the number and quality of your calabashes, the hollowed-out pumpkins, often painted and decorated, which are indispensable for cooking and eating.

Breakfast, and indeed every other meal, consists basically of milk and millet. The long, repetitive process of pounding the millet, usually entrusted to the young girls, is already underway, producing the soft, thudding rhythm that is the heartbeat of so many West African communities. After an hour, sometimes longer, the millet is ready to be mixed with water into the unappetising grey paste that will provide their nourishment for the day.

Céline, who for one summer, at least, has left the lush farmlands of Aquitaine to live with the Wodaabe, tells me that on occasions there is not even enough millet to go round.

'Sometimes they eat only milk.'

She has much admiration for their resilience and her insights into the character of the Wodaabe strike a chord with my own.

'They will not ask anything about you, or take anything from you.'

They have, she says, a free and open attitude to relationships – which can cause problems – but they are not afraid to express shame and regret and accept that life requires patience and tolerance.

This stoic attitude doesn't always do them much good. One of the women has had her fingers broken when a cow stepped on her hand. By the time Pete, who has been on the BBC medical course, gets to examine her, it's clear that the wound is two or three days old and in imminent danger of turning gangrenous. He cleans and binds it as best he can, but it's obvious she needs stronger antibiotics and possibly surgery. We offer to take her to a doctor in Ingal, but she shakes her head very definitely. She will wait until she can walk in with the others. Though she may lose her hand, there is no changing her mind.

Despite hard lives and harsh conditions, the Wodaabe are by no means grey or ground down. Celebration, dance and the pursuit of beauty are important parts of their everyday life and all three come together in the *Gerewol*, an extraordinary Fulani ritual that will be part of their *Cure Salée* celebrations. The young, unmarried men spend hours making themselves look beautiful, painting their faces red, highlighting their eyes with white lines and their lips with black powder. The effect is to make them look feminine and prematurely aged at the same time. The display is combined with a formal dance, at which these richly adorned men vie with each other for the favours of the young girls. The girls make the choice. It's free and open, and whilst it does not have to end in marriage, it does have to end in a night together.

Doulla takes me by the hand and leads me through the bush to a clearing, where a *Gerewol* is in progress. Young men, pouring sweat under aniseed-red make-up, are rising slowly up and down on their toes to the accompaniment of a long, droning chant. Their arms come forward, raising the long decorated sticks that each man carries and which I'm told are symbols of the warrior, whilst their faces perform a pantomime of grinning, eye-rolling and lip-pursing.

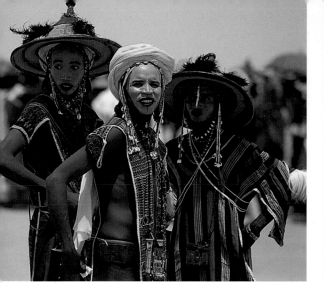

The girls are brought forward, also dressed and made up, one hand shielding the face in a show of shyness and modesty.

The girls turn to face the row of dancing men, bringing the grimacing and eye-rolling to grotesquely bizarre heights, before coming forward, one by one, and choosing their man by a single touch.

What makes this whole surreal performance rather appealing is the similarity to a lot of things we do ourselves. It is basically a ritualised high-school hop or coming-out dance, the difference here being that the sexual motive is not only acknowledged and accepted but actively encouraged.

Later, in my tent, sweltering my way to sleep, I can hear the *Gerewol* still going on, and the insistent thrum of the voices gives way to dreams of tall thin pouting men, their make-up running onto sweet, shy girls. More bromide in the tea for me.

DAY FIFTY-SIX INGAL

Woken early by the sound of donkeys having nightmares and cattle chomping grass inches away from my head. Used to the constant hum of city life, I find these sporadic rural noises quite disconcerting.

Never one of life's natural campers, I'm still getting used to the absence of personal space. My territory extends as far as the flap of my tent, which is about a foot away; beyond that I share Africa with everyone else. I'm pungently reminded of this when, just before dawn, easing myself out of the tent, clutching a trowel and paper for my morning toilet, I step straight onto a freshly laid cowpat.

(The trowel, by the way, is to enable me to dig my own latrine and cover it up afterwards. If I'm really serious about protecting the Sahara I should also take matches to burn the paper, for nothing much biodegrades out here.)

After everyone has eaten, the camp is dismantled and the families set out to walk the last 45 miles through the bush to Ingal. All they ask from us in return for their hospitality is medicine. Eye disease, malaria and chronic stomach pain from tainted water are endemic complaints. As we turn out our medical bags, it's sobering to realise just how much pain they must take for granted.

We squeeze Doulla and Perri and a dozen others into our filming vehicles so that they can go ahead and find accommodation. There isn't much room, so Doulla

volunteers to travel on the roof rack. He seems to have all the makings of a saint, but he shrugs off any credit and reminds me that in Africa no vehicle goes anywhere until it's full, and that means on top as well. This doesn't prevent me thinking of him being flung around above me as we pitch and toss along the rutted un-made track. I comfort myself with the thought that we're reducing his journey time from two days to two hours.

There is relief all round when Ingal's soaring communications mast looms up on the horizon, and a few minutes later we bounce out of the bush and along increasingly busy streets until we emerge onto a huge open area.

At first I can hardly believe my eyes. In the middle of deeply impoverished rural Africa there is a neon-lit showground, screeching distorted announcements, a car park full of gleaming Mercedes, a double-decker tourist bus, women dressed to the nines in sequinned finery, racing camels showing their paces, Touareg chieftains trailing entourages, police and soldiers mingling with ticket-sellers and sharp-eyed boys pushing Coca-Cola sales carts through the crowd. The air is thick with dust and the reek of fuel from humming generators.

'CURE SALEE 2001,' announces a billboard. 'Our Three Themes – SIDA (AIDS), PALU (Malaria), Polio.' It seems much more than a gathering of nomads – a combination of county show and trade fair, school sports day and political rally, Royal Tournament and Boy Scout Jamboree.

The wind tugs at the white, green and orange horizontals of the national flag, unfurled above a group of government-sponsored stalls offering family planning and veterinary advice. The crowd passes them by, intent on celebration rather than self-improvement. Walking through the throng, their ostrich feather headdresses rising above the crowd, are groups of young Wodaabe men, made up like models on a catwalk, preening and effeminate, white rings around their eyes, blackened lips, slashes

166

of yellow across foreheads and down noses, off to dance their own grimacing, eye-rolling *Gerewol*, dressed like girls to attract the girls.

Our little Wodaabe group has fallen silent. They look around with quick nervous glances. The natural ebullience of last night seems to have faded, and as they move off to look for somewhere to stay they seem uneasy and out of place.

As the heat of the day declines the energy levels rise. More and more people mill around, seeing and being seen, greeting and parading. I find myself introduced to an impressive man in white robes, the mayor of Tamanrasset in Algeria, who shouts over the noise that he is hoping we will come and see him on our way north. A moment later someone grasps my hand, a Frenchman who is trying to save the ostrich population of the nearby Aïr Mountains, which is now down to two. He's trying to get them to mate. I don't hear how, as a red-capped policeman on a camel, ghetto-blaster strapped to his thigh, rides between us.

We set up camp at the far end of the flat, gritty strip, but even here, half a mile from the celebrations, I'm kept awake at night by the sounds of amplified announcements, music and the stabbing beams of fast cars roaring away. Where they're going to I've absolutely no idea.

It's all part of the bracing confusion of *Cure Salée*, the party in the middle of nowhere.

DAY FIFTY-SEVEN INGAL

Doulla, Perri and the advance guard of Wodaabe have found some accommodation in town. They've rented two houses with interlocking walled compounds from some Hausa boys. The Hausa, from the south of the country, make up over half the population. Urbanised and opportunistic, they largely control the commercial life of Niger.

Two of them lounge in the shade of the doorway, eyes following us with self-assured curiosity. They're dressed in T-shirts and jeans and wear big watches, and I have the feeling that they can't understand why we should be so interested in a bunch of nomads.

I recall Céline telling me back at the camp that the Hausa-led central government does not have much time for the Wodaabe, being suspicious and hostile, as governments often are, towards those who have no fixed address. So it's not a great surprise to find Doulla and Perri somewhat subdued. They don't like renting and they don't like houses.

Not that this one impresses with its permanence. The mud that binds the building together looks to have been mixed from the contents of a rubbish tip. Shreds of plastic bag, silver paper, bottle caps, glass, fabric and even leather shoe straps protrude from the walls. On the other hand, I can see it's Turner Prize potential. A house made of everyday life.

Accompany Doulla and Perri to buy provisions. In the market, shopkeepers sit cross-legged beneath grass-thatch awnings. Beside them are bowls of sugar, blocks of salt, sacks of tobacco and dried chillies and boxes of green china tea. Staples like millet and kola nuts lie out in the open, piled high on plastic sheeting. After buying the basics, Doulla and Perri get down to what they really enjoy, looking at clothes. They show me the intricate differences in the thread of the indigo blue turban material and the finer points to look out for when buying the loose robe and leggings that form the basic nomad's outfit.

Later, bearing bags of millet, sugar and mint, but with no money left over for new outfits, Doulla and Perri return to their lodgings to prepare for the big night, the first public performance of their *Gerewol*.

We return to our camp site, passing the various shops and stalls on the edge of the showground. One is run by the Niger Post Office, which proves to be boldly internationalist, with colour-soaked special issues devoted to such typically African heroes as Raphael, Rembrandt and Princess Di. Another booth boasts a pair of skis and a snowboard. A dashingly elegant Touareg appreciates my curiosity and tries to sell me a course of sand-skiing lessons. On some of the higher dunes, he says, when the sand is cold and crisp, it can be just like the Alps. He may be right, but the name on his card doesn't exactly fill me with confidence.

'Danger,' it reads. 'Abdul Khadir Danger.'

It's late in the afternoon when we return to the Wodaabe compound. Hairdressing and make-up is already underway as they prepare themselves for their first night at *Cure Salée*. Doulla is having his hair dressed by one of the women. Almost unrecognisable without his headcloth, he has, like most of the Wodaabe, and unlike the Hausa, a surprisingly luxuriant growth, which is being carefully plaited until tresses hang down by his ears like those of a Hasidic Jew.

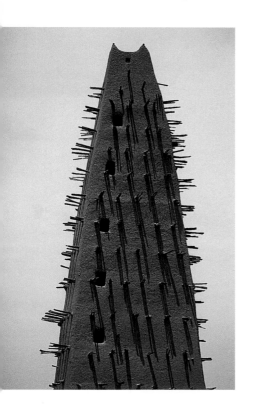

Other young men sit in a line, holding up plastic-framed vanity mirrors, which no self-respecting Wodaabe youth would be seen without. Each one has a sandal on the ground in front of him, which he uses as a palette for the colours. The predominantly yellow base is powder from a stone called *macara*, which they find out in the bush. The black lipstick is from another mineral, called stibnite.

Those already made up are scrambling into leather leggings and exchanging their everyday sandals for elaborate, decorated versions, which they slip on lovingly. Then they tie each other's white turbans, onto which are fixed headdresses of cowrie shells, precious stones and, to cap it all, ostrich feathers.

Once this long and painstaking process is complete, they leave their temporary home and walk the mile or so to the showground. Despite the confidence of their display, they still seem pitifully self-conscious. Country cousins in the big city.

The thudding music grows louder and the red and white Coca-Cola umbrellas draw closer. Our friends sing, not very convincingly, more to keep their spirits up, as their eyes search the crowd for fellow Wodaabe, like new arrivals at an old school reunion. Suddenly I feel that our presence is superfluous. The best way we can repay their hospitality is probably to stay out of the way. It's their show now.

ABOVE *Bristling mud spire of the Grande Mosquée in Agadez.*

168

DAY FIFTY-EIGHT   AGADEZ

I'm standing on the small roof terrace of the Pensione Tellit in Agadez. A hot and hazy sunset is over and night is wrapping itself around the mud-brown walls of this old trading town. Orange lights mark out the network of narrow streets that connect a spread of rounded walls and flat, rectangular roofs. There's only one tall building in town and that's the minaret of the Grande Mosquée, a pyramid of mud, stones and projecting wood beams which rises high above the surrounding town. Anywhere else in the world it might barely be noticed, but this one is the tallest building for a thousand miles and, along with the mosques at Djenné and Timbuktu, it has almost mythic status in Islamic Sahara. I'm staring at it now, as my wife, on the other end of a satellite phone, is describing the almost unbelievable destruction of two other iconic towers, 6000 miles away, in New York.

The news that greeted us all on our arrival at this modest comfortable little whitewashed hotel seems incomprehensibly unreal, but friends and family, contacted by satellite phone, confirm that the attacks not only happened but were seen to happen and are being replayed constantly to those who might have missed them.

They appear to have taken place right across the northeastern United States. The President is in hiding and the country has virtually shut down. Though nobody has claimed responsibility, the finger of blame is being pointed at Arab terrorists and reprisals are said to be imminent.

We eat later, under the stars, beneath a sky which, even out here, seems less friendly than it did last night. All of us are shell-shocked, turning over what we have heard, flailing around for explanations, repeating the facts and trying to fit them into theories, wondering what on earth might happen next.

DAY FIFTY-NINE   AGADEZ to TABELOT

A night of raucous air-con and bad dreams. When I come to write the day's date in my notebook I pause. Yesterday I wrote 'Tuesday, September 11th' without noticing.

Today I write 'Wednesday, September 12th' without conviction. According to radio reports, casualties in New York alone are said to be in their thousands. *Thousands*. Thousands of people, in a city which, apart from Sheffield and London, I probably know better than any other. I flick back the page of my notebook and look at what I scribbled before climbing into bed last night: 'I can think of no parallel act of destructive violence in my lifetime aside from Hiroshima and Nagasaki.'

Out on the tiny courtyard breakfast is laid out. The sky is clear blue, the morning sunlight will soon be tipping over the wall and spilling onto us. I eat bread, two eggs, honey and tea, with which I swallow my malaria pill. The others begin to emerge from their rooms. John has heard the latest news on BBC World Service. Details it's hard to deal with – mobile phone calls from those who knew they were going to die, people jumping eighty floors from the blazing Trade Center. Things you don't want to hear.

But our waiter is the same and the manager is the same and outside in the small square the same cast of characters rise to their feet as we appear, not to talk about terror attacks or the likelihood of a world war, but to sell, cajole and wheedle, exactly as they did when we arrived from Ingal yesterday. The short thick-set man with the rings and silver Touareg crosses: 'I am good friend of the English. I have jewellery. You have come to Niger, you must buy something.' The tall, imposing man with a craggy face and thin grey beard, who stalks me, repeating over and over again, 'You must talk with me. I know Ginger Baker.' A blind woman, hand outstretched, led around by a little girl. Two men on crutches, fleet and persistent. The children, as ever, wanting a gift or some money.

Here in Agadez the world hasn't changed. And why should it? Niger is not a player. It is one of the poorest countries on the planet. Its gross national product works out at $850 per person per year. There are no banks of television screens here pumping out the apocalyptic scenes they're seeing back home. In Niger the literacy rate is barely 15 per cent, and I have not seen a single newspaper or magazine on the streets of Agadez. Life goes on.

We have heard that there is a possibility of joining a camel caravan at Tabelot, a town 50 miles to the northeast as the crow flies, though more like six hours in a vehicle, as it lies deep in the Aïr (pronounced 'eye-eer') Mountains.

I'm excited at the prospect, not just of joining a camel train, but of entering, for the first time, one of the three legendary mountain ranges of the Sahara, the others being the Tibesti in Chad and the Hoggar in southern Algeria.

I'm not disappointed. This is a tortured, twisted, dramatic landscape, created by immense volcanic forces, which have swung the bedrock of the Sahara from the horizontal to the vertical, rolled it over and left it to shatter and splinter in the heat. Rock-fields stretch away into the distance, charred like the rakings from a furnace. Across this untamed surface runs a roughly cleared track. As we shake and sway along, the goatskin in which the water supply is kept, lashed to the side of the car to keep cool, occasionally swings round and taps ghoulishly at the window, as if the goat had come back to life and was asking to be let in.

After five hours we run into Tabelot. It's not much more than a large village, but significantly different from the villages on the plain. The mud walls of the compound are stout affairs, with stone foundations. The tents inside them are more substantial too, with heavy flanks hanging from a strong rattan spine. It all makes sense as soon I step down from the four-wheel drive and feel the pleasant sensation of a fresh, almost cooling edge to the air. We're in the mountains, 2000 feet higher than Agadez, looking across to a mountain peak that's 3000 feet higher still.

Our accompanying team, led by the imperious Mohammed Ixa, a tall, straight-backed Touareg swathed in a yellow robe, slings a plastic cover between acacia trees and vehicles to provide us with some shade. A groundsheet is laid, and as soon as the sponge rubber mattresses are arranged on top of it Mohammed selects one, lies down, closes his eyes beatifically and proceeds to listen to his radio through an earpiece for the next couple of hours. Meanwhile, his minions prepare a late lunch of all the things the guidebooks advise you not to eat – hand-prepared salad (but *whose* hands?),

ABOVE

*Camel-driven
irrigation system at
the oasis of Tabelot.*

watermelon (who knows where the water's come from?) – that sort of thing. Apart from French bread and hard-boiled eggs, it's all there is, so we eat it anyway. A fierce gusting wind snatches at the plastic awning above us, which snaps and crackles but holds fast. This is the *harmattan*, someone says, the wind from the heart of the desert, hot and dry enough to split tree trunks.

Around four the wind begins to drop, and I'm taken to meet Omar, who will be leading the camel train to Bilma. He is a Touareg, around forty years old. Square and almost stocky, he has a wide, friendly face, deep black skin and a thin black beard. He smiles readily, with a shy lowering of the head as he does so.

He's proud of his village and takes us a mile or so away to see the oasis on which Tabelot's survival depends. The water table is close to the surface here and two or three wells feed prolific fields of onions, carrots, maize, millet, and orchards of orange, lemon, fig and pomegranate. In a shady clearing a young boy leads a docile white camel up and down a 30-foot pathway. The camel is harnessed to a rope, which is wound round a wooden pulley and drops down into a 50-foot well, from which it draws water in a glistening black goatskin bag. A funnel attached to the bag flops out like a great tongue, regurgitating the water down a wooden pipe into an elaborate system of mud-walled channels and conduits that carries it eventually into the fields. Every few trips the boy rewards the camel with a mouthful of maize leaves, which it despatches noisily, like a paper-shredder.

As we walk back past freshly tilled onion fields, it's easy to forget we're anywhere near the Sahara. Doves are cooing, streams are gurgling and a balmy and benevolent humidity seems to seep up through the ground.

Omar insists I try dates straight from the tree, which is not as easy as it sounds, for he has to find someone more athletically built than himself to shin up and get them. They appear to grow in white plastic bags. I'm reassured that this is not another GM food trial but a precaution to stop the birds getting at them. And there are birds

171

everywhere: large black birds with white caps, small, noisy, bouncy wagtails, red-dusted firefinches darting in and out of the trees. We move on, munching the dates, which are disappointingly leathery, passing red peppers spread out to dry in groves of grapefruit, grenadine and mango.

We end up at Omar's house back in the village. He lives in a modest collection of straw huts and stone and mud buildings with his four wives and fifteen children,

ranging in age from one month to eighteen years. I ask him if he's rich.

'No,' he replies gracefully, 'but in terms of children, yes.'

When I enquire if there are problems with such a large family, he nods. Shortage of food, medicine, clothing. Wouldn't it be better to have fewer of them, I ask, impertinently.

He shrugs, head on one side. No, he says, with a coy half-smile, he likes a lot of children.

And the wives, do they get on well?

Before he can reply there is a loud guffaw from the youngest and prettiest of them. Judging by the blank looks of the others, she is the only one who understands French.

Omar, who doesn't look like a ladies' man, smiles bashfully and mutters something about '*jalousie*'.

Tonight we are entertained, as is the custom when strangers arrive, by an evening of dancing. In the moonlight, the young women sit together beneath a tree, singing and chanting, while the men form a line opposite them and either singly or in pairs approach the women to dazzle them with their dancing. The beat gradually increases, the movements become wild and flamboyant and inventive, the foot-stomping harder and faster, as each man tries to outdo the other, dancing themselves to the point of hysteria, arms and legs flying, robes stuck to their backs with sweat. The women remain sitting, chanting repetitively and gradually becoming obscured by the cloud of dust raised by their suitors. My eyes sting and a dry, rasping cough catches in my throat, but it's impossible not to be drawn in.

To grunts of approval I'm led forward hand in hand with the man who is going to introduce me to the dance. He watches apprehensively as I improvise a routine that owes less to classical dancing and more to the Ministry Of Silly Walks. Not only am I asked to reprise it, but later I'm paid a high compliment by my sponsor.

'All the forty-year-old women say they have never seen a non-Touareg dance so well.'

DAY SIXTY TABELOT

Uneasy lies the head that wears the crown. Despite accolades from forty-year-old Touareg women, my dreams are more Sunday morning indigestion than Saturday Night Fever, and, waking before dawn, I reach for my head-torch, toilet paper, garden trowel and matches and extricate myself as swiftly as I can from the tent. This is never as easy as it should be, and as I corkscrew my way out into the surrounding darkness I imagine this is what it must be like being born. The sky is clear and dense with stars and the temperature has plunged 20 degrees. It's a good walk to the nearest patch of cover, and as I crouch over my excavations it occurs to me that these are the only times when I'm truly alone in the desert and should be savoured. By the time I'm home and dry, as it were, I have to pull on a sweater to keep warm.

An hour later, the deep lilting cry of Tabelot's muezzin calls the faithful to prayer. Check my clock. It's five. Soon there are sounds of life, soft footsteps passing my tent, grunts of goats and bleats of sheep. There's no such thing as a lie-in in the desert.

Some thirty camels are assembled on a stony stretch of ground surrounded by low houses. Mohammed Ixa, glass of tea in hand, points with languid admiration at the white camels, peculiar to this part of the Sahara.

'*Le chameau d'élégance,*' he purrs, in a Maurice Chevalier sort of way.

For some reason, I've been allotted the most non-white of them. Indeed, his name, Ekawik, evidently means Blackie. There is much laughter from the camel team as I try to pronounce the name, so I'm probably saying something rude by mistake.

Meanwhile, Omar moves quietly amongst them, inspecting a harness here and there and helping one of his eight-strong team to heave baggage, bedding, food and water aboard. The camels endure all this with permanent expressions of weary disdain, as if the whole of the rest of the world is a bad smell they have to endure.

The salt pans of Bilma lie 350 miles to the east and the journey will take almost two weeks.

Omar's plan is to set off this morning and get ahead of us. The first two days will be along mountain trails so narrow and precarious that we shall be unable to get our filming equipment anywhere near. He will rendezvous with us at the point where they emerge from the mountains into the desert proper.

To the accompaniment of rumbling groans and one or two angry roars, the camels are brought to their feet and the tethering ropes removed from their front legs. As Omar hands me the guide rope I'm reminded how big these creatures are. Ekawik's head rises several feet above mine and he observes me through the luxuriant lashes of his heavy-lidded eyes. I smile back with what I hope will convey both friendliness and confidence and pat his flanks, which he doesn't like at all.

As far as camel trains go, ours is modest. In 1922 a Captain Angus Buchanan saw a caravan leave Tabelot with 7000 camels and 1100 men. The train stretched 6 miles from front to back. We have twenty-eight camels, nine men and stretch about 200 yards.

There are no emotional leave-takings and, as far as I can see, none of Omar's four wives or fifteen children turns up to say goodbye. Gingerly attached to Ekawik, I accompany the caravan out of the village and over the first hill. There I hand over the reins and watch them snaking their way off through the rocks, nodding and swaying as if in slow motion.

The Aïr Mountains form such an impenetrable barrier to the north and east that to link up with the camel train we must retrace our steps back to Agadez and take the Bilma road, which skirts the high ground and heads straight across the desert. Mohammed and the drivers are anxious to be on the move, as the clouds grow thicker and greyer above us. In the rainy season one downpour can easily turn roads into rivers. They pack up the camp at speed and we set off at the faster end of safe, stones spinning off the track behind us.

Though the rain holds off, Mohammed keeps an anxious eye on the clouds massing around the 3500-foot summit of Mount Taghouaji, halfway between us and Agadez.

He becomes increasingly concerned when we come across evidence of a recent deluge, and progress is reduced to a snail's pace as our drivers feel their way through flooded ruts and potholes. We narrowly avoid a dried-up riverbed that has turned into a fast flowing stream, 50 yards wide and rising all the time. The sudden power of a desert flood is an awesome sight and Mohammed is persuaded to stop and let us take some film. Then we're back into the cars and racing the last few miles to Agadez, which is, amazingly, dry as a bone.

Back at the friendly little Pensione Tellit, I run into its owner and founder Vittorio, a sixty-five-year-old ex-bank employee from Rome, who first came to Agadez in 1970, fell in love with the place, married a Touareg girl and set up the only Italian ice-cream parlour in the Sahara. He's quietly spoken and looks not unlike an expatriate Roman emperor, with close-cropped white hair and a toga-like African robe. Besides this tiny hotel he has a restaurant called Le Pilier on the main road to Algeria. It's beautifully designed in the Soudan style and serves a very fine spinach and ricotta ravioli.

It's not a great time to be in the tourist business. The economy of Niger is in a parlous state. Income from uranium found in the Aïr Mountains has dried up and the area is only just beginning to recover from the Touareg rebellion of the 1990s. Though the uprising is over, the situation remains volatile. Only two years ago the president was assassinated and most Western governments still warn travellers against going anywhere north of Tahoua, 200 miles south of where we are right now.

When I ring home tonight, however, it sounds as if the rest of the world is much more dangerous than Niger. American airports are still closed. There is talk of war and warnings of further attacks, perhaps on London and Paris as well. Now that the terrorists are known to be Muslim, people back home are worrying that we must be especially vulnerable, here amongst the mosques and muezzins.

In fact, we are, right now, in probably one of the safest places on earth.

DAY SIXTY-ONE INTO THE TENERE DESERT

'How are you, Britisher? I show you something.'

'I must talk with you. I know Ginger Baker!'

'*Donnez-moi un cadeau!*'

As we appear at the door of the Pensione the usual suspects waiting in the shade of the Hôtel de l'Aïr across the street leap to their feet. Today I do not totally ignore the street cries of Agadez. Mindful of what is to come – prolonged exposure to the hottest part of the desert – I negotiate for a turban and am now the proud owner of a 15-foot length of indigo cotton. It seems an awful lot to wrap round a size six and seven-eighths head, but they tell me some turbans are 20 feet long.

As we shall be camping for the foreseeable future, our departure from Agadez is delayed to enable everyone to repack, reducing bags and baggage to the minimum, and to spoil ourselves with an early lunch of *penne arrabiata* with aubergine and a glass of wine or three at Le Pilier.

A couple of hours later, the memory of the meal and the cool, airy courtyard of the restaurant is a distant dream. The Bilma road is a bleak and uncompromising strip of desert dust, defined only by the imprint of vehicles that have passed this way before. The rains have not reached this far south, nor does it look as if they have done so for many years. The ground is hard and hot. Fine green lines, the only hint of decoration in a landscape of sombre browns and blacks, follow cracks in the rocks where a residue of moisture has been trapped. Unbelievably, there are people living here, on the very edge of survival. A thin straw hut bends with the wind. Outside it, children with wild hair and torn blue smocks watch us pass, standing barefoot on the stones, a donkey stock-still beside them.

There are army checkpoints. Whilst Mohammed presents our papers I get out for a breather, only to be hit by a wall of heat unlike anything I've yet experienced. Whatever is the opposite of wind chill, this is it. Air stoked up to 55°C/131°F and driven on by the *harmattan* rakes the desert like a blast from a flame-thrower.

I'm told that in desert as hot as the Ténéré, the human body loses 2 gallons of water a day, which is 9 litres, and 4 gallons if you're on the move, so one should really keep drinking constantly. We have bottles of water with us but they heat up quickly and warm water is so much more difficult to gulp down. J-P has come up with an ingenious answer. He drops a couple of mint tea bags into a plastic bottle, which he wedges on top of the dashboard. The head-on sunlight heats it, the bounce of the vehicle stirs it and the near boiling infusion that results is a lot more palatable than lukewarm mineral water.

The vehicles judder and shudder over a surface that changes with frightening suddenness from hard earth to corrugated rocky ridges. A few miles back we passed a

donkey rolling on its back, enjoying a dust bath. Just now we saw another donkey, stretched out by the side of the road, skin drawn back on its jaw, dead of thirst.

Mohammed Ixa points out four fluted columns, apparently of golden sandstone, 3 or 4 feet high, arranged in the shape of a square. The stones are actually petrified wood and mark a pre-Islamic grave. Which means someone was laid to rest here at least fourteen centuries ago.

As the sun is beginning to sink, we see, coming towards us, what looks like a huge upturned ship, with dozens of people clinging to the wreckage. As it comes closer it's revealed to be a Mercedes truck, groaning beneath the weight of fifty or sixty people, close-packed on top of a cargo of rugs, carpets, blankets and bedding which swells out way beyond the sides of the vehicle. Bags of food, water and provisions hang down its flanks like fenders.

Initially friendly shouts from the occupants turn to angry gesticulations as soon as we attempt to film them.

These are trans-Saharan *camions*, carrying an illegal labour force across the very heart of the desert from the poorer black African countries of the south to the oil-rich countries of Libya and Algeria. The workers generally have no papers or passports, so the *camions* move at night and take considerable detours to avoid checkpoints.

We put the cameras away and watch them recede slowly and ponderously on the twisting track towards Agadez, a fat, swaying silhouette against the setting sun.

DAY SIXTY-TWO   THE TENERE DESERT

We camped last night in complete isolation. Or so I thought until this morning, when, out of nowhere, figures appeared, moving slowly towards us: a group of three women, one with a babe in arms, and a young boy. They were terribly thin and frail. Against the early morning light they seemed almost insubstantial, like wraiths. They didn't speak, just stood and watched us, passive and expressionless. The oldest of the women, who looked seventy but was probably no more than forty, touched her eye and then her leg.

Our drivers looked embarrassed. She was asking for medicine and they didn't have any. If they had, they'd be using it themselves.

We gave them whatever we could, along with some water, and Amadou the cook found some scraps of food. They were still standing there when we drove away.

Most mornings we're quite jolly when we hit the road, but today the mood is muted. It was as if we were all thinking the same thing. That the people who had visited us were starving and there was nothing we could do.

There is more sand about now. Pale, almost white, it gathers at the base of huge black basalt rocks making them look as if they are not rooted in the earth but floating a few feet above it. It blows up against camel skeletons that lie by the road, making graceful streamlined shapes out of bleached corpses.

El Haj, who's driving Basil, J-P and me, is tall, quiet and, I should imagine, quite badly paid. He is a Toubou from the Bilma region and J-P speaks good enough French to get him talking. He's not complimentary about anyone apart from the Toubou, finding the Touareg arrogant and the Fulani, of whom the Wodaabe are a subdivision, too submissive. He cheers up visibly when talking of the Hausa. They're the people everyone detests, he says confidently.

'After all, they're the bosses.'

By mid-morning the mountain range has receded and we turn off the track not far from the site of the celebrated Arbre du Ténéré. Long renowned for being the only tree standing in hundreds of square miles of surrounding desert, the Arbre du Ténéré became even more famous when, in 1973, a truck knocked it over. The bits and pieces have been stuck together and it now resides in a place of honour at the national museum in Niamey.

We turn north now, across country, to the spot where we hope to find Omar and the camel train. The Ténéré, considered by those who know these things to be the most beautiful part of the Sahara, does not make things easy for us. After following a long and ultimately impassable wadi (dried-up riverbed), we're forced to turn back and look for a way through the sand dunes. The first few are low and relatively uncomplicated, but eventually we reach a big one, 100 feet or more and steep. The first two vehicles of our convoy make it, but El Haj doesn't. Revving the engine is fatal, as it just digs the wheels in deeper, so he has no option but to roll rather shamefacedly backwards until he finds level ground.

He lets down the front tyres to increase grip and we put our shoulders to the back of the vehicle as he tries again. Despite all our combined efforts, the wheels spin helplessly, we're covered in flying sand and the attempt is abandoned. El Haj wipes his brow and reluctantly climbs up onto the roof to get down the sand ladders which he probably should have used in the first place. Two of these, placed in front of the back wheels, provide the resistance he needs. But once moving he mustn't stop, and with shouts of encouragement we watch our means of transport hurtle up the dune, pause agonisingly briefly on the crest and disappear over the other side. Our cheers die quite quickly as we realise we have to retrieve the ladders and climb up after him. John Pritchard checks the temperature. It's 56°C/133°F.

After another hour's abortive searching of spectacular but camel-less desert, Mohammed, at the wheel of the first vehicle, suddenly yelps, points and roars off towards a clump of rangy acacias marking a shallow dip in the ground. I don't immediately see the caravan, as it blends so seamlessly into the background, but there they are, Ekawik and his colleagues, fearlessly stripping acacia branches, masticating 2-inch-long thorns to get to the tiny green leaves. Lying in thin shade nearby is Omar and his team.

We make camp in the lee of a 30-foot sand dune and pick our way through another salad, augmented with tuna this time. Before we go out to begin work, I give my increasingly burnt British skin a good coating of sun oil, forgetting as I do so that the wind has peppered my face with fine grains of sand. It's momentarily agonising, like giving myself a facial with an emery board. To avoid any further damage, Omar insists I wear my new turban. He helps tie it for me. I would never have imagined that 15 feet of coiled cotton could make such a difference to my life. Quite apart from protection against the sand, it also keeps me much cooler than a hat. And I look like Lawrence of Arabia. Well, his father, anyway.

DAY SIXTY-THREE   THE TENERE DESERT

The pace of desert life is almost exactly the opposite of the life I'm used to back home. Because of the ferocity of the climate, even the most simple activities must be taken slowly. There is no need to hurry and no benefit in doing so.

For the cameleers, the day follows a timeless, preordained pattern. Prayer, then breakfast cooked over a fire of sticks and branches, then the thick woollen blankets, under which they sleep at night (they don't have tents), are rolled up, secured with twine and laid beside each camel. The camels are brought to their knees and loaded up. Guide ropes are reinserted in mouths stained yellowy-green from cud-chewing, and they are brought to their feet. This provokes a tumult of braying and grunting. I wish I knew what they were saying, for it sounds important to them. Is it passionate protest or is it merely an assertion of team spirit at the start of a new day? Is it 'how many more times do I have to tell you, I'm *not* a beast of burden, right', or is it 'Good morning everyone. Another scorcher by the looks of things'?

Ekawik doesn't speak to me at all. In fact, he doesn't seem the slightest bit interested in making friends with me, despite my sycophantic patting of his flanks and complimentary remarks about the two silver good luck charms hanging from a chain around his neck.

He does, however, honk savagely when asked to carry me. This doesn't help, as I've never felt very comfortable on a ship of the desert. Once perched on Ekawik's hump, I feel about as steady as I would on a surfboard. I've also been provided with a lethal, though aesthetically pleasing, ceremonial saddle with high, spiky prongs and pommels back and front. I may look like some visiting potentate when I'm up there, but when it comes to dismounting, I find it impossible to get my leg over, as it were, and I have to be dragged from the saddle like someone being pulled from a car wreck. Much giggling from the cameleers.

The rhythm of the journey is set by the camels. Normally, they would be on the move at four in the morning, walking for fourteen or fifteen hours a day with two breaks, at midday and late afternoon. Omar tells me that when he's on the road he only has three or four hours' sleep a night.

178

Ekawik and his friends are happiest when performing something steady, simple and repetitive, like walking or chewing the cud. They are superbly adapted to this climate and terrain. Long legs raise them clear of the hot sand, a layer of fat on their backs protects them from the blazing sun. Heat escapes from their big, reassuringly rounded flanks, so they appear not to perspire, and even in this frightening heat they can go for days without any water at all. And their metabolism, as I've learnt from playing with their nuggets, is extraordinarily economical.

Izambar Mohammed, one of the nine-strong team of cameleers, is the *chanteur*, the one who sings and chants and makes up songs to pass the time as we go. He warns me about staying too close to the camels, especially their rear ends. Using fluent mime, he points out the ones that are the worst kickers. Somehow it doesn't surprise me that they include Ekawik.

DAY SIXTY-FOUR   THE TENERE DESERT

Things are better today. I've been taken off Ekawik and allotted a white camel of extraordinary docility whose name I'm told is Ashid. Instead of the VIP saddle, which threatened to castrate me every time I tried to dismount, I now sit astride a less glamorous but much more comfortable roll of bedding.

We have left the mountains behind but are still in a landscape studded with volcanic remains. Fields of cracked basalt rock occasionally break through the stony cover, providing streaks of vivid colour, jet black against the pale straw of the sand. The low ridges make for difficult going. The camels are not happy on slopes, especially if they are covered in soft sand, and Omar has to lead them down with great care, moving forwards at a slow shuffle, testing the ground, as if picking his way through a minefield. The camels slip and slide unhappily in his wake, back legs stiff, straight and awkward, as if this is the first time they've ever been asked to walk downhill.

I'm beginning to get to know the cameleers, though none of them speaks anything but Tamahaq. Harouna is the oldest and is frequently consulted by Omar. Elias and Akide Osman are the youngest, affable but detached. I get the impression that a career in cameleering is not all they want out of life. Izambar's chanting is becoming a bit of a bore, but that could be because I'm not getting the full benefit of his improvised lyrics, which occasionally crack up the entire camel train, probably at my expense. Omar is a good-natured and thoughtful man, unquestionably respected by the others. I've never seen him on a camel. He's always walking, keeping an eye out for loose loads, checking the route ahead. He speaks good French and I like to walk and talk with him, as it takes the mind off the monotony. We talk about the recent war between the Touareg and the government in Niamey. The Touareg, rather optimistically, demanded more funds and less interference. The north of the country virtually closed down for six years, Omar had friends killed and arrested and most of the foreign visitors were frightened away. As he was taking tourists on desert safaris for ten times the money he made from salt caravans, this seriously affected his livelihood. But he never considered giving up and doesn't expect he ever will. He likes walking with the camels. He says it gives him time to think.

By midday he has brought us to a spreading acacia, where we are to lunch and rest up in the heat of the day.

The sight of this single tree, which only survives out here because of root systems which search out water 100 feet or more below the surface, gives an extraordinary lift to the spirits. It's like coming across a house or even a small village.

Everyone gets to work. The camels suddenly become talkative, making their usual sounds of complaint or joy as their burdens are removed. Their front legs are hobbled, but this doesn't stop them shuffling nimbly off to a particularly tempting goblet-shaped bush. Soon they're squeezed around it, feeding, with heads lowered in concentration, like men at the urinals when the half-time whistle has gone.

Those camels that can't find a place at the bush, nibble away at the acacia, impervious to thorns as hard and sharp as small nails.

Today we have a special treat, the Saharan equivalent of a Sunday lunch. And it will be fresh. Omar is sharpening his knife and the two sheep and small black goat which have been brought along from Tabelot are eyeing him beadily. Harouna and Izambar drag one of the sheep over. His companions, far from shying away, follow curiously and have to be chased off.

Whilst Harouna and Izambar hold it down, Omar deftly cuts the sheep's throat. It gasps and shudders as the blood drains from its body. The goat approaches again and this time Izambar throws sand at it to keep it away. Moussa takes over now, skinning and disembowelling the sheep, hanging the carcass from a stout branch and carefully cutting it up. The valuable hide, meanwhile, is laid out and rubbed over with sand to clean it.

Wood has been gathered and a fire lit. Akide Osman is making bread, kneading the dough into a flat disc. Once the embers of the fire are hot enough, he rakes them to one side and lays the bread on the hot sand, first one side, then the other, after which he piles sand and glowing embers on top, creating an instant oven. Omar, meanwhile, slices an onion using a broken razor blade, and Moussa prises open a tin of tomatoes with his knife (memo to enterprising businessman – tin openers for the Touareg), drops them into a blackened cooking pot and mixes them with couscous.

Twenty minutes later, the roundel of bread is exhumed, and, after the charcoal and sand have been dusted off, it's passed down the line. It's not quite what I expected, being much harder, stickier and sweeter than bread.

'*Galette*,' explains Omar, helpfully.

Izambar, who is keen to teach me Tamahaq, the language of the Touareg, points to it.

'*Tagella*,' he says.

'Tagella,' I say, exactly as he's said it, only this time everyone falls about.

'*Tagella*,' he repeats.

'Tagel-la,' I reply, this time with extra care. Everyone falls about again.

This pantomime goes on until we're all laughing hysterically. Clearly my pronunciation does not mean bread. It probably means the private parts of a goat, or personal attributes of my mother, but whatever it is, it proves that there's nothing like a bit of incomprehension to bring people together.

I am honoured to be the first to taste the mutton stew. The meat is a little tired, but it had been walking in the sun for four days. Thankfully, the Touareg do not insist on my rolling the food up into a ball with two fingers of my right hand before popping it into my mouth. Out here in the desert they know how to live. I'm handed a wooden spoon, one of four that we share between us.

Izambar teaches me '*isan*', meaning meat, and '*izot*', which I think means 'this is very good', but induces more mirth when I say it.

There is some laughter too when I take off my turban, or *tagelmoust* in Tamahaq.

'You have a blue head,' says Omar, and I laugh indulgently. It's not until someone holds up a mirror that I realise I do indeed have a blue head, a stripe of indigo following a perspiration line right across my forehead.

DAY SIXTY-FIVE THE TENERE DESERT

Omar tells me that camels only need two hours sleep a night, and having got up to commune with nature in the early hours I can confirm that the majority were up and grazing in the moonlight. Two were lying flat out on their sides and three or four others were kneeling, with their long necks bowed and heads resting on the floor like wilted plants.

Breakfast this morning is the remains of the mutton, reinforced with rice and macaroni. Heavy and almost indigestible, but as the next meal may not be for ten hours there's no question of not eating it.

By mid-morning, having completed shots of departure from camp, the crew and gear are taken on in vehicles to the next stopping place. I could go with them, but I've not walked much with the camels in the heat of the day and I feel I must try it. I fill my water bottle, and take another litre, which Omar insists on carrying for me. We set off, twenty-six camels, eight cameleers, me, Omar, one sheep and a small black goat. No-one is striding out. The overriding consideration in this climate is to conserve energy, and I fall happily into the steady even pace. The only sound, apart from the soft rustle of moving camels and the flip-flopping of Omar's sandals on the ground, is an occasional burst of song from Izambar, which rises, hangs in the air and blows away into silence. All that matters is the present. The past and future cease to exist.

Omar and I fall to talking about the health of camels and what threats they face out here. He says parasites, insects and particularly spines in their feet can easily cause

infection (which is ironic, having seen them crunch 2-inch thorns in their mouths without blinking). One esoteric piece of information is that if a camel eats a praying mantis it will die. The camel, that is, not the praying mantis.

I stop to jot down this little gem, and by the time I've put my notebook back in my bag, Omar has moved ahead, his well-worn light blue robe billowing out to reveal deep blue cotton leggings beneath. Several camels have passed me. I've lost Asid and am alongside a camel I don't recognise. I look up to see Akide lying flat out on top of it. He grins down at me. I hope he's impressed that I've opted to walk with them, but I'm pretty sure he thinks I'm completely mad.

A tiny lizard, shockingly naked and white, pops its head out from a stunted clump of grass, takes one look at us and darts back in again.

The wind changes direction and starts to blow grains of sand directly towards me. I glance sideways up at the camels, but they seem completely unaffected, long lashes down, protecting their eyes from whatever is thrown at them.

I take a swig of water, trying not to break step as I do so. Omar is even further away now, and I'm almost halfway down the camel train, alongside Izambar, who returns my smile but, for once, says nothing.

I look down. The desert floor has changed yet again and is now covered in a series of crusty flakes, like fragments of eggshell. Like dew, dried and hardened.

I look back at my footprints. They're quite deep, much deeper than the camel prints beside them. Their broad feet work like snowshoes, distributing their weight and leaving barely a mark.

The classic description of a camel is a horse designed by committee, but it's not quite fair. I see it more as a horse designed by rival universities, all of whom got a grant for different parts. Technologically, it is far more interesting than a horse; it's just that the whole lot could do with some co-ordinating hand.

Time for some more water. I've almost drained my water bottle, but I notice none of the cameleers has taken a drop. We're walking along a wadi and Omar is up on top of a low dune, scanning the land ahead. As we draw level I raise my bottle and he comes down towards me and fills it up again.

Then he leads us out of the wadi and onto the dune, beautiful to look at but murderous underfoot. My feet slip down into the sand and for the first time on the walk I feel faint alarm. By the time we're at the top of the dune I can hear my heart thudding. I slither down the other side and find myself in a long curving bowl between two ridges, dotted with tussocks of *krim-krim* grass and the bleached white branches of dead trees.

Elias Abrokas, swathed in a multicoloured scarf, draws water from a green plastic container into a stainless steel bowl and walks up the line with it. No-one seems to take more than a couple of gulps, and the camels don't stop.

The sight makes me thirsty and I take out my bottle. It's nearly empty again, and by now I'm level with the last three camels. Tuck my bottle back in my bag, put my

184

head down and concentrate on catching up. Mercifully, there is harder sand down here and my boots can get some grip.

After a few minutes of concentrated effort I look up and see Omar as far ahead as ever. I redouble my efforts, setting myself a target to pass three camels in five minutes, but make no headway at all. I've lost the rhythm, the beat, whatever it is that moves camels so easily across the sand. If I pause for a breather I know I shall only slip further back. To shout for help seems pathetic. I look ahead of me. The camel train moves on remorselessly. Akide is still lying peacefully across his camel's back; Izambar has nodded off. Omar is taking the same small, regular paces as when we started. So how have I got down here?

The last camel comes level and passes me. My mouth is dry but I've no more water. The stories I've heard around the campfire spring, unwelcome, into my mind. Of vehicles breaking down and guides dying of thirst as they went for help; of the stranded French couple who gave their six-month-old baby their own blood to drink and still perished.

In only two hours, the joy of solitariness and contemplation has become the fear of isolation and abandonment. Marine metaphors come constantly to mind. I'm out of my depth.

Like a man overboard shouting after a receding ship.

Then Omar turns and motions that there is something up ahead. I wave my bottle as high as I can, neck downwards. He doesn't move but watches the camels pass until I reach him. He hands me what's left of the water and enquires, wordlessly, how I am.

'*Très bon, merci, Omar,*' I lie.

There, in the distance, is a tree, and, below it, a ring of four-wheel drives and Pete cleaning the camera and, almost certainly, Mohammed Ixa lying on his back, listening to the radio.

DAY SIXTY-SIX THE TENERE DESERT

A new arrival at the camp this morning. A baby gazelle, no more than a day old, has been found abandoned by its mother, possibly frightened by the arrival of the camel train. It is a tiny, spindly, shivering thing, with its coat all mussed up; confused, lost and breathing hard. Its legs are as thin as matchsticks, its eyes big, black and searching, its ears as long as a rabbit's. The news that Amadou is to take care of it worries me initially. He is, after all, our chef. But I'm assured that this delicate little beauty will not end up in the pot like the two sheep and the goat, now *one* sheep and a goat, which accompany the caravan. Later, I see the gazelle being held in the massive hands of El Haj, whilst Amadou tries to get her to take milk from the end of his finger.

The camel train moves into spectacular desert today. '*Désert absolu*', as my *Guide Bleu* describes it. The *krim-krim* grass, acacia scrub, even the ubiquitous desert melon bushes, whose fruit is tempting but inedible, have all disappeared. This is landscape reduced to its barest essentials, a rippling, rolling, shadeless surface purged of every living thing.

The immense emptiness quietens everyone. Progress is slow and steady, although

such is the lack of distinctive landmarks it sometimes feels as if we're walking on the spot.

In the middle of the morning, several hours out from the camp, there's a sudden commotion up front, voices raised, a quite un-desert-like sense of urgency and emergency. The camels have come to a halt, so it must be serious. I hurry up the line to find Moussa and Amadou skipping round, shouting and pointing down at the sand, as Izambar runs in with a stone and proceeds to beat at something in the sand. There's great excitement, halfway between fear and fun. Eventually, to gasps of mock horror, Izambar raises above his head a small, white, and, by now, entirely lifeless snake, about 18 inches long. He moves it sharply towards me and I duck back involuntarily. Encouraged by the response, he pretends to eat it, provoking howls of delighted disgust.

Omar, who has been watching all this clowning with the mildly indulgent smile of a teacher on a school outing, tells me that this is the much-feared *vipère du sable*, the sand viper, whose bite, relatively harmless for humans, can cripple a camel. The desert is clearly not as empty as it looks.

As if to rub this in, Mohammed, normally so languid and laid-back, gives a sharp cry as we lie on the mats after lunch. He's been bitten by a scorpion. I'm lying next to him and move pretty smartly out of the way, as someone grabs my boot and deals the scorpion a fatal blow. Like the snake earlier, the scorpion looks a pale defenceless little creature, the last thing in the world to cause trouble, but even after the poison is sucked out and sedatives administered Mohammed is clearly in serious pain, and says he will be for another four hours.

The excitements of the day are not yet over. Shortly after darkness has fallen, distant headlights stab the gloom and soon we hear a rapidly approaching vehicle and, at the same time, a high-pitched drone in the sky above us. There is some nervous speculation that we have been mistaken for Osama Bin Laden and American Special Services have come to deal with us, but the reality proves to be a pair of French paragliders. First the ground support arrives and minutes later, once signal lights have been set up and vehicle headlights switched on to pick out the landing strip, an Icarus appears, strapped to a motor attached to a wheel-like frame and swinging on the end of a yellow mattress parachute. After two or three low passes over the camp this surreal figure hits the ground to a burst of spontaneous applause.

Renaud Van De Meeren is the flyer and François Lagarde the ground crew. As they join us around the single lamp it's hard to distinguish features, but François is clearly the older man. Wiry, tall, with a boyish flop of fair hair, he has flown his machine all over the world but still regards the Sahara as his favourite desert.

'It's still alive, you know. There is authentic life, here.'

188

He talks about the paraglider like a boy with a new toy. The whole kit folds down into two bags and can be carried with them as accompanying baggage. Yesterday they were in Paris. And the experience of flying it? Smooth and solid.

'Like swimming in oil.'

Their theatrical arrival is upstaged by the clutch of Western newspapers and magazines that they have brought with them. These contain the first pictures we have seen of the attacks on America eight days ago. Since then we have all carried our own separate mental pictures of the destruction, made up of descriptions from families and friends at home, BBC World Service reports and individual imaginings. Now, by the light of a flickering lamp in the heart of the Sahara, we share with the rest of the world, for the first time, the classic images that will come to define the tragedy; bodies falling through the air, black smoke blotting out Lower Manhattan, dust clouds racing down the streets.

By the time I climb into my tent it's nearly eleven. This is very late for the desert, where darkness rules and we're usually in bed by half past nine, yet for once I can't get to sleep. The arrival of the paragliders, with their papers and their magazines reminding us of where we came from and what we shall soon have to go back to, has broken the spell, compromised our isolation, drawn us back into the wider world just as it was becoming soothingly irrelevant. Much as we might want it otherwise, life in the desert is a diversion and the blazing skyline of New York is the reality.

And that's not all that's keeping me awake. There are persistent scratchings on the side of my tent, as if the wind is blowing something against it. But there is no wind.

BELOW

Ancient and modern. The camel train pauses as a French motorised paraglider invades their space.

ABOVE

*Divided loyalties.
Izambar, in indigo
robe at far right of
picture, and Omar,
next to him, watch
as I try to tear
myself away from
the team. A sad
and happy leave-
taking, after almost
a week together.*

Heart beating a little faster, I pull the zip open and peer out, but there's nothing there, and indeed what could be there, in the middle of the Ténéré? Apart from camels. Oh, and snakes. And scorpions. And gazelles. And paragliders.

DAY SIXTY-SEVEN THE TENERE DESERT

The noises in the night prove to have been the work of little black beetles, and judging by the network of tracks around my tent they had put in a full night's work. There are over 350 species of black beetle in the Sahara, but I haven't seen so many in one place since we watched the camel train come into Timbuktu. They bustle around as I pack, full of curiosity, wanting to get into everything, as they had presumably wanted to get into my tent last night. Nor was I the only one to have been kept awake by them. J-P, dark-eyed and dishevelled, became convinced that hyenas were prowling around and has barely slept a wink. I can understand it. In such a soundless environment the slightest noise can become weirdly amplified. And he had had a brandy or two.

Renaud, whose speciality is aerial photography, is also up early to take advantage of the light at sunrise. Lashed to the wheel of his paraglider like some mediaeval penitent, he runs into the wind, but there isn't enough to fill his parachute, and he has to keep on running, trying to find the elusive lifting breeze. He disappears behind a dune, engine revving away. There's a pregnant pause, and a moment later the sound of an engine cutting out, followed by a short splintering crash.

Renaud is fine, but his machine is a write-off. Later, François manages to get his craft airborne and the morning's travelling is enlivened by his appearances over the dunes, sweeping down across the camel train, filming with one hand, steering with the other.

To get the right pictures the camels have to be led backwards and forwards over

190

the same ground, which emphasises how, in a way, things have changed. Omar and his team are following us instead of us following them. Whatever relationship I might have assumed I was forging with the Touareg has been subsumed by Western technology.

In the evening I have one last meal with the cameleers. In a recklessly generous act of hospitality they cook the remaining sheep, preceded by a tasty mix of crusty-topped goat's cheese and dates. We sit round the fire and go through my Touareg vocabulary for the last time.

'*Tagel-la.*' (Roars of laughter.) '*Izot!*' '*Issan!*'

As we raise our glasses of mint tea I teach Izambar some useful English in return. I advise him that the English say 'Bottoms Up' when they raise a glass.

Izambar is a very quick learner, though his first faltering attempts – 'Bott-erm erp' – give me a chance to get back for all the *Tagel-la*s.

The main thing is that we laugh a lot. Almost like old friends.

DAY SIXTY-EIGHT OUT OF THE TENERE DESERT

Breakfast on the side of a long stony slope with no cover other than a few boulders. Ekawik, perhaps sensing my imminent departure, is very frisky and when Elias has finished loading him he breaks away, scattering his cargo and skipping about with joyful abandon. For his pains he gets a ticking off and a very severe kick up the bottom (not an easy thing to do to a camel).

'*Méchant. Très méchant,*' mutters Omar, but he can't help smiling.

I want to give Omar something for his help and good company, but all he will take is my bottle of eye-drops. Eye problems are the most common complaint in his village and he will keep these till he gets back. It feels a pathetically inadequate thanks, but I think he has enjoyed himself. We have been on the move with the camel train for five days. They have adapted their movement to our own and would normally, by now, be over halfway to Bilma. As it is, we have moved only about 100 miles from the mountains. We must leave them to go on at their own pace and I must strike off, north, to the Algerian border.

191

ALGERIA

DAY SIXTY-NINE   I-N-GUEZZAM

I approach Algeria with a certain amount of trepidation. The second largest country in Africa, and the tenth largest in the world, has, since 1992, been sidelined to the fringes of the international community, a nation synonymous with trouble. Information is

hard to find. My Lonely Planet guide apologetically devotes only ten pages to it. 'Due to its continuing problems,' they explain, 'Algeria was the one African nation we were unable to visit.'

The BBC advised against operating there, and the Foreign Office insisted that if we go we should take armed bodyguards. Even the artesian well at the border, marked so hopefully in blue on my Michelin map, has the word *'sulfureuse'* alongside it.

The country that fought a bloody civil war to win its independence from France in 1962 is currently involved in another, just as bloody, which began in 1992, when the military-dominated, socialist regime cancelled an election which they feared was going to be won by an Islamist opposition party. The opposition militarised itself as the GIA (Armed Islamic Group), and it is estimated that in less than ten years more than 100,000 people have died on both sides.

Everyone tells me, however, that the worst of the trouble is confined to the north, where 85 per cent of the population lives. Everyone, that is, but the driver who is at this very moment carrying me across a swathe of flat, gritty desert (*reg* as opposed to *erg*) towards the border town of I-n-Guezzam.

His small talk features mouth-drying accounts of the extreme lawlessness of the Sahara. Smuggling is a way of life. Mostly cigarettes, made illegally in Nigeria and brought north by the truckload. Governments have little influence in isolated areas still controlled by local warlords.

Had I not heard of Mokhtar ben Mokhtar, alias Louar, the One-Eyed One?

I shake my head, '*Qu'est-ce qu'il fait?*'

My driver can't believe his luck. '*Qu'est-ce qu'il* fait!'

He's stockpiled thousands of illegal weapons, stolen several hundred four-wheel drives and shot down an aircraft. He has a fleet of vehicles equipped with satellite navigation, armed with AK-47s and refuelled from dumps deep in the sand. An entire Dakar Rally had once been diverted to avoid going through his territory.

'Which is where, exactly?'

My driver gestures, a circular motion of the right hand that leaves little room for doubt. Wherever it was that Mokhtar ben Mokhtar operated, we're in the middle of it.

'I was told it was Islamic fundamentalists that stopped the Rally.'

He shakes his head. 'Mokhtar works for himself. And for the freedom of the South.'

'South?'

'Of Algeria.'

The car slides to a halt.

'There it is!'

My driver points to two metal posts stuck in the sand.

There always seems something faintly absurd about borders. One stone belonging to one government and the stone next to it belonging to another. In the immense void of the desert, marks of sovereignty seem gloriously irrelevant. Yet here they are, confirmed in a plinth at the base of a 6-foot-high oval steel tube.

'*F. Algéro–Nigérienne 27/11/1981*'

The clipped inscription has been crudely applied, picked out by a finger whilst the concrete was still wet.

Next to it is a shorter triangular steel post, which my driver tells me is an upright for the *palissade,* a fence which the authorities hope will one day make this a serious border and stop the likes of Mokhtar ben Mokhtar treating Algeria's desert like his own private fiefdom. This could be the fencing contract of all time. Algeria's Saharan border is nearly 2000 miles long.

There is one other marker at this desolate spot. It's a small concrete trig point left behind by the French. Detailed measurements and the words '*Nivellement Général*' are inscribed in a clear, legible and ornate inscription. This was the work of people who intended to stay in Algeria for a long time.

Nearby, the shells of two abandoned cars lie in the sand, as if, like marathon runners breasting the tape, the effort of getting to the line was all they could manage. Jettisoned tyres, a carburettor and an un-rusted cylinder head are scattered about.

Across the border our Algerian hosts wait to greet us. Said Chitour is a journalist from Algiers who has worked tirelessly for this day. He's a stocky, busy man in his early forties, anxious and exuberant at the same time. With him is our security man, Eamonn O'Brien, with a broad smile and the reassuring physique of Action Man, and an assortment of uniformed attendants. Gendarmes in green, border police in black.

BELOW LEFT

At I-n-Guezzam, described to me as the Siberia of Algeria, the national flag is raised. My guide, Said Chitour, stands to the right, saluting.

BELOW

On the road to Tamanrasset we pass what's known as the 'Cemetery', a graveyard of hopes that driving across the Sahara was easy.

All are armed. Said reminds us that no walkie-talkies or satellite phones are to be used while we are in Algeria. Security, he says, with a quick shrug and a smile, before turning to the drivers.

'Come! We go!' he shouts, a touch manically. Engines rumble into life and, accompanied by our substantial entourage, we head across the two or three miles of no-man's-land that separates the end of Niger from the first town in Algeria.

The crescent moon and green and white verticals of the national flag flutter above the sub-prefect's office in the main street of I-n-Guezzam. Construction is going on to turn this dirt strip into a dual carriageway, but work seems desultory. Two rake-thin guards, rifles slung over their shoulders, stand outside the office where our papers are being checked. As we wait, Said confides to me that I-n-Guezzam is considered the end of the earth, and a posting here is usually a penalty for past mistakes. I like Said. He is clearly proud of his country and impatient with it at the same time, like a father with a delinquent son.

He apologises that there are no hotels of sufficient quality in I-n-Guezzam. We have been invited instead to spend the night on the roof of the mayor's house. This is a two-storey brick and plaster building with a small garden tucked away behind high walls. The downstairs rooms are full of people, mostly family I assume. The mayor, a tall slim Touareg, wears a yellow turban, matching *gandoura* (an Arab kaftan), leggings in cream and red check and a pair of thin scholarly glasses. Our presence is clearly something unprecedented in I-n-Guezzam and he is for ever bringing people up to the roof to meet us. The commissar, a short stocky man in T-shirt and Umbro training pants, shakes hands all round, followed shortly by someone introduced to us as the Surgeon of Police. I think they're all quite keen to hang around and party, but we cross-Saharan travellers are by now desperately in need of food and sleep.

194

DAY SEVENTY   I-N-GUEZZAM TO TAMANRASSET

I should be used to the gripping chill of the desert nights by now, but I still find myself reaching for a sweater in the small hours. I find I've laid my sleeping bag beside a small drainage hole in the wall, through which a blast of gritty wind is blowing straight into my face. Stuff my towel into the hole, wrap my turban round my head and settle myself back to sleep. It doesn't come easily. There is a constant subdued roar coming from somewhere, as if planes are warming up for take-off (I'm later told it's the town generator). I can't wait for the dawn.

ABOVE

Mirage effect on the horizon. The massive rocks look double the size, as if reflected in water.

It is a beauty. The sun rises as a pulsing red ball, glowing like a hot coal before softening into a peachy glow which fills the sky with benevolent promise. (I keep making a mental note to myself not to describe any more sunrises, but some are majestic and, jaded travellers though we are, we never ignore them. They raise the spirits like nothing else. Apart from a cold beer.)

The mayor and the commissar and the surgeon of police all gather around as we load up. They're candid about the problems down here at the frontier. There is no oasis and no water for crops, so all their food must be brought in from Tamanrasset, 250 miles away.

The mayor unpicks a stick from his teeth and gestures at a row of new houses across the street.

'The people are poor, but very conservative. We build new houses, with floors, and they still want to sleep on the sand.'

As Said puts it, they mistrust the 'chair culture'. They remain nomads at heart, so everything expendable is dumped in the street for the goats to sift through.

'And the women,' the mayor shakes his head, 'you don't see them. Some of them never leave their houses.'

As the time comes for yet another goodbye, the mayor and his friends are warm and courteous, but I sense they are already switching off, preparing to return to the reality of their isolation. They know that almost anywhere else is better than here and yet it is their home. To survive it must require a particularly indomitable spirit.

The road to Tamanrasset follows one of the oldest trade routes across the Sahara, from Nigeria to Algeria, across the very heart of the desert. It is still a sand piste. There are signs of a hard-top being laid north of I-n-Guezzam, but it runs beside us, tantalisingly unfinished. The surface, by no means free of rocks and boulders, is generally firm, but there are softer patches where wheels cease to grip and the cars begin to swing.

This is a main road without garages or tow-trucks, so virtually everything that breaks down is left to the mercy of the sands. It was between I-n-Guezzam and Tamanrasset that Margaret Thatcher's son went missing in the 1980s. He and his girlfriend were rescued after a long and expensive search. Not everyone was so lucky. A few miles off the main piste is an undulating area of fine sand and basalt boulders so strewn with old car bodies that it's known as the Cemetery. Quite what happened to all these wrecks is difficult to tell. Some are twisted out of recognition, others seem just to have been abandoned, one door swung open, as if someone had decided to get out and walk. Anything that could be removed from them has been removed. The wind, a constant companion in the desert, catches at their metal skeletons, making them twitch and vibrate as if not quite dead. An old Deux Chevaux, painted all the colours of the rainbow and half filled with sand, adds a touch of colour to the wreckage, a reminder of the part deserts played in the hippie dream. There is no shelter here and not a cloud in the way of a sun which is sending temperatures beyond 38°C/100°F.

The wonder is that any of these cars got this far.

Seven hours after setting out, we arrive in the well-kept streets of Tamanrasset. The town feels as if it has just had a makeover. Kerb-stoned sidewalks, concrete arcades, lines of shade-giving trees, walls and buildings decorated in what seems to be a regulation shade of blood-brown. Even the razor wire has been painted in Tamanrasset.

DAY SEVENTY-ONE TAMANRASSET TO ASSEKREM

Around 10.30 the four rusty flagpoles on the forecourt of the Hotel Tahat recede into the distance as we take to Tamanrasset's gloriously smooth and comfortable roads. Within a mile we throw an abrupt right onto a track so ferociously jagged that for a moment I fear we might have been hijacked.

It does not get much better. Every now and then we come to a stretch that is merely rutted earth, but these are few and far between. Generally, it is a bed of broken and solidified lava, over which the vehicle judders and shudders as if possessed. A puncture offers some brief respite, then the whole painful process begins again. But it is a price almost worth paying for magnificently dramatic scenery. We are in the Hoggar Mountains, which, with peaks rising to 10,000 feet, are amongst the highest in the Sahara. They're formed by the hard cores of ancient volcanoes, eroded into a series of weird and wonderfully shaped towers, plugs and pinnacles.

Some have incised vertical surfaces, as if they've been clawed, others are so deeply scored that their sides look like organ pipes or massive petrified tree roots. On one the

LEFT

In the Hoggar Massif. Rock formation like a petrified starburst.

RIGHT

*With Tom
Sheppard, doyen of
the desert.*

scarring runs in all directions like a starburst captured in stone. There are knobs, spires, needles, arcs and bluffs, rocks standing four square on plinths of rubble, resembling mediaeval castles. Tenacious tufts of grass cling to the defiles and gullies; otherwise, this is a land of rock and stone. The Touareg know it by the suitably Tolkien-ish name of Atakor.

Just as I'm constructing romantic notions of mythological lands, a squat white Mercedes jeep bounces down the track towards us. Not unbelievable in itself, but quite a shock when I see it has British number plates. It pulls up and out gets a bony, angular man of late middle age, with a flick of fair hair and a quick, elfin-like energy. With mutual exclamations of surprise we introduce ourselves. His name is Tom Sheppard, a well-known traveller with books to his name.

Like many twentieth-century Englishmen, from T. E. Lawrence to Wilfred Thesiger, he has a passion for desert, and particularly this part of the Algerian desert. He's been coming here for forty years, following tracks marked on the old French maps.

'The Hoggar's very special.'

He likes the compactness of the area, and that there is, within 1000 square miles, such an extraordinary combination of mountain and dune.

'Pristine dunes, quite untrodden by anyone at all.'

He hasn't seen another human being for eight days, one of which was his sixty-eighth birthday. He describes it with almost military relish.

'I had a really special meal on that one. Meat and two veg. Chilled grapefruit for goodness sake. Damp kitchen towel, wrapped around the tin, the dryness of the air makes evaporation and you get cooled grapefruit segments. What more could you ask for a birthday?'

Life has been made much safer for him since the advent of satellites.

'God bless the Americans for putting them up there.'

He enthuses about something called EPRB, Electronic Precision Recording Beacon – basically a distress signal, which bounces off a satellite to centres all over the world. He's had to use it in Libya recently.

'And they were on to it, just like that, eleven minutes after starting transmission.'

I'd like to talk a lot more, but Tom politely turns down our offer of lunch. Though he exudes conviviality, his pleasure is in going solo, and as his dust-covered Mercedes, as compact and self-contained as its owner, crunches off down the track, I find myself distinctly envious of the man.

Having covered the next 50 miles in a painful four and a half hours, we catch sight of a tiny hut silhouetted on a ridge high above us, a refuge built by the ascetic French missionary Charles de Foucauld ninety years ago. After a few more agonisingly slow hairpins we pull up at the gates of a compound below the hut, where there is a hostel maintained by the town of Tamanrasset.

The accommodation is basic mountain stuff: an uncompromising stone-walled building, with two outside lavatories (quite far outside), three dormitories and a communal meeting room, with rugs and cushions, chairs, tables and an open fire. After our meal we sit in here with Arouj, the administrator, a heavily turbaned, moustachioed Touareg, probably a devastatingly handsome man in his youth, now a little fleshed out. Business doesn't look good. There's room here for 150, but apart from ourselves there are only four other visitors tonight. One is a young German biker, who set out to cross the Sahara with two friends, both of whom have had to return home after arguments with sand dunes. Arouj orders some mint tea for us all. He's pleased to see us. Very few British ever come here, he says. Germans, yes, Italians (for the rock climbing) and Spanish.

French?

He wobbles his hand. *Some* French.

I feel for him. The locals have put a lot into this place. There is an airstrip at Tamanrasset, and the Hoggar mountain area is a national park, protected by UNESCO. But as long as Algeria remains better known for its civil war, places like Assekrem will remain a well-kept secret.

I make my apologies and get off to bed. We're to be up at five tomorrow to walk up to the refuge. Arouj hands me his card. It has his website marked.

DAY SEVENTY-TWO ASSEKREM to HASSI-MESSAOUD

An alarm sounds in our dormitory, followed by total silence. Then a rustling of sleeping bags, a muffled curse, a cough, a variety of yawns and silence again. We've all been very well behaved in the night. No raucous snoring, farting or too many trips to the toilet. I know, because I've been awake most of the time. I never sleep comfortably if there's an unusually early start in the offing. My body knows it's in for a shock and stays on red alert for most of the night. A torch is switched on, the first light of the morning.

Pull myself reluctantly from my sleeping bag, which has had more use in the Sahara than on all my previous journeys put together. I keep thinking I won't need it any more, then up comes a night like this. Middle of the Sahara and cold as a Scottish winter.

Bleary, grunted greetings. Queue for the lavatory, faces washed with a splash of bottled water. Tea has been made by someone, God bless them. Then out onto the mountainside. The mass of bright stars, normally such a delight, seems to be almost hostile this morning, the cold already intensified by a wicked little wind. The top of the hill is a few hundred feet away, up a steep zigzag footpath. Nigel and Pete set the pace, weaving up like mountain goats, despite carrying more than anyone else. Maybe

Nigel, a well-established quinquagenarian like myself, felt an urge to prove himself after yesterday's encounter with the boyish sixty-eight-year-old Tom Sheppard.

By the time we've reached the top of the path and the broad flat plateau on which Père de Foucauld built his refuge, we're above 9000 feet and gulping gratefully at the chilly air.

There is still three-quarters of an hour to go before sunrise, but the stars are fading slowly and a faint lemon-magenta glow is shading the eastern horizon. Up here the mountains are all below us. Only one summit, that of Tahat, away to the north, is superior, and that by a few hundred feet. Even before the sun comes up the view is breathtaking. The misty pre-dawn light compresses the spaces between the mountains, giving the appearance of a solid range to what we know to be a collection of eccentric individuals.

Said whispers in my ear.

'This is third best sunrise in the world, after Fiji and Ceylon.'

He pauses a moment for me to take this in.

'The purity of the air here is recorded by the meteorological station and sent back to the United States. To measure carbon and ozone in the atmosphere.'

(I'm not altogether sure about this purity of the air bit; it brings to mind something less reassuring that I recently read in Jeremy Keenan's book *Sahara Man*. At In Ecker, less than 60 miles northwest of here, the French tested their first nuclear weapon. According to Keenan, there is anecdotal evidence of poisonous emissions and mysterious deaths immediately afterwards.)

A bitter north wind drives me to take shelter in the refuge. Above the doorway of this plain stone construction is a white marble panel. It reads '*Charles de Foucauld, juillet–décembre 1911*'. Inside, a narrow passage leads to a small chapel, where there is a picture of a lean Frenchman with a well-trimmed beard dressed in a white monk's habit, and, above it, the emblem of a red heart with a cross rising from it.

Fifty-three years before he built this refuge de Foucauld was born in Strasbourg, a *vicomte* from a privileged and wealthy background. He joined the French army and was posted to Algeria, where he lived a playboy life, doing little but splash his money around on parties and mistresses. Then, suddenly and quite drastically turning his back on the easy life, he travelled North Africa disguised as a Jewish rabbi, joined a Trappist order at the age of thirty-one and, twelve years later, entered the priesthood. His work brought him to the Touareg of the Hoggar Mountains, amongst whom he gained considerable respect, not only learning their language but also producing the first French-Tamahaq dictionary.

He accepted, indeed revelled in, the isolation of the desert. There is a shelf beside the chapel on which a book of his writings lies open at the place where de Foucauld gives his own account of what has brought us here: 'The beauty of the view defies description or even imagination...it is marvellous.'

There's not much I can add to this as I watch the sun rise over the Hoggar Mountains, giving each peak form and colour and revealing the spectacular proportions of this strange and unforgettable landscape.

The Sahara's fearsome reputation for ending people's lives prematurely was enhanced by the murder of de Foucauld, who was shot and killed in Tamanrasset five years after building this refuge. The order he founded, the Little Brothers of Jesus, continues his work, supported by Algeria's Muslim government. The current incumbent, Brother Edward, offers tea to ourselves and two other tourists who've struggled up to the sunrise. He tells us that Père de Foucauld, far from being forgotten, is in the preparatory stages of canonisation and will very soon be made a saint.

He also asks if we wouldn't mind taking down to Tamanrasset a Korean acolyte, who has just spent forty days and nights on his own up here. We pick him up later in

BELOW

With Brother Edward of Les Petits Frères de Jésus, *successor of Charles de Foucauld at the remote refuge at Assakrem, over 9000 feet above the Sahara.*

the car park, an incessantly smiling, patient man, jauntily dressed in fishing hat, windcheater and jeans. It looks more like he's spent four hours in Banana Republic than forty days in solitary.

We're back in Tamanrasset by midday. Snatched rudely from the sublime to the ridiculous, we find ourselves struggling to negotiate forty-odd bags through an overcrowded airport with 'Feelings' playing over the Tannoy. Nor does the culture shock end there. We are soon aboard a 737 bound for Hassi-Messaoud. It has taken us four hours to drive the 40 miles from Assekrem; the next 700 miles of our journey will take less than ninety minutes.

As we take to the air I can't take my eyes off the panorama of peaks spread out below me like tombstones, and even when the Hoggar Mountains slip away to the south, the desert landscape remains hypnotically beautiful. A series of round black circles, the traces of spent volcanoes, cover the surface like blisters, before giving way to a wide flat tableland eroded into a series of long twisting terraces. This in turn gives way to the glorious salmon pink of the Grand Erg Oriental, part of the sand sea that swirls across the centre of Algeria in long languid curves.

As we begin our descent the unbroken stretch of virgin sand becomes increasingly tarnished. Straight black lines cross the landscape below, connecting up a series of tiny installations, making the surface of the desert look more like a printed circuit board. The lower we get the more depressing it becomes. The sand sea is riddled with roads, pipelines, clusters of low huts surrounded by smeared black pits, at the centre of which, like the totems of some ancient religion, are towers spouting flame. This is Algeria's Aladdin's Cave. Within a 300-mile radius of the rapidly approaching oasis of Hassi-Messaoud are sufficient reserves of oil and gas to make this embattled country the third richest (after Libya and Tunisia) in the Sahara.

In an already security-obsessed country the oil and gas production facilities are fortresses in themselves. No vehicles are allowed up to the airport buildings, and we have to carry all our equipment 300 yards down the road, through a narrow checkpoint and across into a car park surrounded by a 10-foot-high razor-wired steel fence. Behind the bars of the car park are more white faces than I've seen on our entire journey. They stare out from minibuses and four-wheel drives, company coaches and private saloons, their gazes neutral and incurious as they wait to be driven away. These are not the faces of people glad to be here; they're the faces of people who have to be here. They're the oil men.

We are in turn collected and driven to our accommodation in *bâtiments durs,* long low huts, like grey steel tents, put up by the French in the 1950s. A television is on in a small communal area just inside the door of the hut and a rugby match between Ireland and England is playing.

The crew, lured by beds and bathrooms, crash out in their rooms, and I'm the only one to witness England's defeat and Eamonn O'Brien's unconfined joy.

DAY SEVENTY-THREE   HASSI-MESSAOUD

I feel thoroughly disorientated. I saw with my own eyes last night that we were in the middle of the desert, but this morning I step out of our hut to find it surrounded by tall swaying trees. Green lawns and flower beds border the road to the communal dining block. Hassi-Messaoud means 'the well of the man called Messaoud', and I can't imagine he would recognise his watering hole since the oil men got here. A network of electric pumps works round the clock to bring water up from hundreds of feet below the surface, enough to support 15,000 trees and 40,000 people. This tiny postage stamp of greenery, this blip in the wastes of the Sahara, has flocks of ducks and herds of goats, palm trees producing the very finest *deglet noir* dates, cows producing four barrels of milk a day, tennis courts, schools, swimming pools, fountains and a cinema.

This eerie similarity to a piece of provincial France is not accidental.

When oil was first discovered in the desert in the 1950s, Algeria was an integral part of France, not a colony, but a series of *départements*, as much a part of the mother country as Aveyron or Vaucluse. The French purred with pleasure at the news of this first-ever discovery of oil on its territory and immediately put in the investment needed to retrieve it, creating, amongst other things, the man-made oasis of Hassi-Messaoud.

At almost the same time, however, the Algerian uprising began and by 1962 France was forced to grant full independence to its most obstinately defended African possession. The French dream of a Saharan equivalent of North Sea oil finally died in 1971, when the Algerian oil industry was nationalised, without a cent of compensation to the French government.

Nevertheless, French influence still clings to the place. The VIP dining room is called the Salle Bleue and is decorated with a nice touch of Gallic surrealism, featuring nets, fish tanks, underwater grottoes and other watery themes. At lunch, to which I'm entertained by the executives of Sonatrach, the Algerian state oil and gas company, French is spoken and there are many courses: salad, hard-boiled eggs with caviar, carrots, lettuce and tomato, grilled swordfish, lamb chops, omelette, lemon tart with cream, fruit and coffee.

'We eat well before Ramadan,' jokes one of my hosts.

The only thing missing is a bottle of Beaujolais, but the ban on alcohol is, I'm assured, a general rule in all drilling areas, anywhere in the world.

The Algerian executives seem comfortably westernised. The head of the base refers to his countrymen as 'Mediterranean people' and dinner-table conversation revolves around such bourgeois topics as children's education, keeping fit, summer holidays and life in Algiers, to which most of them return for three weeks leave, every four weeks. I ask them the reasons for the high level of security at Hassi-Messaoud, the massive fences, the armed guards, the watchtowers. Do terrorists strike this far south?

A few swift glances are exchanged around the table, a wordless debate as to how much I should be told. Oil workers were killed in 1992 but since then it's been safe. The boss man leans back, dabbing his mouth with a napkin. Apart, that is, from 'Glass Eye'.

Glass Eye? Some nasty infection carried by blowing sand?

No, Glass Eye is a bandit who steals vehicles and reads Islamic tracts to his captives.

Ah, this is beginning to sound familiar. Does he ride around at the head of a fleet of Land Cruisers full of armed men?

General nodding. That's the man.

Also known as Louar, the One-Eyed One?

They seem awfully impressed with my information. I'm awfully impressed by Glass Eye's range. We're 800 miles from the border, where I first heard of him.

To be honest, they're happier talking about hydrocarbons than one-eyed bandits. This doesn't make for jolly banter, but it's interesting to learn that the oil which has paid for Hassi-Messaoud, the Salle Bleue and this six-course dinner is no longer the biggest money-spinner for Algeria. They currently produce less than Britain's North Sea fields. Natural gas reserves, I'm told, put her fourth in the world league after Russia, the USA and Canada.

Our hosts are determined that, before we move on, we should visit the gas production plant, 200 miles northwest. There is a plane that leaves every morning, at half past six.

Irresistible.

DAY SEVENTY-FOUR   HASSI-R'MEL

One advantage of being up at five is to witness the industrialisation of the Sahara in its most dramatic form. Dozens of flares blaze away in the desert, creating the eerie illusion of a false sunrise. The rigs, hung with arc lights for round the clock production, are dotted about in the sand, buzzing with the might and menace of rockets at their launch pads. This, you feel, is the work of the gods.

Barely visible in the glare from the working lights are the dim, huddled Bedouin encampments outside the security fence, a reminder of what it must have been like here before oil was discovered, when the nomads and their families came to find water at Messaoud's well. The only way they can get close to it now is to take on some menial work inside the base, but they're removed from its green and pleasant avenues at the end of the day.

Hassi-R'Mel is cooler and fresher than Hassi-Messaoud, and its airport cleaner and less frenetic. We're given a VIP welcome, which means tea and biscuits on arrival at the airport and a turnout of executives, including my host for the morning, the impressively titled Head of Quality and Quantity Control. His name is Salah Benyoub, an amiable and unassuming middle-aged man, dressed in striped shirt and wearing a baseball cap over a hairless scalp, which, he readily tells me, is the result of recent chemotherapy. He has worked here for thirty years and speaks good English, which, he says, is the lingua franca of the oil and gas business. It's an international business too. Salah has been to Texas and vacationed in Vegas.

'Did you lose any money?'

'Of course. That's what you're meant to do isn't it?'

Once tea and polite introductions are over, we're driven over to the heart of the operation, the CNDG, the National Centre For Despatching Gas. This proves to be a huge and rambling complex of multicoloured pipes (yellow for natural gas, brown for liquid nitrogen, green for composite), looking more like some computer-generated model than the real thing. Gas from far below the surface comes up in molten form, is treated and eventually chilled to minus 170 degrees, at which temperature it is sent through one of two pipelines, either west to Spain, under the Strait of Gibraltar, or east to Italy, under the Mediterranean. When it reaches the other end of the pipeline it is warmed and expands to 600 times its volume. Every cubic foot that leaves Hassi-R'Mel turns into 600 cubic feet at the receiving terminal.

It's all a bit much for me to take in, but I do like the thought that the yellow paint

LEFT

Salah Benyoub at the CNDG at Hassi- R'Mel. Natural gas that will cook lunches from Milan to Mannheim to Madrid is prepared here and despatched along sub-Mediterranean pipelines.

205

on the pipe at the back of my cooker matches the yellow paint of the 4-foot thick pipes rearing above my head in the middle of the Algerian desert.

One thing I will remember from this froth of facts and figures is that by 2005, at the cost of $5 billion, there will be another route across the Sahara. It will be laid at a minimum of 6 feet below ground and will connect Europe to the gas fields of northern Nigeria. This will mean a lot more yellow pipes at Hassi-R'Mel and add a new name to the long and not always illustrious list of cross-Saharan trade. Gold, salt, slaves and, now, natural gas.

DAY SEVENTY-SIX IN AMENAS

It's ironic that, given the mighty size of Algeria, the first trace of the oil that transformed the country was found within strolling distance of Libya, near the village of In Aménas. Since then, natural gas has been discovered too, and there are four big fields running along the border, being jointly developed by Sonatrach and BP-Amoco. In Aménas now has an airport, maintenance depots, storage yards and a lot of Brits.

I'm driven out to a drill site at the base of one of the steep, flat-topped, sandstone escarpments south of the town, accompanied by an Algerian from the BP/Sonatrach partnership. His name is Tobba, a geologist by profession, who came out here in 1983. He's a genial man, small and wearing a BP cap.

He's the first Algerian I've met, apart from Said, who's been to England and I ask him for his impressions. He was struck, he said, by the contrast between the beauty of the countryside and the ugliness of public behaviour. He was with his wife and children and found the sight of embracing and kissing in the street very hard to deal with. The same with drinking. He didn't mind bars but was embarrassed by people drunk on streets where he was walking with his children. As Tobba is clearly an educated, decent man, neither severe nor prudish, these criticisms hurt. Arabs generally behave with dignity in public, and in a society which takes no alcohol, there is a marked lack of that unreasoned, aggressive posturing that flares up so easily back home.

The drill site is a square patch of ground, fortified by an 8-foot-high sand wall, known as a berm, and heavy security paraphernalia, including a wall of lights outside, a chicane at the entrance, guard towers and a protection force of gendarmes. I later learn there are fifty of them. This is how important the gas is to Algeria.

A board at the entrance lists the personnel on site, along with their job titles. It reads like a cast list in a theatre programme. There's Tool Pusher, Company Man, Chief Mechanic, Driller, Assistant Driller, Derrick Man and (very Shakespearian this) Roughnecks and Roustabouts.

We seem to have arrived at a bad time. The site is being dismantled and the 180-foot-high derrick lies on its side awaiting collection. A small group of British workers is supervising an Algerian workforce of loaders and drivers in blue boiler suits and turbans. Willy Wallace, a roly-poly Scot with a Viva Zapata moustache, fingers the stiff creases of a tight and suspiciously pristine outfit.

'They made us wear these. Must have known you were coming.'

OPPOSITE

(ABOVE) *The scale of Hassi-R'Mel shows the hidden potential of the Sahara. Soon the first ever trans-Saharan pipeline will bring natural gas here from northern Nigeria.* (BELOW) *One exploration site that didn't live up to expectations. I talk to Willy Wallace as the derrick is dismantled.*

207

Willy's life seesaws between down-to-earth domesticity and the almost recklessly exotic. He's been on rigs in the North Sea, Colombia, the Congo, China and Kazakhstan. Colombia was 'scary'. He was shot at and, as he put it, 'had to hide under the desk a few times'. Kazakhstan was the only place in the last nine years where he didn't need any guards with him. The other half of his life is back home in Scotland, with his wife, a son at Stirling University and a different set of drinking buddies, for whom Coca-Cola is no longer the strongest thing on offer.

He waves vigorously as a 50-tonne truck toils slowly by, the driver waving back from a cab high above our heads.

They've been on this site for sixty-two days. Working round the clock, it took them thirty-two of these days to drill over 8000 feet down into the desert. Gas was found but not at sufficient pressure to make production worthwhile. They're moving on to another site, identified for them by the geologists after a three day seismic test in which 600 miles of the Sahara was wired up and an artificial earthquake created.

According to Willy, expenditure on the ultimately fruitless work has been augmented by certain below-the-line items.

'We had a visit from Glass Eye. Took 60,000 dollars worth of surveying equipment.'

We drive back into In Aménas. A few huts and palm trees linger on the outskirts, a dusty hint of what the village must have been like before it was engulfed by the oil industry. Now it's dominated by compounds full of storage tanks and drilling equipment, watch-towered and double-fenced. The wind scythes across the desert, tearing at a foliage of plastic bags caught on the razor wire. A filthy sign welcomes us: 'Throw Your Litter Away For A Clean and Beautiful Village.'

Tonight the Brits working here have laid on a party for us. As Mike Batley, our portly, solicitous host, cooks sausages on the patio of a bungalow, we could almost be back in Maidenhead. Except that we are on the equivalent of an industrial estate, with the steel walls of a maintenance shed rearing up behind us.

Mike has worked abroad for much of his life and makes me feel like a novice at this travel thing. He, on the other hand, envies our freedom to move about Algeria. Oil workers are virtual prisoners in their camps, and he bemoans the fact that we have seen more of the country in seven days than he's seen in seven years.

Beers appear from the fridge, and a bottle or two of Algerian wine loosen tongues around the table. Everyone seems to like the desert. Mike notices how it sharpens the senses.

'We're spoilt for smell,' he says. 'Smell a rose in the desert and it's much more acute and intense.'

Sue, a drilling engineer from Aberdeen, finds the desert different, unusual, exotic, whilst John, a geologist from Holmfirth, is passionate about sand dunes. South of the site we visited today there are some of the biggest he's seen. Five hundred feet high.

When the conversation turns to the wider picture, the geo-politics of oil, the subject becomes murkier. Someone makes the point that the USA has vast petrochemical reserves, but it knows that the longer it can keep them in the ground the better, so American foreign policy is led by the need to find cheap energy sources beyond its boundaries.

It all seems academic here, full of sausages and red wine, under a huge sky in the serene silence of the Sahara, but a few thousand miles away, in Afghanistan, another desert is being blasted by B-52s, and no-one knows what fury this might provoke.

DAY SEVENTY-SEVEN ON THE LIBYAN BORDER

Roads are rare in the Sahara. They are usually built to exploit resources of some sort, and once they reach those resources they stop.

So it doesn't surprise me that the road to Libya, after winding its way across a grubby oilscape of grit and shale, littered with pipes, empty cable spindles and rusting Portakabins, comes to an abrupt halt at the top of a cliff. The debris also comes to an abrupt halt. Instead, there is a magnificent view of towering, shining dunes, soothed by the wind into graceful, sensuous contours and stretching out to the east as far as the eye can see. This is Libya.

Between the dunes and the edge of the cliff is a flat and sandy valley floor, about a mile wide, and in the middle of this is a single acacia tree. This marks the border.

There is no fence or wall or guard-post or flagpole or barrier to be seen. Just the tree and, beneath it, an indistinct cluster of white dots. I'm told by one of our tireless escorts that the tree is a famous meeting place, where people on both sides of the border, Libyans and Algerians, get together to take tea and exchange news and gossip.

We drive down off the *falaise* and I join a group of them for local dates and strong mint tea. The sun slowly declines, turning the colour of Libya from gold to russet. It is a grand, remote, spectacular spot and for once a border lives up to its romantic expectations.

BELOW LEFT
The Libyan frontier near In Aménas is marked by a single tree. This spare, uncluttered, beautiful spot was one of my favourite places in the Sahara.
BELOW
Algerians and Libyans gather beneath the tree to take tea and exchange local gossip.

LIBYA

DAY SEVENTY-NINE   TOBRUK

It's a warm, clammy evening on the north coast of Libya. A coach has disgorged a number of elderly Britons at the door of the blandly modern Al-Masera hotel. Once in their rooms, they will be able to push aside the net curtains and look out over the sea, where a sharp curve of the coastline has created a perfect harbour. It will mean more to them than the average tourist, for sixty years ago they nearly died defending it.

At Tobruk, the Sahara meets the Mediterranean Sea and we are less than 250 miles from the Greek mainland, closer to Europe than at any time since leaving Gibraltar. A hundred and fifty miles the other way, to the south, is the Great Sand Sea, a massive wilderness of parallel sand ridges, hundreds of feet high, rolling across the desert like waves in a hurricane. In the Second World War, the battle for control of Egypt and the Suez Canal was confined to the area between these two seas, a thin strip of land, whose only outlet was the port of Tobruk. The fighting was fierce and Tobruk itself changed hands five times between 1940 and 1942. But for eight crucial months, between April and December 1941, despite being surrounded by the enemy and bombed from the air, Allied troops clung on to Tobruk and kept open a vital supply line. The siege cost many lives, and the men filing into the hotel, some shuffling in on the arms of others, some with sticks and some in wheelchairs, are returning, one last time, to the place where they lost so many friends.

Considering theirs is an eight-day trip and they've already done the battle site of El Alamein earlier today, the veterans are holding up well at the supper that's been laid on for them. It could be something to do with Avril, Lady Randell, a vivacious woman with short-cropped blonde hair and unquenchable enthusiasm, who has organised many of these reunions. It could also be something to do with the fact that being together again reminds them of happy as well as hellish times.

I find myself sitting next to a smart, tweed-jacketed man called Ray Ellis, with thick white hair and a ruddy face. His regiment, the South Nottinghamshire Hussars, were trapped by the Germans in a corner of bleak desert known, ironically, as the Knightsbridge Box. They had already been in the desert for a year, without a day's leave, when, under heavy attack, they were given orders 'to fight until the last drop of ammo'. Ray it was who fired the last shot, before being captured, taken to Tripoli and put aboard a coal-carrying cargo ship bound for Italy. This journey, which he spent crammed together with all the other prisoners in a sealed hold, with one meal a day and the constant fear of being blown up by British air and sea patrols, was, he admits, more terrifying than anything he'd endured at the siege of Tobruk. On arrival, he and his colleagues, filthy and emaciated, were paraded through the streets of a small town near Naples. He was at his lowest ebb, when, out of the jeering crowd, came a young girl, who ran up to him and pressed a peach into his hand. He pauses here, not for breath but to let the emotion register, as if the peach had just that moment been handed to him. He nods gently at the memory, and goes on.

He escaped and was on the run for nine months, hidden by Italian families. He still sees them and has written a book about his experiences, which will soon be published in Italy, though not, it seems, in the UK. Ray has a bit of a double act with another South Notts man, Harry Day. Harry was a medical orderly – 'Never a proper soldier,' Ray chips in – who has given me a booklet issued by the Ministry of Information in 1941 called *Destruction of an Army*. It's full of wonderful sepia photos of the Libyan campaign, as fought by decent chaps who smoked pipes a lot.

Ray nods sagely. 'It's 100 per cent propaganda from start to finish.'

He's not the only one who's written about his experiences. Frank Harrison, once of the Royal Signals, is a painter and a poet as well as an author. Partly disabled after a recent stroke, he's here with his wife. He talks almost lyrically about the appalling conditions they endured. Any guidebook I've ever read about desert survival emphasises the vital importance of drinking several litres of water a day. Frank and 25,000 others like him were expected to live, work, and, if necessary, fight on one cupful.

'And that was for everything.'

Far from complaining, Frank suggests they developed a sort of evolutionary adaptation to the conditions.

'The surprising thing was, none of us grew beards. I don't know why, but it's true. I don't think I had a day's illness in the nine months I was in Tobruk. We were fit. We were terribly fit.'

They didn't have tents and mostly lived in holes, like shallow graves, that they'd managed to dig out of the compacted mud.

'We loved our holes,' says Frank, eyes wandering briefly into the middle distance. 'That's why we won the name rats. Desert Rats.'

The Desert Rats have more stamina than I. Leaving them burning the midnight oil, I retire to my eccentric room. The bathroom is like a Laurel and Hardy set, with a shower that sends out spray from every point apart from the head and a lavatory flush that requires both hands and one foot against the wall to operate. Over many years of travelling I have acquired the habit, though I often regret it, of checking the state of the bed sheets. I'm pleasantly surprised to find my sheet at the Al-Masera is as clean as a whistle, but as soon as I climb in my foot goes right through it. This is not the time to have a go at hard-working attempts to improve tourist facilities, but there are certain basics, like non-splitting sheets, that someone ought to have noticed. Tourist brochures are another. If you really want to bring in the visitors it is surely not too much to employ a translator who knows their language. The leaflet in my room invites me to visit 'scenes of the Second World Ear', and has a lot of trouble with the word 'snacks'.

'Lunch is mainly takeaway snakes. Dinner is the major meal. It is a full one consisting of different Slacks...' It concludes with a wonderfully loopy passage about Libyan beaches that could have been written by the late, great Stanley Unwin: 'You may enjoy the moon-lighted nights and sleep smoothly on the sea waves songs in your tent.'

Clutching the two halves of the sheet around me, I at least drift off to sleep with a smile.

DAY EIGHTY TOBRUK

ABOVE

(LEFT) *The standard of the Desert Rats of Tobruk is paraded at the Acroma-Knightsbridge Cemetery.*
(CENTRE LEFT) *With Ray Ellis in the cemetery – all ranks and nationalities have exactly the same size gravestones.*
(CENTRE RIGHT) *Preparing for the last ceremony of the day: the floating of a wreath on the waters of the harbour that the Rats defended for so long.*
(RIGHT) *With the Australian memorial rising behind them, Lady Randell comforts relatives of Australian and Maori war dead.*

A busy day ahead for the vets. Already, groups are gathering in the lobby. In one of them is a Maori woman who lost her brother at Tobruk. Twenty Maoris were killed here, she says.

'For what?' She spreads her arms. 'Senseless. We've tried to come to terms with it. We cry, then we laugh.'

Rex, a New Zealander a little younger than myself, is here to try to find the grave of his uncle, Owen Gatman of the New Zealand Division. He and eleven others were killed when the Panzers overran their position. Their grave has never been found. Rex has now moved on from searching files and archives to searching the desert with a pick and a sledgehammer. Though he says he found 'a couple of promising mounds', the hard ground has yielded no secrets so far. But he won't give up.

Stephen Dawson of The Royal Horse Artillery, who served throughout the siege, is eighty-nine, tall and thin, with sunken El Greco cheeks. Part of the agreement with the Libyans is that uniforms should not be worn at the reunion, so Stephen is dressed for the day ahead in a bobble hat, a windcheater and trousers a little too short. Slung across his chest is an old bag, webbing blancoed and frayed, which he carried throughout the war.

'I was completely technically incompetent,' he observes cheerfully, 'so I was put on signals.'

The desert held no terrors for him.

'I'm an agoraphiliac. I loved it.'

A bagpiper, kilted and sporranned, walks behind him, causing Libyan heads to turn, and the young bugler, a boy from the Royal Green Jackets and the only one here who's actually still in the army, looks around, pursing his lips nervously. I reckon he's at least sixty-five years younger than the rest of the soldiers.

The Acroma-Knightsbridge Cemetery is a few miles outside Tobruk, in an area of stony ground and occasional fields, in which small birds dart and dive amongst resilient cornstalks. It is looked after, on behalf of the War Graves Commission, by a Libyan, Mohamed Haneish, and his wife. He's a soft-spoken, courteous man with

short-cropped grey hair, who calls the dead his 'boys'. Mohamed has worked here for eighteen years and his father tended the graves for thirty years before that. He complains about the salinity of the water and the difficulty he has making things grow, but you wouldn't know it. The place is immaculate. Enclosed within a well-built sandstone wall, with an arched gatehouse entrance, are 3649 graves, every one of identical size, set in neat rows on perfectly tilled ground, interspersed with trees and enough flowers to bring butterflies dancing around the headstones.

I wander down the lines. On closer examination, these apparently identical stones reveal rich diversity: Jewish stars, New Zealand ferns, inscriptions in Afrikaans and Urdu, French, Yugoslav, Polish and Arabic. Mohamed points out two VCs, one of whom, we learn from his inscription, was a chartered accountant, and only one woman, Janie Beryl Wright of the Nursing Reserve. The dedications range from the affecting 'Good Night Little Brother' to the conscience-tweaking 'Fight to build as we have fought to destroy'. The effect of these ranks of white stones, set in the pale red sand, is terribly moving.

The service of remembrance gets underway as the weather deteriorates. It's cool and feels like rain. The vets process in, led by Douglas Waller, wearing a beret and gripping the Rats of Tobruk standard for all he's worth in the strengthening wind. As the trees swing about above the headstones, which seem to stand out more vividly now the sky has darkened, the words of Laurence Binyon's poem, 'For the Fallen', are quietly but firmly recited by the living on behalf of the dead.

'They shall not grow old as we that are left grow old:
Age shall not weary them, nor the years condemn.
At the going down of the sun and in the morning
We will remember them.'

Then the piper plays, and, after prayers have been read, thanks given and wreaths laid, Paul, the bugler, sounds the Last Post.

There are, I notice, four Libyans buried in the Commonwealth cemetery at Acroma.

ABOVE

The Rats of Tobruk, sixty years on. They took their name from the propaganda broadcasts of 'Lord Haw-Haw' in the Second World War. 'Come out of your holes you rats!' he taunted. And they did. (Left to right): Francis Cload, Douglas Waller, Leslie Meek, Frank Plant, Peter Vaux, Frank Harrison, Harry Day, James Pearce, Stephen Dawson, Ray Ellis.

On their graves, instead of 'Rest in Peace', is an Arabic inscription. Translated, it reads 'He is forgiven'.

On the way back into Tobruk, we pass the sombre bulk of the German war memorial. It is a replica of a Teutonic castle, on whose dark protective walls the names of the dead are inscribed, unaccompanied by details of rank or regiment. It is simple, powerful and completely different from the cemeteries we saw earlier. The contrast reveals a lot about national character and the myth and legend by which it is expressed. The Allied dead lie in gardens, as if in a state of Eden-like, prelapsarian innocence, as far away as could be imagined from war and suffering. The Germans lie in a different kind of sanctuary. A castle, a bastion, a place where warriors who have fought the good fight sleep with the gods. Both sorts of memorial show, sadly, that our ability to create order and dignity for the dead greatly exceeds our ability to do the same for the living.

The afternoon programme includes a reception at the hotel laid on by the Libyan government. Before the reception there are speeches by a group of distinguished figures. One is introduced as Brigadier Suleiman, 'commander of all the forces in Eastern Libya'.

'Strong Gaddafi man,' Stephen Dawson whispers in my ear.

He is impressive in a suit, with a droopy grey moustache and a confidently authoritative manner, much of which is lost in translation. The interpreter is the complete opposite of the brigadier. He's a sullen civilian in a suit two sizes too big for him. He's also completely useless, and there are long periods of silence between his halting translations. At one stage he turns to the audience and shrugs his shoulders sulkily.

'It's just too many words.'

Finally, the brigadier's patience snaps and he fixes the translator with a terrible eye.

'Do not have breakfast with my language!' he roars, before going on to deliver the rest of his speech in perfectly good English.

This knockabout disguises quite serious material. The gist of the brigadier's message is that Libyans are still being killed and maimed by mines left over from the Second World War and he and his government want maps of the minefields handed over and a big international effort made to clear them.

At the side of the stage are display boards, which are so universally ignored that I feel duty bound to have a look. They don't make comfortable viewing. Alongside photos of mines being laid by Germans and Allies alike are photographs of Libyans mutilated by them sixty years later.

A ceremony was to be held down at the waterfront, at the point where the defenders of Tobruk were finally relieved, but Lady Randell had found that this was now a sewage outlet, so it's relocated to a small patch of open ground with the harbour on one side and a building site on the other. There is something about the banality of the surroundings that makes this last little piece of drama all the more affecting. As the blustery wind flicks at the yellow standard of the Tobruk Desert Rats, a message from the Queen is read out, and a wreath is tossed into the harbour. As it drifts away the eighteen octogenarians are brought to attention and marched off, one last time, in the direction of Tobruk.

'Eyes left!' Heads turn towards the British ambassador, who takes the salute, standing in the grounds of a half-finished house.

BELOW

At Acroma-Knightsbridge Cemetery. Mohamed Haneish and his wife keep the place immaculate, working wonders with limited resources. Water is scarce and, because they're close to the sea, it's brackish and salty. Mohamed, whose father taught him the job, calls the dead 'my boys'.

DAY EIGHTY-ONE   TOBRUK TO BENGHAZI

ABOVE

Apollonia.
Remains of a
2000-year-old
mosaic flooring,
showing palm
trees and wild
animals.

This morning we part company with the Rats of Tobruk. They are going east, to Egypt, and we are turning west, across the northern edge of the Sahara, all the way to Tripoli and the Tunisian frontier, 1200 miles away.

Our coach is big and pink and accommodates not only ourselves but also a half-dozen Libyan escorts, including two government minders and a video cameraman whose job it is to record our every move. The staff from Apollonia Tours are attentive, regularly plying us with refreshments, coffee, tea, water, biscuits and sweeties, when really the only thing we want them to do is to turn off the Richard Clayderman tape.

Once we're past the port of Darnah, the immaculately surfaced, virtually empty road rises and falls and snakes around pretty bays, as we run along the knuckle of land that brings Libya to within 250 miles of mainland Europe. Almost at the apex of this chunky headland are the remains of Apollonia, once the port for the Roman city of Cyrene, high up on the hills behind it. I'm not a great one for archaeological sites – I think I lack the patience required to imagine so much from so little – but Apollonia is enchanting. A strong offshore wind has swept away the murky humidity of Tobruk and turned the Mediterranean a glamorous, white-flecked blue. Beside it, along a mile of coastline, rise a series of graceful ruins. One of them, the Eastern Basilica, is especially elegant. A grove of slender columns made from green and white cipolin marble outlined against an azure sky. Between them are traces of a superb mosaic floor, with images of Africa, wild animals and palm trees. Such treasures would be dazzling enough in a museum, but to find them, intact and largely unspoiled, where they were laid 2000 years ago is almost unbelievable, and has me worrying immediately that they are not sufficiently protected. Not that there are any crowds here. A scattering of Italians, a few Dutch, otherwise we have it to ourselves.

Further on, looking out over the sea, is one of the most perfectly located theatres I have ever seen, and in excellent condition too. Time seems frozen as I climb on the stage, waves thumping against the rocks a hundred yards behind me, the steep stone tiers rising and curving around in front of me. Test the acoustics with a few lines from Julius Caesar, not long dead when this was built, but am booed off by the crew.

As the road winds up the hill behind Apollonia, it passes a complex of ancient tombs and catacombs extending right across the hillside, most of them fallen into a romantic state of disrepair. Those classical carvings, vaults, decorated lintels and bits of sarcophagi that haven't already been looted lie around in staggering profusion, visited mainly by flocks of sheep and herds of goats picking away at the scrubby grass that covers them.

The extent of this burial ground gives some idea of the importance of the city of Cyrene, much of which still stands, built into the folds of the hills. Two mighty propylaea, a colonnade and several headless deities with exquisitely sculpted robes adorn the old Greek settlement, erected in the seventh century BC. A cluster of elegant baths and fountains show the preoccupations of the Romans, who grafted their own architecture onto the Greek original. I'm poking around them when I find a goat in the hypocaust. Quite a shock, but a good name for a volume of archaeological memoirs. A Goat in the Hypocaust.

Following the railway tracks laid by the Italians in the 1920s to help them excavate and restore the site I come across the eye-catching Fountain of The Nymph Cyrene. With its carved statue of a young girl gracefully ripping open a lion's mouth, it's an ingenious way of telling a story and creating a water outlet at the same time. In Greek mythology, Cyrene so attracted Apollo with her animal wrestling skills that he sent a chariot to pick her up and take her across the water to the fertile highlands of northern Libya, in which green and pleasant land they consummated their relationship and she bore him a son.

BELOW

Abdul Gerawi, our chief Libyan guide (in the well-cut Western-style clothes worn by most professional Libyans), watches filming in the magical Roman theatre at Apollonia, rediscovered only forty years ago.

The land that Apollo chose for his tryst with Cyrene is known nowadays as Jebel Akhdar, the Green Mountain, and it is quite an extensive upland area, its scenery not a lot different from Provence or even at times, where the roads narrow and the limestone walls crowd in, of Dorset. Annual rainfall up here is about the same as London's and wide and fertile cornfields stretch away on either side of the road. It was grain that brought the Romans to Africa, and vast quantities were shipped across the Mediterranean, earning Libya the title of the breadbasket of Rome.

Cyrene was continuously occupied for over 1200 years, until the Arab invaders of the seventh century, not much interested in classical cities, let it fall back gradually into oblivion.

The Italians returned to the province of Cyrenaica in the 1920s but met spirited resistance to their colonising from a local leader called Umar al-Mukhtar. In 1930 General Graziani was sent out from Rome to deal with the opposition. Mukhtar was captured and hanged, and those who resisted Graziani's policies were rounded up in concentration camps.

So hated did the Italians make themselves in this short period that there is now almost no indication they were ever here on the Green Mountain. Al-Mukhtar, on the other hand, is still remembered as a hero and received the ultimate accolade of being portrayed on screen by Anthony Quinn.

As we descend from the plateau towards Benghazi, the olive groves, junipers and stands of cypress and Aleppo pine grow fewer and the number of roadblocks increases.

Like Tobruk, Benghazi is a city of infrastructure, girdled by a network of underpasses, ring roads and flyovers, all largely free of traffic, and as the road signs are only in Arabic it's impossible to tell where they're going. The woods and fields of Jebel Akhdar seem like a dream as we cruise slowly through a bare and featureless cityscape to come eventually to rest before the concrete and glass terraces of the Hotel Tibesti. I would have said at the doors of the Hotel Tibesti, or even at the portals of the Hotel Tibesti, but the architects of this magnificent late 1970s pile miscalculated the height of the concrete roof above the entrance and all tourist buses have to park and unload in a nearby road, making it a good walk to the hotel lobby through a taxi rank, a small garden, past ornamental fountains and up a substantial flight of steps.

DAY EIGHTY-TWO   BENGHAZI

In the lobby of the Hotel Tibesti hang neat placards with quotes from Colonel Gaddafi's *Green Book*. To us sophisticated Westerners, for whom talking about political theory is about as uncomfortable as talking about piles, it seems pretty odd to have 'Committees Everywhere' hanging up in a place of hospitality and entertainment, not to mention the even less catchy 'The Social i.e. National Factor is the Driving Force Of Human History'. But that's how it is here in the Jamahiriya, the 'state of the masses', where Muammar Gaddafi has run the show for the last thirty-one years. After he and fellow army officers got rid of a monarchy backed by America and Britain, Gaddafi made sweeping changes. Private enterprise was banned, foreign

influence discouraged and the country reorganised around people's committees and congresses. Alcohol was banned.

Bankrolling the revolution was not a problem, Libya being in the enviable position of having the world's third largest oil earnings and a population less than that of Greater London.

Gaddafi's survival owes much to his ability to reinvent himself. He's been at various times scourge of the West and leader of the Arab world; currently he is the great Pan-African. The change can be charted on the billboards.

It's not quite the old communist-style cult of personality, but there is a lot of him about. The standard image is full face, aviator shades, pillbox-style *chechia* perched on thick black curly hair, skin creased by deep, but reassuring, Jagger-style grooves. None of the Soviet-style hard man here. He looks every inch the entertainer (and is almost the same age as Mick). On one rapidly fading billboard I saw, above the words 'American aggression', Gaddafi, fist raised, defying the bolts and arrows of missile attack (fifteen years ago his adopted daughter was killed in the American air attacks on Benghazi and Tripoli). Around this centrepiece were depictions of the caring Colonel, visiting children in schools and hospitals. On more recent posters he's likely to be seen emerging from a map of Africa, shedding a halo of golden rays across the continent. The parallel that comes irresistibly to mind is with Cecil Rhodes and his dream of spreading the red of the British Empire from Cape to Cairo.

The redirection of Gaddafi's foreign policy towards Saharan Africa should not perhaps be a surprise. He has always identified with the nomads and still prefers to live in a tent rather than a palace. There are few leaders these days who care much about the Sahara and I would very much have liked to have met and talked to him about his policy.

So far our advances have met with no success. The Libyan authorities remain deeply mistrustful of Western media and today we have to content ourselves with another closely guided tour.

ABOVE

Sweeping gaze.
Plenty of brushes,
but where are all
the people?

ABOVE RIGHT

The mosque of
Jami' Osman, with
Ottoman-style
dome, is one of the
few old buildings
left in Benghazi,
which was heavily
bombed in the
Second World War.

Abdul and Mohammed collect me in their car. Abdul is our chief minder from the Government Media Department, while Mohammed, slimmer, younger and already a father of five, is an air-traffic controller in Benghazi. This, apparently, is not a full-time job; he's also a plumber and a painter.

'One thousand, nine hundred kilometre beach begin here,' announces Abdul, waving his arm at a flat milky-green wasteland studded with cones of freshly tipped rubbish. I'm taken to meet a friend of theirs who runs a tourist village. Photographs are taken. Along another meaningless swirl of motorway into the centre of the city. A number of Italian colonial buildings remain, including a Venetian-style governor's residence, now the headquarters of the local committee. It's a Friday and there aren't many people in the streets. Those that are about seem to favour Western dress. There are more sharp, Italian-style suits than there are *tarbooshes* and *djellabas*.

Lunch is long and formal. The tables are big enough for a peace conference, and conversation is in the polite international style, with bursts of animated misunderstanding punctuated by longer periods of silence. Afterwards we prowl around two good-looking mosques, and a small square dominated by a classical copper-domed cathedral, now also a mosque. I climb the wide stone steps that lead to the portico, only to find the massive west door bricked up. Perhaps anxious to correct any bad impression we might have got from the boarded-up cathedral, Abdul takes us to a Catholic church and mission run by Franciscans, closed in the early years of the revolution and reopened in 1976 after a Catholic-Islamic pact was signed in Tripoli. Seven priests and thirty-five nuns keep it open all week, and offer mass in five languages, Arabic, English, Italian, Polish and Korean.

The bishop of Cyrenaica, a short, genial Maltese, explained this eclectic mix. Poles work on a lot of the urban construction projects and the Koreans on the Great Manmade River Project, Gaddafi's epic scheme to bring fresh water from underground aquifers thousands of feet below the desert to irrigate the coast. At one time the project used Filipinos, very good Catholics.

'There were thousands of them,' sighed the bishop, wistfully.

Our day in Benghazi may have lacked sparkle, but the night is memorable for one of the most dangerous journeys I've ever undertaken. Our hosts had organised a trip to a local restaurant, not by car or pink coach, but in horse-drawn buggies. Though a battle-hardened film crew are perhaps not the best people to take advantage of such romantic transport, it all started well enough, until we turned off the quiet street, up a slip road and onto an eight-lane motorway. At one point it seemed as if our driver, who obviously thought his place was in heaven, had panicked. The horse certainly had. He swung his head from side to side, eyeballs staring manically skywards, nostrils pumping away like pistons as the traffic roared by.

Eventually, we found sanctuary in the crawler lane, and remained there for what seemed like hours, before we found our exit. The food was as good as anything we've had in Libya, but I did miss the alcohol that had been my only hope of surviving the journey home.

DAY EIGHTY-THREE BENGHAZI TO SIRTE

No sign of the horses this morning, which is a relief, as we have the best part of 400 miles to cover. The pink coach is once more at our disposal and Farsi, the video cameraman, is back in action, recording our walk from the lobby to the door and the door to the coach, whilst Abdul photographs him photographing us.

In the middle of a roundabout on the outskirts of Benghazi is a huge installation commemorating the Great Manmade River Project. Its centrepiece is a circular stack of pipes embedded in concrete looking like a giant metal cake. Around it, the cardinal points of the compass are marked by 30-foot-long pipe sections. I climb inside one of them.

About 13 feet in diameter, it feels more like a small Underground station than a water pipe. A quarter of a million of these sections were used in the first phase of the project alone, and apparently the number laid now would stretch from the southern tip of Italy to the Orkney Islands. There have been unforeseen problems, however, one of which is the high saline content of the underground water, which is causing corrosion and leakage that is either very serious or little more than expected, according to who you talk to. Abdul, not surprisingly, is of the latter opinion. A group of passing schoolboys sees us filming and pandemonium and excitement break out. They point, shout, laugh, until their enthusiasm is cut short by our driver, Faraj, who climbs down and gives them a terrific scolding. Their faces fall and I can see momentary fear in their eyes. It's a pity, as this is the first time we've seen any reaction from Libyans on the street and I was rather enjoying it. We're herded back onto the pink coach, sedated with

BELOW
*Benghazi
schoolchildren stop
to watch the
filming.*

Richard Clayderman and driven south, into increasingly dry, hot, stony desert.

Instead of trees, there are electricity pylons and instead of wheat fields, there is scrub grass interspersed with pipeline, the occasional flaming head of an oil well, trailing a dirty black slick along the horizon. Near Brayqah, concrete holding tanks, into which the Manmade River disgorges, nestle in the gritty sand, each one as big as two football pitches. A little further on, a metal arch with Gaddafi's likeness painted on it marks the entrance to a massive dusty white complex, where the giant pipes are made. By now the Clayderman tape has reached 'Tulips From Amsterdam' for the fifth time, and cries for a lunch stop, or even an engine failure, are increasing. Thirty miles later, Abdul and Faraj spot three trees, close enough together to qualify as a picnic spot.

The picnic lunch is a big disappointment. And I mean big. Jumbo-sized white boxes reveal salad, chicken and cold chips. And it looks as if we might be here for some time. Whilst attempting a tricky and not strictly necessary three-point turn, Faraj has run the back wheels into soft sand and the coach is spread across half the carriageway like a beached whale. Various passing vehicles are flagged down to help, including a lorry with twenty kneeling camels in the back, all nodding away gently like toys on the back shelf of a car, but none has any towing equipment. The police arrive with a chain. It snaps. By now we have an expectant audience of fourteen people, twenty camels and a small car park of vehicles. Faraj looks as whipped and chastened as the little boys he screamed at this morning.

Eventually, a low-loader with a bulldozer on board, heaves us out and we carry on our way.

Mile after mile of salt scrub numbs the senses, but Mohammed has a treat in store for us. An in-coach movie. It turns out to be *Lion Of The Desert*, a Hollywood biopic of the great national hero, Umar al-Mukhtar. The irony of the Libyan national hero being celebrated by the Great Satan doesn't seem to worry them, and we settle back to a truly blood-drenched couple of hours. If the Libyans are happy to have Anthony Quinn portray their hero, then presumably the Italians would have been relieved that the villain of the piece, Colonel Graziani, is played by Oliver Reed, and Mussolini by a stratospherically over-the-top Rod Steiger.

By these standards, the casting of Sir John Gielgud as a Bedouin was pretty obvious. *The Lion Of The Desert* brings us safely to the birthplace of The Guide Of The Revolution. Besides being Gaddafi's birthplace, Sirte is a potential new capital of the Great Socialist People's Libyan Arab Republic. Modest outskirts of low mud and brick houses give way to a complex of hotels and government offices. Landscaped towers of white stone and black glass could be a corporate HQ in California, until you get inside and find the decorative style is pure Arabian Nights, festooned with spangly curtains, brass lamps and throne-size chairs which take three people to move. A Pan-African conference is to be held here soon, but at the moment, as with so much of 'official' Libya, this grand and expensive campus is deserted. Abdul finds us some food, though once more it's Western rather than local, but at least there is a bowl of *harissa,* the hot pepper paste, to breathe life into our hamburger and chips.

DAY EIGHTY-FOUR SIRTE TO TRIPOLI

As we set off for another long day's drive up the coast I ask Abdul if there's any serious alternative to driving or taking a camel. Wouldn't a railway help? Indeed, he says, and Colonel Gaddafi is very keen on railways, but there aren't any in Libya. The national airline has been badly hit by the continuing American embargo on aircraft spares. Motor car spares are equally hard to find, causing many unnecessary road deaths. The Colonel has tried to deal with this by 'inspiring' a new design of five-seater vehicle. With glare-free headlights, non-exploding tyres, high-impact bumpers and all round air-bag protection, it would be the world's safest car. It's to be called The Rocket of the Libyan Jamahiriya. Now that's a proper name for a car. Well, better than Cherry anyway.

Nigel is losing his patience with the camera. Not his, but the Libyan government's. I actually heard him this morning going on about how he hates being followed by a camera. Well now he knows what it's like. I ask Farsi, the cameraman, what they are going to do with all this footage of us entering and leaving hotels. He seems quite aggrieved by my question.

'There's only six hours.'

BELOW
Camel delivery service stops to offer assistance.

A few miles short of Tripoli is Leptis Magna, the richest and most magnificent of all the Roman cities in Africa. We pile out and take the tour. It is indeed wonderful, much more grand than Cyrene and much bigger too. A paved street, the Via Colonnata, runs for almost half a mile, and to walk its well-worn slabs is to feel yourself in the heart of a great city. The smaller details stick in my mind, like the beautifully carved dolphins standing on their heads in the market, probably the sign of a Roman fishmongers' stall, but the massive interior of the new Basilica at Leptis is hugely impressive.

It was used as a law court and standing in it, dwarfed by the mighty Aswan granite columns, is to experience an almost palpable sense of the brute force of Rome.

Next to it, the 300-foot-long, 200-foot-wide Imperial Forum is like a vast mad monumental mason's yard. Columns, capitals, decorated friezes, plinths, pendentives, bas-reliefs and massive heads with curls like eighteenth-century wigs lie around as if an earthquake had just struck.

The sumptuousness of Leptis Magna may look very European, but it would not

have been built without Saharan money. The bread which Libya so copiously supplied to Rome could not in itself have provided sufficient revenue for excess of this scale. The difference was made up of the wealth of gold, ivory and slaves, brought here on caravans from across the Sahara Desert.

There is a parallel here with the wealth of present-day Libya, which also comes from the desert. Gaddafi's oil, which is not only copious but also of very good quality, keeps the West going, the same way Libyan grain kept Rome going. Who needs who most?

DAY EIGHTY-FIVE TRIPOLI

Our last day in Libya. From the balcony of a monstrous hotel I look out over the harbour. A ferry is loading, one of six or seven ships in port. It's a hazy, warm day, and the wind that sends the green flags fluttering carries a faint tang of sulphur from the chain of chemical works and refineries that dot the coast. Below me is a green and white-domed mosque, squeezed in by the side of the surging highway that leads towards the skyscrapers of the city. The centre of Tripoli, a wide, open meeting place called Green Square, lies beside the castle, at the place where the old medina and the newer, largely Italian streets meet. The green louvered shutters of the houses remind me of Gibraltar. I still feel frustrated. Abdul, Mohammed and the others have treated us well, but I feel we've also been strong-boxed. It's been hard to meet people beyond the pink coach.

So I'm surprised when a youngish Libyan man approaches me in Green Square. He extends a hand and asks, in good English, what I think of the country. I murmur the usual praise and we shake.

'I won't tell you what I think,' he says bitterly, and is gone.

TUNISIA

DAY EIGHTY-SEVEN DJERBA

Seventy-five miles across the Tunisian border is the island of Djerba. It claims to be the Land of the Lotus-Eaters, celebrated in Homer's *Odyssey*. In one of history's most famous examples of R and R, Odysseus and his crew put in here for a while and surrendered themselves to the soothingly narcotic fruits of the lotus.

These days it's hard to find the lotus or its fruit, but there is a heady local preparation called *boukha,* made from fermented dates or figs, which seems to have pretty much the same effect. After Libya, where fermented anything was forbidden, the sudden proliferation of hotels offering every sort of inebriant from Baileys to Bloody Marys is a profound shock to us all and a lot of surrendering goes on.

Nor is this the only shock. The sheer numbers of lotus-seekers thronging the north coast of Djerba is in bewildering contrast to where we've just been, and indeed with almost anywhere else on this journey. German, Dutch and Swedish seem to be the native languages here.

This sudden return to a world of wine lists and multi-channel television produces an odd sinking feeling and an unexpected upsurge of nostalgia for those trips into the desert in the wee small hours, armed only with trowel and toilet roll.

BELOW
Like rows of open oyster shells, sunbathers flank the pool of one of the big hotels on the lotus-eating Isle of Djerba. In Tunisia, tourist revenue makes up for the lack of oil earnings with which neighbours Libya and Algeria have been blessed. Or cursed.

DAY EIGHTY-EIGHT DJERBA

The design of our hotel, a huge U-shaped wall facing out to sea, tries hard to create a feeling of all-embracing exclusiveness, an ample concrete bosom of pleasure, where all your needs will be attended to, where food, drink, recorded music and thalassotherapy are always at hand.

Try and get away from this fortress of fun and you will find twenty or thirty others, right next door, all offering similar versions of what you've got, and before long you realise that wherever you are is just like where you've come from.

Somewhere outside the fortress walls is Djerba itself, an offshore island, 18 by 16 miles, flat, dry and agricultural. Compared with the desert we've come through, it looks almost lush, but the reality is that rainfall is low, only 8 inches a year, and the water saline. The dates from Djerba's palm trees are only suitable for animal feed and the olive groves yield low returns. The island's most productive pastures are the shallow waters that surround it. Fishing here is a traditional industry, carried on by traditional methods.

On the dockside at Houmt Souk are stacked rows of turnip-shaped, terracotta pots. These elegant little amphorae, about 18 inches high, are not for tourists to take home; they're for catching octopus. Each one has a rim at the top, around which a string is tied, attaching it to a long line of pots which are then dropped into the sea a few miles offshore. For some reason, octopuses are irresistibly drawn to the pots, curling up inside them and presenting a perfect gift for fishermen. It's a technique that's been used since the Phoenicians came this way 3000 years ago, and the octopuses still haven't caught on.

We've wangled ourselves aboard one of the brightly painted, low-tech fishing boats, which is setting out to check its lines.

Once out of the harbour, we run into a lively sea, licked up by a freshening wind. The stubby, wooden-hulled boat bounces all over the place as we search for the line they put down a couple of days ago. So competitive is the fishing out here that they mark the line as discreetly as possible, and it's only after a half-hour search that they detect the green plastic bottle to which the line is attached. By now the boats are bucking all over the place as the pots are hauled up from the sea bed no more than 12 feet below us. I'm hanging on for dear life as we hurtle up and plunge down the waves, but the fishermen are balanced only by knees against the rail as they inspect the pots. There are fifty on this line. One after another contains only sand and seaweed and is tossed back into the water. Not an octopus to be seen. It's early in the season, they say.

We head for another line. The wind is strengthening and the boat tossing ever more violently, but the third pot they pull out produces a great cry and the pink rubbery mass inside is tipped out unceremoniously onto the deck.

Then another and another. All hands are at the pots and I'm given the job of keeping the catch in a large blue plastic tray. This isn't easy. The octopuses are not at all keen to stay on the tray and once they get a leg outside it their suckers clamp on to the wooden deck. By the time I've loosened one leg, the other seven are stuck fast. Clinging to the octopuses with one hand and a piece of superstructure with the other, I succeed in wrenching them off, only to be flung across the boat, octopus in hand and fast latching on to my arm.

Keeping the octopuses in the tray becomes like a routine invented for a Japanese game show, but it seems to cheer the fishermen up no end. Meanwhile, I've become quite an admirer of these tenacious creatures and am thinking of starting an Octopus Protection League.

Knowing the British, there probably already is one.

In the late afternoon, as the shops are opening, I walk through the souk, which seems well stocked with goods, mostly aimed at the tourist market. Rugs, tiles, lamps, hands of Fatima, pieces of Rose du Sable (natural sculptures of crystallised gypsum found in the desert), hubble-bubble pipes and the like. There are some superior items in a shop owned by a man known as 'El Haj', including a Turkish carpet woven with a million knots per square metre. El Haj (an abbreviation earned by anyone who has been on the haj, the pilgrimage to Mecca) is a short, scholarly man with a neat moustache and thick glasses, wearing a cream *gandoura* over a tartan shirt. He speaks

LEFT
There Must Be Easier Ways To Make A Living, Number 24: wrestling freshly caught octopus.

English well, and five other languages too, but almost apologetically, looking down as he does so.

Though tourism supplies 70 or 80 per cent of his trade, he is not entirely happy with its impact on the island. Local families won't walk on the beach any more because of the number of naked and semi-naked tourists, a phenomenon which he thinks is encouraging some Muslim youths to drink alcohol and sell themselves for casual sexual encounters.

Sex tourism, in Djerba?

He nods. 'When he sees a nude lady on the beach, he thinks it means she is looking for adventure. They should respect our culture, our religion. They can come for the sun but they don't have to take all their clothes off and walk.'

When he was a boy, the north coast was wild and deserted. Now there are a hundred hotels there. They attract a large workforce from outside the island, which has to be absorbed. Thankfully, he says, Djerbans are traditionally tolerant.

'I think this is the only place where you find Jewish and Moslems living together.'

Peacefully, he must mean.

'We have the oldest synagogue in North Africa. I think 586 before Christ it was built.'

Many of the Djerban Jews have gone to France, often running corner shops known simply as '*le djerbain*', but many come back to marry. There are 2000 of them in Houmt Souk.

'I take my car to a Jewish man, I buy my jewellery from a Jew, a number of my neighbours are Jewish and I'm a Hajan practising Islam, and there's no problem with it.'

On our way back, between the outskirts of Houmt Souk and the first hotel, there is a surprisingly tranquil stretch of national park. The air is now so still that sky and sea merge seamlessly, one reflecting the other like a continuous sheet of glass. In front of which, as if in a mirage, oystercatchers, herons and flocks of flamingoes are feeding. But the hotels are getting awfully close.

DAY EIGHTY-NINE DJERBA TO EL HADDEJ

Before I set out on this Saharan journey southern Tunisia was the closest I'd ever been to the desert. That was in 1978 and I came here to be crucified. Security problems in Israel and an appetite for biblical epics had created a lucrative role for Tunisia as a stand-in for the Holy Land. Not only did Tunisia look right, it was also both friendly and stable, and when the producers of Monty Python's *Life of Brian* approached the local authorities they agreed to let us use locations in Monastir and Sousse for urban Jerusalem, whilst the scenes set outside the city were to be shot in the bleaker, more desolate south, around Matmata on the edge of the Jebel Dahar mountains.

A wide bend in the road and a hill with a long flat-topped ridge spreading out below it has a curiously familiar feel, and as the bus climbs I remember, with a shock of recognition, that this is where we filmed the Sermon on the Mount. That day in November 1978, very similar buses, in which several hundred of our extras had been brought up earlier, appeared on this road halfway through the afternoon's filming. The extras, who had been forced to stand around watching Englishmen do silly things all day, saw this as a sign that it was all over and began to stampede off the Mount and down to their buses. Terry Jones, our director, raced after them, urging them to come back. Unfortunately, he was dressed as the virgin Mandy at the time, and the memory of this black-clad old crone screaming at 500 joyful Arabs is an image of the Matmata hills which will give me pleasure on many a cold day.

So it is that, soon after lunch, in a flat hazy light, I find myself standing above the village of El Haddej, almost twenty-three years, to the day, since I hung on one of two dozen crosses, tapping my feet and singing 'Always Look on the Bright Side of Life'.

BELOW

Return to the crucifixion scene. Walking round a troglodyte home in El Haddej. Both Life Of Brian *and* Star Wars *were filmed in this unique, moon-like landscape.*

El Haddej looks much as I remember it. It's set in a landscape of low, yellowing hills scored by deep gullies, as if it had just dried out after a mighty flood. In fact, it has not rained here for three years, and the land is bone dry. There are the usual hardy bushes, a few palms, their lower fronds discoloured by drought, and on the side of a hill an old man is watering a single young olive tree, which won't give fruit in his lifetime.

These hills were settled by Berbers over 2000 years ago. Finding little cover above ground, they took to the caves below, and to this day their descendants still live as troglodytes.

From up here their homes look like a series of lunar craters, some with cars or pick-ups parked on the rim, others barely visible in the folds of soft, friable rock around them.

The troglodytes of the Matmata hills are experiencing rapid change. The combination of a well-organised tourist industry and the choice of one of the caves as Luke Skywalker's birthplace has, as in Djerba, brought lucrative tourist business to a poor area. Some caves have been turned into hotels, but when these proved too small to accommodate tour groups, hotels were built to look like caves.

I start to walk down the hill, passing a small dog, which barks ferociously at a line of sheep but rushes away in terror at the approach of a black plastic bag slowly twisting in the wind. I look down into two or three dwellings which appear to have been abandoned. Holes some 60 feet across and 30 feet deep, have collapsed in on themselves. To add a final indignity, rubbish has been dumped inside them.

There is one cave which is still occupied and rents out rooms, or cavities, perhaps. The only entrance is through a dimly lit tunnel. It's some 30 yards long, and smells of fur and dung. At its darkest point I run slap into a donkey, which is quietly munching away at some straw. Emerging into the soft grey light of a courtyard, I see an elderly man and two women waiting to welcome me. The man's name is Bilgessou. He stands straight-backed, wearing a fine red skullcap and a knee-length brown overcoat, his bearing matching a military-style silver moustache. Next to him, in brightly coloured Berber stripes, are his wife Manoubia and their daughter Jemila. They stand almost motionless, like a tableau waiting to be photographed.

After we have introduced ourselves, they pull aside a palm wood door and usher me into a side room off the courtyard. The roof is a low, smoke-stained vault, lit by a single bulb (there is electricity here, but water has to be fetched from the well). Bilgessou sets to work making tea on a calor gas stove, Jemila sits down, revealing a bright and well-holed pair of yellow stockings, and she and her mother set to work rubbing the skins off peanuts and dropping them in a bowl. A rangy black and white cat appears from the depths of the cave, is shooed away but holds its ground, eyeing the preparations.

Once the tea has been made and poured, as it is throughout the Sahara, with a flourish from as far above the glass as possible, Bilgessou takes the bowl of nuts and scatters them onto a roasting tray, which he lays on the fire. Most of this is done in silence, as none of them speak French and I don't speak Arabic, but Jemila has a sweet understanding smile and somehow it doesn't feel wrong to be silent.

However, once the first glass of tea has been taken, Bilgessou begins to talk, in a powerful voice, with a lot of barking, back-of-the-throat sounds.

The young don't want to live in the caves any more, he says. They're moving above ground, tempted away by ready-made houses in New Matmata. The authorities don't understand. They've shown little interest in preserving the troglodyte way of life, except for the tourists. He extends an arm towards his wife. She has never left El Haddej in her life. She can't be expected to change just like that.

I'm handed a biscuit and a cotton cloth to put on my knee to catch the crumbs.

Anyway, he goes on, these troglodyte houses make sense. They're safe and secure, warm in winter and cool in summer. The soft rock is easy to excavate, and, unlike the timber round here, there's plenty of it.

LEFT

Taking tea with Bilgessou and his wife and daughter. Refusing to move from the cave he's lived in all his life, he makes money by providing accommodation for curious travellers.

When he stops, the silence returns, thick and heavy, deadened by the weight of the earth around us.

They show me my room. It's across the courtyard and up a flight of irregular stone steps, cut from the clay. The coffin-shaped entrance has decorated stone dressings and inside is a vaulted space, some 20 feet deep, with just enough room to stand straight at its centre. The walls have been plastered and painted white at some time, but that's faded now. A mattress is laid along one side where the wall slopes down quite sharply. Dangerous if you wake suddenly in the night.

Not far from here is a tantalising example of the old way of life that Bilgessou fears is disappearing for ever – an underground olive oil press, set into the side of a hill. Inside the cave is a circular chamber, consisting of a platform, around which is just enough room for a donkey to walk. The oil-maker tips a basket of olives – stalks, leaves and all – onto the platform. Then the donkey, harnessed to a pole, and wearing a pair of pointed woven blinkers that look like a large wicker brassiere, starts to plod round. The pole turns a spindle, which rolls a cylindrical stone block over the olives, reducing them to an inky mulch.

The mulch is then stuffed inside pancake-sized rattan discs, which are stacked one on top of the other, fourteen at a time, and squeezed in a wooden press. Every 100 kilograms of olives produces 35 litres of oil.

The reek of olives is quite heady and every inch of this dark, cramped, glistening chamber is thick and sticky with accretions, like the inside of an immensely ancient cooking pot.

Walk back to Bilgessou's cave. What's the address I wonder? What would I ask for if I were lost? Number 43, The Mountain? The family are in the courtyard, in exactly the same positions, Bilgessou standing like an old soldier, Jemila and Manoubia sitting on stones. Their life encompassed by this pit of crumbling red rock.

And later, as darkness falls, I find myself doing exactly the same thing, just sitting there, on the steps outside my room, looking up at the stars. It's not that there's nowhere to go, or anyone's stopping me taking a walk out of the tunnel to see some other folks on the hill, it's just that once you're in here the outside world ceases to mean very much. There is no view but upwards.

Before I go to sleep I get out my portable DVD player, watch myself being crucified and feel better.

DAY NINETY EL HADDEJ TO SOUSSE

As we pick our way through the spare and stony cover of the Matmata hills I realise that this is the last I shall see of the desert for a while. The final leg of my journey will take me north and west to see the other side of the great desert countries like Tunisia and Algeria. The side where people live, where capital cities lie, where the great trans-Saharan trade routes began and ended, where the Sahara was talked about, its wealth evaluated, its various conquests planned.

It's no coincidence that Libya, Tunisia and Algeria, the three richest countries of the Sahara, share a Mediterranean coastline. Their capitals are all much closer to the markets of Europe than those of Africa. The remains of so many Greek and Roman cities show how close the historical links have been. Yet all three are firmly Arab and Muslim countries. Together with Morocco and Mauritania they're collectively known by the Arabic word Maghreb, the land of the West, and their political alliances are currently with each other, through the Maghreb Union Treaty of 1989, rather than with Europe. Libya, it seems, doesn't mind this too much. It's looking back into the desert. The conferences that were being prepared in Sirte and Tripoli are, some consider, the first step to Colonel Gaddafi's goal of a United States of the Sahara. Will Tunisia and Algeria go along with this or might they be ready to look north again?

The last sand seas may be behind me, but the intellectual, cultural and political heart of some powerful Saharan countries lies ahead.

From Gabès the main road north follows the coastline, running between the sea and the railway, along avenues of eucalyptus with enormous olive plantations stretching away in long straight lines on either side of the road.

The industrial port of Sfax is signalled by a plume of black smoke trailing out across the Mediterranean, and for several miles we pass through a wasteland of spoil heaps and phosphate factories. I couldn't help noticing the name of the road: Boulevard de l'Environment.

By lunchtime we have reached El Jem and are able to eat beside one of the finest sights in Tunisia, the honey-coloured walls of the third biggest amphitheatre the Romans ever built.

It's a powerful presence. Fourteen hundred feet in circumference, it could accommodate over 30,000 spectators.

Gazing unhurriedly at it over a lamb kebab, I'm struck by the boldness of the design. The massive blocks of stone not only had to be hauled in from quarries 20 miles away, they also had to be stacked in an elliptical wall 100 feet high, supported entirely by its arches. No buttressing, no concrete, just a precisely calculated balancing act.

El Jem itself is a modest market town, whose entire population could fit in one end of the colosseum, and, like flies round an elephant, the locals get on with life

apparently oblivious to the monster in their midst.

Unless, of course, they're in the tourist business, which is not looking too bright at the moment. The shadow of September 11th means horses and carts go by unoccupied and there are plenty of spare tables to be had. Guides saunter about, but no-one looks desperate, or in any way resentful of our being here. One man in a striped robe, skullcap and dark glasses spies us and breaks into a broad grin.

'Allô, allô, my friend, 'ow are you? We are the Taliban. Only joking.'

Tunisia is the smallest and most compact of all the Saharan countries, and as we've been used to driving two or three hours between trees, let alone towns, our surroundings seem to be changing with indecent haste. Within half a day we've been from troglodytes to amphitheatres, and an hour later we're at the gates of one of the largest and best-preserved Arab fortresses in North Africa, the Ribat of Harthouma in Monastir. Its towers, turrets and battlements stand proudly beside the sea, rich cream against azure blue. It may lack the majesty of El Jem, but it has a more subtle appeal, the quiet dignity of a fortress that has survived 1200 years of conflict. How, then, were we ever allowed to shoot *Life Of Brian* here? A party of schoolchildren is listening dutifully to an account of the history of this venerable building. I find myself longing to take them on an alternative history tour, to show them where John Cleese had a boulder dropped on top of him, where Brian leapt from a tower only to be rescued by a flying saucer, and where 500 Tunisian extras laughed at Biggus Dickus.

The truth is that the Ribat is now so squeaky clean that it's lost a bit of character. Lew Grade's Jesus of Nazareth set, which once loomed up beside it, has long gone, replaced by ornamental gardens, and where we lounged around between takes, being rude about each other's beards, is now paved and swept clean as a whistle.

Our art department and the current restorers were both in the same game, trying to bring an ancient, partly ruined fortress to life, and to be honest I think we did a better job. The Ribat is still a good place to visit, with high walls and battlements completely, indeed recklessly accessible, but I preferred it with the market stalls, ex-lepers and writing on the wall.

We spend the night in nearby Sousse at another big, comfortable holiday factory by the sea. Though business is down by 50 per cent since September 11th, it's still as busy as a railway station, and what it must be like at full capacity is terrible to contemplate.

I meet up in a local café with a group of Tunisians all involved in the tourist industry. Around us are tables full of men playing cards. Some football flickers away, largely ignored, on a wall-mounted television. El Mejid, a pale-skinned, squarely built

Tunisian, who looks more Irish than Arab, runs Berber evenings six days a week out at an old olive oil factory. Belly-dancing, bareback riders, waiters with bottles on their heads, a meal and all the wine you can drink for 13 dinars a head, roughly £6.75. One of his friends puffs on a *chicha*, a hubble-bubble pipe; another, wearing a tracksuit, arrives late after a work-out. He looks tired and his back is giving him trouble. He's the only one who breaks ranks and expresses any doubts about the benefits of tourism. He worries about the growth of the cities, with a corresponding break-up of family life and threat to traditions.

'The wedding,' he says, 'the traditional wedding used to be about one week. Now it's only one day or two days.'

His colleagues shake their heads. They seem willing to pay almost any price to bring in the visitors. I ask if they see any point in limiting the new developments.

'No limit, I think. We used to receive three millions and now about five millions. Maybe in ten years ten millions.'

Ten millions. On current figures that's more than the entire population.

DAY NINETY-ONE SIDI BOU SAID

Sidi Bou Said is next door to Carthage and both are salubrious suburbs of the capital, Tunis. The town is up on a hill, and our hotel looks out over the green and swaying trees of the coastal plain, towards the Gulf of Tunis and the 2000-foot mountains of the Cap Bon peninsula. It's a grand and comfortable view, full of colour and pleasant rambling houses dotted about. The only similarity with the bald slopes of the south are the small white-domed marabouts, tombs of holy men, which are scattered through the country. Sidi Bou Said was himself a holy man ('*sidi*' in Arabic is equivalent to 'saint' or 'master'), who, after a trip to Mecca at the end of the twelfth century, settled on this hill and lived a much respected ascetic life.

Several centuries later, Sidi Bou Said's fine location seduced a quite un-ascetic set of Europeans, led by a rich Frenchman, Baron Rodolphe d'Erlanger, who built an anglo-oriental mansion which is still here today. He created an international appetite for these picturesque cobbled streets on the hill and, rather like Tangier, Sidi Bou Said was near enough to Europe for writers and artists to pick up the scent, Paul Klee, August Macke and André Gide amongst them.

It's still a highly fashionable, moderately bohemian enclave and its centre is the celebrated Café des Nattes.

It stands in a dominant position at the top of Sidi Bou Said High Street, and even when you've climbed up the hill there's still a score of steep steps between you and the door, so you're guaranteed to enter breathless. The wide, but intimate, rectangular room was once part of a mosque and dates back to the fourteenth century. There is a well-used feel to it, a definite sense of layers of history, behind the black and white horseshoe arch of the doorway. It's a bit self-consciously traditional – very woody, with striped pillars and roof beams painted red, white and green, song birds in filigree cages, old wireless sets, black and white archive photos of Sidi Bou Said on the wall and a man behind the counter with a sprig of jasmine behind his ear. Wise old waiters in green and black striped jackets serve a largely young, international clientele sitting cross-legged on woven straw mats, the *nattes* that gave the place its name.

I order a thick, rich Turkish coffee and a glass of *thé aux pignons*, tea with pine nuts, for my companion Moez, a Tunisian film producer and director. Several people are puffing contentedly at bubbling *chichas,* so we order one to share. Moez says there's an extra intensity to the smoking, since Ramadan began two days ago, forbidding the taking of anything by mouth during the hours of daylight. Not that this produces a drastically slimmed-down nation. Apparently, the month of fasting results in such indulgence during the hours of darkness that people come out of it having put on weight.

The *chicha* is brought over by the waiter and set with courteous formality on a green baize table beside me. It's the size of a small vacuum cleaner, and comes with various accessories, like a silver tray of fresh charcoal and a pair of tongs. My breath draws the smoke from the coal down through the tobacco and it cools as it passes the water chamber. It gurgles pleasantly and is completely legal. According to Moez, the sound is an important part of the relaxing process. The other is breath control. An accomplished smoker can keep the pipe going for an hour or more.

'It's not easy,' Moez cautions, as I start puffing away like a steam engine. 'Both of us would burn the tobacco in ten minutes.'

We talk about his work. He's making a film about the Tunisians who died in the Second World War. From the war movies I remember, you'd be forgiven for thinking any Tunisians were involved at all.

Plenty of big foreign epics have been made in the country, including *Star Wars*, *The English Patient* and *Raiders of the Lost Ark*, but Moez prefers to work on local subjects.

'We need to see our images, you know. The audiences here like to see Tunisian faces, Tunisian stories, Tunisian jokes.'

DAY NINETY-TWO   SIDI BOU SAID

Out early. Sidi Bou Said is very walkable. It's spotlessly clean with almost every wall and house and building painted white and cerulean blue. Bougainvillea and morning-glory burst out of tight, green gardens and spill over into the streets. The national flag is everywhere, red and white crescent and stars wrapped round lampposts and on bunting hung across the street. Tomorrow is the fourteenth anniversary of what the

Tunisians celebrate as '*Le Changement*', the day in 1987 when the great founding president, Habib Bourguiba, was declared senile and unfit to rule and power was painlessly transferred to his deputy, Ben Ali.

Ben Ali's likeness is everywhere. A fleshy, pleasant-looking man staring glassily down from the posters and wearing a purple sash. He is almost as popular as Bourguiba and credited with bringing in young well-educated technocrats to modernise industry and business. Ben Ali and the Technocrats may sound like a 1960s rock band but they are hailed here as the new saviours of Tunisia.

One of those Tunisians who has benefited from all this lives nearby, in a sprawling 100-year-old mansion next to a golf course in Carthage. Three seriously impressive satellite dishes sprout from the roof. Leaves blow across a tennis court and gather in the swimming pool. Over the hedges there's a glimpse of orange orchard, and at least a dozen oddly assorted dogs caper about beneath palms, pines and cypress trees at the top of a long drive. All it needs is a shooting party and a crowd of Tunisian country gentlemen to complete the picture. In fact, one small middle-aged woman emerges from the front door to welcome us. She's short and compact with thick dark hair and a strong broad face. Her name is Hyett Alouami. She's fifty and has two children. Her husband died of an aneurysm at the age of forty-six.

From the moment she greets us it's clear that this is the sort of formidable woman who doesn't do things by halves. She has not one but twelve dogs, all of them from a shelter which she herself started. She also has three cats and four transport companies.

She introduces us to the dogs, which have names like Café, Chocolat and Vodka. One she's particularly fond of is just called Back.

'Because he keeps coming back,' she explains.

She gives instructions to an elderly manservant in a fez and green wellies, slipping her hand through his arm as they walk together through the garden. Then we repair to the waterfront to talk, for most of her life has been spent in the shipping business.

She was born on a farm near Sousse, but began work in the port of Bizerte, not as a clerk in an office, but actually on the dockside, in the resolutely male world of stevedores.

'It was hard for the first five or six years, sure. There were always little things. I always had to open the gates for myself in the morning.'

She speaks effusively of her country's debt to President Bourguiba. Without his insistence on a secular state, free universal education and equal opportunity for

239

women, she would never have had the chance to go into business, let alone run companies. She is not alone. She reckons there are at least 1000 women of her generation who are entrepreneurs. All of which makes Tunisia quite exceptional in the Arab world. I ask her quite why this should be. The Tunisians, she points out, are a mixture of many races, including Romans, Phoenicians, Turks, Greeks; even the Normans came down here.

'It's a melting pot and that makes the nation a little bit different from other Arab countries.'

How different?

She nods, then stares out across the bay for a moment, before delivering a trenchant, if heretical judgement on the Tunisian male.

'They are educated, they are sweet.' She watches me for a moment. 'But he's quiet, he's not a fighter.' She breaks into a smile. 'We say the Tunisian men are women.'

The smile becomes a surprisingly deep throaty chuckle.

'I mean, I prefer that they are women rather than be men and kill each other.'

I ask her if Tunisia itself feels threatened, a slip of a country sandwiched between the oil- and gas-rich giants of Libya and Algeria. Again, her reaction is not quite what I'd expected. Her eyes seem positively to shine at the prospect of not having oil.

'We are lucky. We are lucky to be in a small country without oil. Oil...is a mal-addiction. God continued not to give us oil so we have to work hard to survive. In a way we feel a little bit more proud than the Libyan and the Algerian. We, not we, I mean Bourguiba, has invested a lot in education, health care and women. And women are leading the country, actually.'

DAY NINETY-THREE   TUNIS TO ALGIERS

The electric train service into Tunis is clean, efficient, regular and stops at Carthage, which may have been laid waste by the Romans 2000 years ago but is now the smartest place to live in Tunisia. A sign of its significance is that there are no less than five Carthage stations listed between here and Tunis. I get on at Carthage Hannibal, partly because station names don't come much better than that, and partly because I've always had a fondness for anyone who stood up to the Romans. Hannibal's dramatic invasion of Europe and his spectacular feat of transporting an entire army over the Alps made him their enemy number one and resulted in the eventual destruction of the Carthaginian empire. As a symbolic gesture of this destruction the Romans ploughed up the fields and sowed them with salt.

At Tunis Marine we disembark and take the tram a short way through the city to the main station in Place Barcelone, from where the Trans-Maghreb express leaves for Algiers.

We pull out, on time, at 1.10 pm. Six blue and white coaches run by SNCFT, Société Nationale de Chemins de Fer Tunisienne, the name itself an indication of how comfortably Tunisia has dealt with its French colonial past. A hundred and twelve miles, and three hours away is the border with Algeria, where things are tragically different.

Jamina, the girl sitting opposite me, is studying in Tunis and going back to see her family at the weekend. She speaks English well, but with the over-deliberate emphasis of someone who has taken the learning of it very seriously. Jamina gets off the train at Ghardimaou, less than a mile from the Algerian border. I watch her go, confident and self-possessed, on her way to see her mother, who was illiterate but whom she and her sisters have taught to read and write.

She has a spring in her step, a belief in herself and her country, which is a sharp and poignant contrast to the apathy and resignation I've seen in so much of the Sahara.

ALGERIA

DAY NINETY-FOUR ALGIERS

Eamonn O'Brien is walking me through the lush gardens of the Hotel El Djazair, Algiers, formerly the St George, known to the Victorians as 'The Leading Hotel of North Africa'. An elaborate network of paths winds past beds in which hibiscus, rose and flowering cacti seem to grow in profusion, undaunted by prolific fronds of banana and palm trees. The paths, together with occasional colonnades, pergolas and ornate ironwork screens, show that this bosky little Eden has not grown wild. It was laid out by the British, who built the hotel in the 1880s, when the warm Mediterranean air, sheltered by the mountains from the harsh dry winds of the interior, made Algiers a favoured destination.

LEFT
Every home a balcony, decreed Napoleon III, and the apartment blocks of Algiers, with louvered shutters and neo-classical details, are a reminder that for more than 100 years, until independence in 1962, Algiers was as much a part of France as the Lyon or Marseille it resembles.

The hotel, with its rambling mix of European and Moorish styles, looks much the same as it does in the century-old black and white photos on its walls. But one thing has changed. There is no equivalent now of the crowd of smiling, heavily dressed foreigners photographed taking cocktails under wide umbrellas. Neither the British, nor anyone else for that matter, come to Algiers these days to enjoy the balmy warmth of a Mediterranean winter. It is, as Eamonn is telling me, just too dangerous.

Sitting together on a bench between two ornamental columns, like characters out of a John Le Carré novel, Eamonn tells me the grim reality of present-day Algeria. An estimated 100,000 people have lost their lives in the civil war, which began ten years ago when the government cancelled an election that a radical Islamic party was poised to win. Since 1993, all foreigners have been under a fatwah, a sentence of death, and over 100 have been killed. As the aim of the rebels is to cause maximum embarrassment to the government, those with a high public profile are particularly at risk. I'm not exactly Tom Cruise, but I appreciate Eamonn paying me the compliment of scaring me stiff.

Four members of the SPS, the Service de Protection Spéciale, will be with me every time I leave the hotel. With Eamonn, that's five, so we've almost doubled our crew already. And that's not all. In certain high-risk areas like the casbah, another six members of the SPS will be drafted and men from the Commissionaire de Police of the casbah, the Casbah Cops as Eamonn calls them, will throw a *cordon sanitaire* around us.

Having never had a *cordon sanitaire* thrown anywhere near me before, I suppose I should feel faintly flattered, but I feel bound to ask Eamonn if it's all absolutely necessary.

BELOW
Light and darkness on the roof of the Villa Suzini. Behind me, sunlight across the city explains why the French called it Alger La Blanche, the White City. Below me, in the cellars of this pretty Moorish villa, Algerians who resisted French rule were beaten, tortured and often killed during the independence struggle in the 1950s.

His reply is terse and to the point.

'You're a public figure. You're a guest of the Algerian government. And frankly, if I lose you, I lose my job.'

Pure James Bond.

My immediate security team, four lean young men in suits with two-way radios, are affable and approachable. I learn from them that the French for walkie-talkie is *talkie-walkie*. That cheers me up a bit.

I'm also reunited with Said Chitour, who takes me first to the Villa Suzini, a handsome Moorish house from whose roof there is a fine panorama of the city, laid out across wide, sometimes steep slopes curving round a generous bay. The French called it Alger La Blanche, and it is still a brilliantly white city, laid out like Lyon or Marseille, with tiers of imposing terraces, breaking down into the less regular outlines of the old town, the casbah, on the western arm of the bay.

To the east, the skyline is dominated by a towering monument of 300-foot palm leaves, built of reinforced concrete, and dedicated to the martyrs of the revolution. Martyrs are very important to the Algerians, though there have been so many claimed by different sides that the word has become almost meaningless.

Unlike other countries of the French empire, such as Tunisia, Senegal, Mauritania and Mali, Algeria's independence was won at considerable cost. Hundreds of thousands of French settlers had made their lives here, and, rather than accommodate the demands for self-determination that swept through Saharan Africa in the 1950s and 1960s, they decided to make a fight of it. Their battle to turn back the tide of history ended in ignominious failure in 1962, when General de Gaulle, heavily influenced by world opinion, finally handed over the country to the nationalist FLN (National Liberation Front).

The elegant old Villa Suzini played a particularly sinister part in all this. Down in the cellars, below the Carrara marble floor and the mosaic tiles and coloured glass of the central courtyard, are rooms into which the sun never shines. Plaster peels off the walls and there is a sour smell of damp. It was down here that the French paras interrogated their suspects. Torture was routinely used. Electric shocks were administered to various parts of the body through serrated pincers known as 'crocodiles'. Some of those who died of their beatings were buried in the garden or thrown down a well at the back of the house. The Villa Suzini was, until two or three years ago, used as an office, but now, apart from a sallow-complexioned caretaker and two or three dogs, it is deserted. No-one will work here.

'Too many ghosts,' explains Said.

Near the villa there is a funicular railway, and we take a car down the hill into the working-class district of Belcourt, where Albert Camus, winner of the Nobel Prize for Literature, was brought up, and about which he wrote in an unfinished autobiographical novel, *Le Premier Homme* (*The First Man*).

ABOVE

In the room in which Albert Camus, the Nobel prize-winning French Algerian writer was brought up. The balcony looks down on the streets of Belcourt, which he wrote about so well.

ABOVE RIGHT

A wall in Belcourt is covered with football slogans. The English contribution, though misspelt, is not forgotten.

He made much in his book of the different levels in Algiers, both literal and metaphorical, with the poor crowded down by the port and the big houses with gardens higher up the hill. It's like that still. In one short ride in a bruised and dented cable car, the atmosphere of the city changes, from villas to tenements, from well-swept streets to open ground strewn with drifting rubbish. Though the streets are meaner, they're full of life and bustling activity. One of them borders a cemetery, whose outer wall is an open-air clothing store, hung with dresses, nighties, headscarves, coats, trousers and huge brassieres, with one section entirely devoted to football strips. One of the young boys wears a Manchester United shirt, but the strips on sale are mainly those of the big Algiers club, CRB Belcourt. Various international team names have been painted on the wall, including one which just reads 'Holygans'.

The Camus family apartment at 93, Rue Mohammed Belouizdad (formerly the Rue de Lyon) is still there, above a photographer's shop. There is nothing to commemorate the fact that a Nobel prize-winner lived here, but then Camus was a French Algerian, one of the European settlers they called the *pieds noirs*, and he was as critical of the Marxist revolutionaries of the FLN as he was of the French colonialists. But it does mean that the room in which he worked is very little changed, apart from a sticker in Arabic on the door, which reads 'In the name of God and Mohammed his messenger'. It's small, maybe 15 by 18 feet, with grey-blue French windows opening onto the street with its neatly clipped shady trees. It faces west and even now, in November, I can feel the force of a midday sun that must have made life unbearable in the long hot summers.

The modest two-storey house may be unheralded, but it's certainly not unused. It's owned by an old but sprightly Algerian, who lives there with his wife, three sons and their wives and children. Eighteen people altogether.

One of the sons says that we are the first people to visit since 1998. I'm quite moved to be here and linger by the window for a while, looking out at the children's wear shop opposite, the milling crowd, the line at a bus stop, the ordinary everyday life of the city which Camus observed so carefully.

DAY NINETY-FIVE ALGIERS

Judging by the headline in *Liberté*, this might not be the best day for our visit to the casbah. '*Algérie en Colère!*' it screams – 'Algeria in Anger!' – but for once it isn't a massacre or another killing that's responsible. The anger this time is directed at the inadequacy of public services, and especially the water supply, which has remained unchanged since the French left. After another long dry summer, water in some areas is now rationed to one day in five, and there are reports of a typhoid outbreak in the poorer parts of the city. We're told on no account to drink tap water.

Before entering the casbah we rendezvous with the local police outside the white walls of the Barberousse prison, named after the Barbarossa brothers, two Turkish corsairs brought in by the ruler of Algiers to fight off Spanish invaders in the sixteenth century. It stands at the top of the hill looking balefully out over the narrow, crowded roofs of the casbah. Because of the heightened security and the momentousness of our visit (the first foreign film crew to be allowed in for several years), we're all a touch jumpy, and when, with a sudden blaring of horns, a convoy of cars bursts round the corner, we instinctively rush for cover. Much mirth on the part of the security men, as it turns out to be nothing more than a wedding procession, in the middle of which is a portable band – six musicians in fezzes, white cotton tunics and red waistcoats, sitting in the back of a pick-up truck. With a salvo of car horns they move past down the road.

So thorough have the security forces been that when Said and I at last cross the road and enter the network of descending alleyways, the casbah is like a ghost town. Five hundred years of human traffic may have worn down the old stone steps and cobbled passageways, but there are no traffic jams today. I catch glimpses of faces at black-grilled windows, set high in the walls above us. Doors scrape into place just before we reach them, and I can hear the hum of voices behind them. I have the feeling that the casbah is only holding its breath until we've gone.

It doesn't surprise me that UNESCO has named the casbah a World Heritage Site. It is undeniably atmospheric. The buildings crowd in on one another. Some of them, judging by their elaborately detailed stone doorways and patches of decorative tiling embedded in cracked white plaster, must be substantial inside. Many houses have upper storeys cantilevered out over the alley and supported by rows of wooden poles, so they almost touch at the top. They have mains water and electricity now, but some houses still rely on the old system of collecting rainwater on the rooftops. Litter drifts

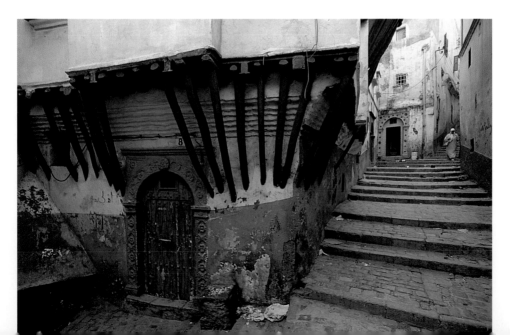

LEFT *In the casbah, Algiers. This is the oldest part of town and dates from long before the French arrived. It's also the heart of anti-government feeling. The houses are squeezed tight along narrow alleyways, making it easy to defend and very difficult to attack.*

about and there is a pungent smell of wet plaster and drains. Said confirms my suspicion that everything is going on the other side of the walls.

'It's overpopulated. Sometimes you find six families in the same house. It's too much people.'

'How many?'

'Sixty people sometimes.'

The house where Ali La Pointe and three other resistance heroes chose to be blown apart by the paras rather than surrender (a story powerfully told in the film *The Battle of Algiers*) has been rebuilt. On the wall an Arabic inscription details the circumstances of their deaths on 8 October 1957.

I can understand now what made the casbah such a superb defensive position and why the resistance, the 'freedom fighters' as Said always calls them, were able to hold out for so long against crack French paratroops. Sophisticated weapons and modern vehicles are useless in streets the width of a loaded donkey, or on roofs which act as another thoroughfare for those who know their way around them.

As we near the main road at the lower end of the casbah there is a milling throng. Eamonn walks beside me, casting wary looks, but everyone seems to be either friendly or preoccupied.

I feel that we have barely touched the real world of the casbah, which, as in all Arab communities, is private and inward-looking, so Said takes me round to the shrine of Sidi Abderrahmane, a holy man of great powers who lived here in the sixteenth century. The sound of female voices rises from inside as we approach the domed building surmounted by a tall balconied minaret.

This is traditionally a place for the women to come and invoke the help of the saint in childbirth or with problems of infertility, but the imam is happy for us to join them. Remove my shoes and enter in reverent silence. I needn't have bothered. The small chamber is less like an English parish church than a kindergarten at collection time. Small children sit and play as their mothers worship in their own way. Nothing is formal. One woman hugs the side of the tomb, singing plaintively, another bows to Mecca, another has brought her new-born baby to touch the wooden casket that contains the saint's remains. It's the first place, she declares proudly, that he's ever been taken to. Brightly coloured texts run round the walls, heavy cut-glass lamps hang,

undusted, from the ceiling, and in one corner is a heavy-duty industrial safe, with a slit for offerings. Said tells me that the poorer women sometimes stuff chewing gum in the slit and come back later to collect money that hasn't gone down.

By now I've completely forgotten that I might be a target. The *cordon sanitaire* has been discreet to the point of invisibility and the people of Algiers as cordial and curious as anywhere in the Sahara.

DAY NINETY-SIX ALGIERS TO ORAN

A peerless morning. The only cloud in the sky is caused by an enormous flock of small birds, which plunges us into shadow as we wait in the hotel courtyard for transport to the station. More and more birds seem to join all the time, crying and calling, until their numbers reach a critical mass and, as if on a given signal, they execute a dizzyingly precise banking turn and disappear southwards. Our coach driver tells me they're swallows, migrating from Europe to winter in the Sahara. They regroup here on the mountainous shoreline before starting the final leg of their journey.

We who are migrating the other way, out of the Sahara and into Europe, are also on the last leg of a journey. Today we catch the train to Oran, second city of Algeria, which is less than 300 miles from where we set out all those months ago.

Eamonn is anxious. Travelling from Algiers to Oran by train is, in security terms, an out of the frying pan into the fire situation. He has trawled his dictionary of doom this morning. Over the last ten years this has been the most bombed railway line in the world; it passes through an area known as the Triangle of Death (not mentioned in the timetable) and terrorists have been known to board the train and kill people ' in awful circumstances'.

It all sounds theatrically exaggerated on this brilliant, life-enhancing morning, as we drive down through the city for the last time, past the grand arcades, the long straight thoroughfares, the great domed Post Office – built by the French in 1913, but so Moorish in its inspiration that it looks like a mosque – and the long white walls of the apartment blocks, flecked with the bright colours of a thousand sun blinds.

Our train was once the romantically named Algiers-Casablanca Express, but the land border with Morocco has been closed since 1995, after disagreements over security, and it's now terminated at Oran, 300 miles and five hours away. The silver-ribbed aluminium shell of our coach is studded with small holes, and I'm just about to bring these to Eamonn's attention when a group from Algerian Railways arrives to welcome us aboard and generally look after all our filming needs. One of them is a dark-haired lady with long, lustrous hair and a brisk, efficient manner which barely conceals a palpable nervousness.

She dismisses any current problems on the line.

'It's all much better now,' she assures me confidently, rather spoiling the effect by adding, '*touche bois*'. Touch wood. *Inshallah* would have been more appropriate.

The train rolls out on time and I push aside the flimsy green curtain to take a last look at Alger La Blanche, which I doubt I shall see again for a long, long time. The morning sun catches the roofs of the casbah and the city finally slips away behind a succession of tunnels and flyovers.

The railway runs through a poor area consisting of cheap new housing blocks, separated from the line by a corridor of concrete walls and steel fences which rise on either side of the train. This grim barricade continues into open countryside, where fields, apple orchards and vineyards stretch away towards the grey-green foothills of the Atlas Mountains. The fields around Blida were once renowned for their roses; now the town is part of the aforementioned 'Triangle of Death', which is marked by Blida in the west, Bouira in the east and Algiers in the north. It was in this deceptively benign

landscape that the GIA used to stop trains by putting an accomplice on board to pull the communication cord. As the train came to a halt they would board and either kill their victims there and then or take them away and murder them. There are no communication cords on the trains any more. Even the nice friendly PR team from the railway cannot disguise the problems here. The woman with the lustrous hair lost her voice for three years after seeing some soldiers, who were guarding one of her stations, murdered. Like many other victims of the GIA their throats had been cut.

Once beyond Blida, the continuous protective wall stops, but heavy security remains in place, with block-houses and pillboxes at

ABOVE On the Algiers-Oran express, one of the most frequently attacked trains in the world. Fellow passengers keep a watchful eye.

strategic points like bridges or tunnel entrances.

The worst of the attacks peaked around 1995 and recently the government has experimented with an amnesty, which seems to have reduced the levels of violence.

The damage nowadays is more likely to be inflicted by bored teenagers throwing stones, which happens all the time and explains not only the number of Plexiglas window panes but also the scattering of dents on the bodywork which caught my eye as I was boarding.

We're climbing now, through a long tunnel and into a station called Ain Torki. The only people on the platform are soldiers wearing camouflage, but in the distance, my eye is caught by a procession of women leaving a graveyard, scarves and veils streaming behind them, plumes of colour in a hard brown landscape.

At Chlef, two and a quarter hours into the journey, our guard is changed and no less than eighteen black-clad members of the Gendarmerie Nationale, wearing body armour, squeeze aboard. Eamonn casts a professional eye over them and notes that one or two have Simonov precision rifles.

'*They're* serious.'

The soldiers settle down behind us, but when Nigel raises the camera they all move away and hide.

The last few miles into Oran are particularly sad. An arid landscape of stony ploughed fields is covered with blowing rubbish and drifting plastic bags. The stations, once trim symbols of French civic pride, are falling apart, with gaping holes in pantiled roofs, windows smashed, red-brick walls stained and grafittied. It pains me to say so, because our Algerian hosts are charming, co-operative, friendly and above all desperate to please, but this is a vision of callous decay.

And, perhaps, a perfect metaphor for post-colonial Sahara. The old owners have been thrown out and the new ones still haven't decided what to do with the property.

Oran Station emphasises the point. It is a magnificently stylish example of the Mauresque style, full of height and light and space, set off by ornate wood mouldings and iron-work screens. It's been kept in very good condition, but not so the Hôtel Terminus next door. Beneath the layers of dust, the broken lighting and the holes in the ceiling, the grand vision of the French railway builders is unmistakable. Solid Moorish arches rise from the mosaic floor, a fireplace in massive blocks of grey marble is incised with the initials P. L. M., the Paris, Lyon and Marseille Railway. Above it is a mirror 9 feet high. Everything is intended to elevate and inspire, but this purpose has sadly been forgotten. No pastis here now, no freshly opened bottles of wine, no apronned waiters bustling amongst tables buzzing with gossip from Paris and Algiers. Instead, there's Coke or Fanta and a handwritten sign above a lifeless bar: '*La maison ne fait pas du crédit.*'

We are eating later at the Comet, a plain old-fashioned restaurant, whose wine list and entrecôtes go a long way to making up for the Hôtel Terminus, when the flow of conversation is interrupted by the chanting of a crowd outside. It sounds like football supporters celebrating, and Said, who goes outside to check, confirms that this is the case, Kabilya JSK having defeated AC Africa from Côte d'Ivoire, to win the African club soccer championship.

The hooting and shouting grows louder and more vociferous and seems no longer entirely to do with football. I'm sure I hear the word '*Assassins!*' repeated over and over. The proprietor pushes his windows shut, which doesn't do much good, and, if anything, urges the crowd on. There seem to be only two words they're chanting now.

'*Pou-voir! Assa-ssins! Pou-voir! Assa-ssins!*'

Said goes to the door, but peers out a lot more warily. For the first time I begin to

wonder where my *cordon sanitaire* has gone. Probably been given the night off for getting us to Oran safely.

After a few more minutes, during which the stamping and shouting rises to a frightening intensity, the crowd moves on.

I ask Said what it was all about.

Don't worry, he reassures me, it wasn't directed at us. Kabilya, where the winning team comes from, is a mountainous region of eastern Algeria, not Arab but Berber. They are a strong-willed, proud and enterprising people (the actress Isabelle Adjani is Kabilyan) and have their own quarrel with the government over suppression of their language and culture. After a recent protest march in Algiers, forty young men disappeared, and the word is that they were taken away on police wagons. The military-backed government is known by its opponents as *Le Pouvoir*, The Power, hence the shouts of '*Pouvoir*' and '*Assassins*'.

In Algeria it's quite common for football teams to be used for political protest.

'Were you as worried as I was?' I ask Said.

'If this had been in Algiers, yes.'

DAY NINETY-SEVEN ORAN

The good news is that my hotel overlooks the sea. The less good news is that between me and the sea is a warehouse, a grain silo, two fuel storage tanks, a stack of containers and a chimney. The positively bad news is that at six o'clock this morning I was bent double with stomach cramps. Since my emetic experiences in Western Sahara I've kept a bottle of Pepto-Bismol nearby and am gulping the thick chalky fluid every hour on the hour.

I don't think I'm the only one with problems. The hotel itself looks distinctly off colour. My bathroom ceiling has been partly removed to provide access to a water pipe, and every now and then strange, animal-like cries issue from the gaping hole. The tap on my basin coughs and splutters in a horrible parody of my own lurchings and strainings, and I can find no taps on the bath tub at all.

I make my way gingerly to breakfast. I'm on the tenth floor but I haven't used the lift since I saw the owner banging the control panel to make the light come on, so it's a long walk down. As I pass the third floor I have to step over a stream of water, which is running down the corridor from beneath the door of Room 306.

As if things aren't delicate already, my first walk through Oran reminds me that this is the city immortalised by Camus in his novel *La Peste* (*The Plague*).

In it one of the characters actually keels over and dies of the plague on the stage of the Opera House. This splendidly florid edifice still stands at one side of the Place du 1ᵉʳ Novembre 1954, formerly the Place d'Armes. It makes for an interesting culture clash. Brazenly bare-breasted women loom large at the top of the Opera House, whilst a statue in the middle of the square bears a quotation from the Koran: 'And Victory is from God and God is merciful.'

This then is the end of the road. It looks as if the only way from here to Morocco might be by sea, and, given the current state of relations between Morocco and Algeria, even that could be tricky.

Back to the hotel. Get talking to a tall, rather striking Algerian with a family in Stockholm. He is curious to know what I think of the bombing of Afghanistan. Something in his manner rubs me up the wrong way and instead of expressing my doubts I dither indecisively. He thinks it will only strengthen the hand of the Islamists. I shift the discussion to something that has worried me ever since I came to Algeria. What happened after the glorious armed struggle against the French? How come the freedom fighters of the FLN became the oppressors? How did the anti-colonial legacy of the 1960s become today's '*Pouvoir*', a military state almost wholly dependent on oil and gas exports to the West?

He looks witheringly at me.

'A hundred and forty years of colonialism cannot be destroyed right away.'

He shrugs and reaches for his briefcase.

'Mistakes will be made.'

DAY NINETY-EIGHT   CEUTA

There is an alternative to Morocco. Two hundred and sixty miles east of Oran, tucked in at the foot of the mountains at the point where two continents almost meet, is a low-slung town occupying a narrow isthmus between two peaks. Neither part of Morocco nor Algeria, it belongs to one of the less well-known African countries – Spain.

The heavily fortified town of Ceuta has been Spanish sovereign territory since 1580. It's one of two Spanish towns barnacled onto the coast of Morocco, ensuring that the transition from Africa to Europe is not as clean as one might romantically like it to be. It's reachable by a combination of ferries, and I duly find myself spending my last night in the Dark Continent at a Parador hotel drinking Rioja and eating *jamón serrano*. Very confusing.

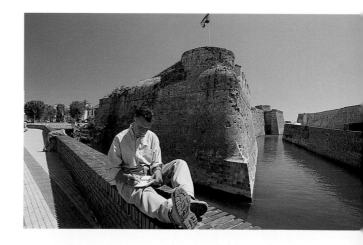

BELOW

The Portuguese-built bastions of what is now a piece of Spanish territory in Africa, the city of Ceuta.

251

In my experience, hotel brochures, especially of the aspiringly glossy variety, always feature a room spectacularly better than the one you're in and a swimming pool you can never find. In the case of the Hotel La Muralla, Ceuta, I do find the pool, which is similar in every respect to its photo except that the one in the photo has water in it. The brochure is gushingly enthusiastic about Ceuta's history. In fact, I can't imagine why I've never heard of the place.

'Phoenicians, Romans, Arabs, Visigoths, Portuguese and Spanish successively took control of the ancient city.'

Good harbours, like the one I entered last night, so close to the Mediterranean gateway, meant trade, security and wealth. Under its Arab rulers Ceuta had all three, but couldn't hold onto them against the determined and expansionist Portuguese. In 1415 they conquered Ceuta and took their prize seriously enough to build a powerful fortification, La Muralla (City Wall). It remains in place, solid and imperturbable, and I enjoy a good walk around the sturdy, elegantly angled walls, crenellated and studded with barbican towers, which slide down into the clear green waters of a moat. Felipe II united Portugal and Spain and in 1580 Ceuta became a possession of the Spanish crown, and has remained so ever since. Though it has the look and feel of a European city, the central square is nevertheless called the Plaza de Africa. It contains a small church dedicated to Our Lady of Africa and a monument commemorating the Spanish invasion of Morocco in 1859.

In the gardens of this quiet square, sitting on the grass or pacing the neat hedge-lined paths that radiate from the monument, are a number of young men. All Africans, they range from tall loose-limbed Blacks to paler Arabs, some in Western dress and others in flowing robes. They look like me; a little awkward, strangers in a foreign land.

I ask one of them where he's from. His English is not so good, and he prefers to talk in French. He's from Mali, on the other side of the Sahara, and has made his way here to try to find work in Spain and once in Spain, any of the European Union countries. He points out an Algerian, a group of Mauritanians. They're here to pick up scraps of information, about who's going where and how, about deals, about boats crossing the Strait, about how they can take the final step on their long journeys. They've come to the Plaza de Africa because they want to get out of Africa.

I ask how they survive in Ceuta. Most of them, it turns out, are in a holding centre run by the Spanish authorities on behalf of the European Union, where they are given food and accommodation until they can be found work in Europe.

Later in the day we visit the centre, a bright, freshly painted, concrete encampment up in the hills, surrounded by a grove of mournfully swaying eucalyptus trees. Here in the Centro de Estancia Temporal de Imigrantes are gathered 335 men, 42 women and 13 children, waiting for permits and, in some cases, asylum papers to enable them to get work 'up in the Peninsula', as they call Spain and Portugal.

The place is newly opened and is clean, orderly and antiseptic; an institution in which no-one has anything wrong with them, like a hospital in which all the patients are well or a jail in which everyone is free. It's full of Africans but unlike any African village I've ever seen.

Despite an educational programme, offering language tuition and some job training, most of the inmates stand around or pace the compound with an air of displaced restlessness.

The director is a decent man, who takes some pride in the fact that fifty-nine of them have been found work in the previous six months, but most of those I talk to dispute that. A Nigerian in a Cardinals baseball shirt has been here five months. His journey sounds like ours in reverse. Up through Mali and Senegal and Western Sahara to Morocco. As Moroccan government policy is to send all immigrants back, I ask him how he got through.

'On a Zodiac (a small rubber dinghy) across the sea.' He adds bitterly, 'I thought they were taking me to Europe.'

Another Nigerian has come across the desert, 1000 miles or more. He nods bleakly and repeats the word 'desert' as if at some infinitely painful memory.

He made it to Ceuta as a stowaway on a ship from Morocco. It cost money, though not as much as the $1500 a Mauritanian paid to make the same journey. The stories tumble out, and the resentment too.

'Ten months! Ten months we have been here!' shouts a woman with hair in braids. She has left her children behind in Sierra Leone.

'Help us! Tell the world!' shouts a young man as we leave.

On a clear day the hopeful immigrants in Ceuta could see the green hills of Spain with the naked eye. They could certainly see the man-made forest of wind turbines running over the crest of the hills, propellers spinning on top of giant white stalks. If they had a strong enough telescope they could see telescopes looking back at them from the hills above the town of Tarifa. Tourists come here to be thrilled by the prospect of the sheer rock walls of Morocco, and the sight of the Strait of Gibraltar, no wider than a Swiss lake. They buy postcards and take photographs of the 9-mile distance between them and Africa.

For some it might jog memories of unsettling newspaper photographs of couples sunbathing on a Spanish beach beside the huddled body of someone who drowned trying to get to Europe. What the tourists will not know is that some evenings, hundreds of Africans will set out to cross the Strait and land a half-mile away from where they're standing. They will have paid a lot of money to risk their lives, travelling in unlit boats, without lifejackets or maps of any kind, across one of the busiest and most unpredictable stretches of water in the world. Some will never make it. Over 3000 have died attempting the crossing in the last three years.

There is heat still left in the afternoon as I reach the Spanish mainland and walk along the beach at Tarifa with Belinda Whaley-Braithwaite, a traveller herself, who rode from here to Paris on a horse called Dragon and wrote a book about it. Now she and her husband live most of the year in a pretty house with six guest rooms a mile or so across the fields.

The beaches are long and full of fine white sand, and in the creamy blue-black breakers kite-flyers, surfers, swimmers and fishermen try to stay out of each other's way.

Then we come across a red and blue-striped fishing boat, no more than 20 feet long, broken and embedded in the sand. It looks quite picturesque, until you realise why it is here and who it has brought.

'Sometimes they can be up to 700 in a night, and the police may only catch 200, so the rest are in the countryside. If they're Moroccan there's an agreement, so they'll be sent back, but the people who've come from Chad or Senegal...'

'From Black Africa?'

'Black Africa, yes, there isn't the same agreement, so they're quite happy to be caught.'

Belinda, perhaps being something of an adventurer herself, talks with a sort of shocked admiration for what they go through. Boats the size of the one we're looking at may have forty bodies in them, including pregnant women who want their children to be born in Europe. Other boats never make it to the shore, leaving their charges to swim in over the reef. Unscrupulous skippers lie to them, telling them they're a hundred yards from land when in fact they're still half a mile out.

The lucky ones who do get ashore bring waterproof bags with a change of clothes.

Some speak only Arabic and clutch pieces of paper with contact names and numbers. One came to Belinda's door and asked her if she might help her contact a Spanish Internet address. The name she had been given, but didn't understand, was a very sick joke. It was two Spanish words, *'puerto muertos'*, literally 'the port of the dead'.

As we walk back to her house, through dunes littered with cast-off clothes that may well have protected people on mighty journeys across the Sahara, Belinda explains why she thinks the best way to deal with the immigrants is to allow them a short-term visa.

'Then at least they could come and try it out. I think a lot of them actually come over here and don't like what they see. It's more expensive to live here, they can't get a job, so they're actually happy to go back to their families.'

She pauses and looks out the way we've come.

'But you know, when all your family and friends have clubbed together to get this ticket for you to Paradise...How do you go back?'

It's dark by the time we reach Gibraltar. There's a queue to get in. Our driver grumbles about the usual Spanish prevarication. But there's a lot more for him to grumble about since we left here all those months ago. The British and Spanish

254

governments have been doing the unthinkable – talking joint sovereignty. Though they've been assured that nothing will be decided without a referendum, the folks who live on the Rock are very angry. Joint sovereignty may mean the end of this bickering at the border, but the very suggestion of a Spanish flag flying on Gibraltar, even alongside the Union Jack, is seen by some here as the first rumbling of betrayal, the beginning of the end.

For me, for all of us, this *is* the end. After nine countries and some 10,000 miles of travel we've made it back to the reassuring armchairs of the Rock Hotel. By tomorrow we'll all be back home, worrying about the price of car insurance and why the plumber hasn't called.

I've had a few beers of celebration and I'm a little light-headed as I stumble out onto my balcony at midnight. I look out over the star-lit Strait towards Africa and try to think big thoughts about what I've learnt from all this, other than that nowhere is Paradise.

AFTERWORD

I'm glad to be home, but in the all-moving, all-talking mayhem of modern life, my restless thoughts go back to that great place of silence and apparently infinite space. I need to be reminded of its special qualities, but, like keeping up with an old friend, that can be hard work.

Even checking the weather (sad person that I am) isn't easy. The likes of Nouakchott and Bamako rarely show up on a list of world cities.

A few scraps of news have come out of the desert since we finished our journey. A United Nations report blames high-tech foreign fleets for destroying Mauritania's fishing industry. The Polisario has released 115 Moroccan soldiers, held in their desert jails for twenty-five years (they never told me about them), but Saharawi independence looks as far away as ever as the UN discusses an American-backed compromise proposal for Western Sahara. Nancy Abeiderrahmane has had her attempt to sell camel cheese in Europe turned down, because the camels are not mechanically milked, and the drought in Algeria ended savagely and dramatically soon after we left, with hundreds drowned by flood-water in the capital. Dave Hammond, the British motorcycling hope in the Dakar Rally, was in twentieth place with only two stages left when he fell into a hidden chasm on the blind side of a sand dune. He spent many weeks in a Paris hospital but is now back home and recovering. As I write, the British and Spanish prime ministers are meeting to discuss plans for the Rock, whilst the government of Gibraltar is putting ads in British newspapers to ask for support.

Otherwise, the mystery of the Sahara remains largely intact. Except in my dreams, where it still springs vividly to life.

Michael Palin, May 2002

BACKGROUND READING

I gratefully acknowledge a number of other people's efforts, including the *Rough Guide to West Africa*, Lonely Planet's *Africa on a Shoestring*, the Footprint guides to Morocco, Libya and Tunisia, Barnaby Rogerson's *Cadogan Guide to Morocco* and *A Traveller's History of North Africa*, Ross Velton's *Bradt Guide to Mali*, Kim Naylor's *Discovery Guide to West Africa* and James Wellard's *The Great Sahara*. Hollyman and Van Beek's beautiful book on the Dogon is one of the best on a difficult subject. Sanche de Gramont's *The Strong Brown God* and T. Coraghessan Boyle's *Water Music* were essential River Niger reading. I found the Eland edition of Mungo Park's *Travels into the Interior of Africa* indispensable and Quentin Crewe's *In Search of the Sahara*, Jeremy Keenan's *Sahara Man*, Richard Trench's *Forbidden Sands* and Martin Buckley's *Grains of Sand* informative and inspiring. Hachette's *Guide de Sahara*, Chris Scott's *Sahara Overland* and Simon Glen's *Sahara Handbook* are all good chunky guides that get right to the heart of desert travel.

First published in the United Kingdom in 2002 by Weidenfeld & Nicolson

Text copyright © Michael Palin, 2002
Photographs copyright © Basil Pao, 2002
Design and layout copyright © Weidenfeld & Nicolson, 2002

The moral right of Michael Palin to be identified as the author of this work has been asserted in accordance with the Copyright, Designs and Patents Act of 1988

A CIP catalogue record for this book is available from the British Library
ISBN 0 297 84303 6

Quotation on p17 from *Their Heads are Green* by Paul Bowles, published by Peter Owen; on p126 from *Travels into the Interior of Africa* by Mungo Park, published by Eland Editions; on p153 from *The Strong Brown God* by Sanche de Gramont, published by Houghton Mifflin Co.; on p213 from 'For the Fallen' by Laurence Binyon

Design Director David Rowley
Editor Claire Marsden
Designed by Bobby Birchall / DW Design, London
Artwork photography by Martin Norris Photography
Map on pp10–11 by Stephen Conlin

Printed and bound in Italy by Printer Trento

Weidenfeld & Nicolson
Wellington House
125 Strand
London WC2R 0BB

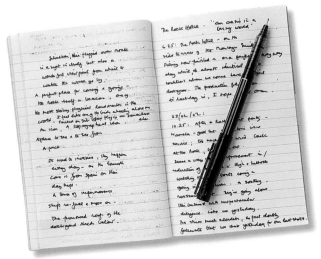

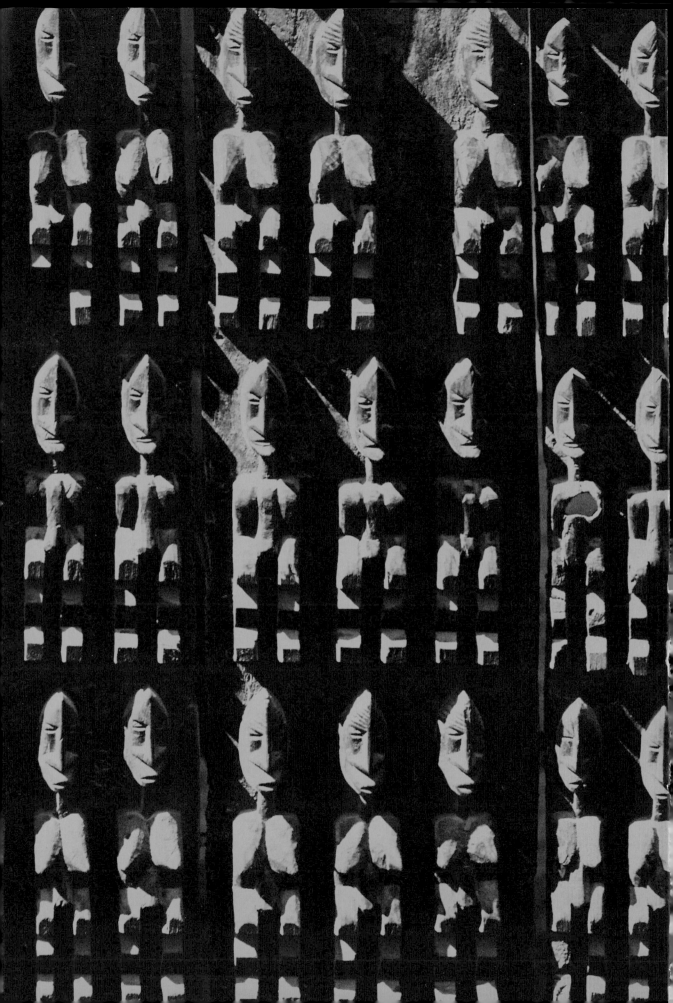